HELEN M^cNAB

To Eric,
with kind regards,
from
Helen

I survived 10 years as a High School Scripture Teacher

teach
pray
love

Ark House Press
PO Box 1722, Port Orchard, WA 98366 USA
PO Box 1321, Mona Vale NSW 1660 Australia
PO Box 318 334, West Harbour, Auckland 0661 New Zealand
arkhousepress.com

Unless otherwise stated, all Scriptures are taken from the New Living Translation (Holy Bible. New Living Translation copyright© 1996, 2004, 2007, 2013 by Tyndale House Foundation. Used by permission of Tyndale House Publishers Inc., Carol Stream, Illinois 60188. All rights reserved.)

Cataloguing in Publication Data:
Title: Teach Pray Love
ISBN: 9780994194152 (pbk.)
Subjects: Biography
Other Authors/Contributors: McNab, Helen

Design by initiateagency.com

Contact the author via email: helen_mcnab@bigpond.com

For,

SRE teachers to help and encourage you

those who enjoy a romantic comedy

and

fellow travellers who need some inspiration for the journey

With thanks...

Thank you to David Wallace, and Mark Tough, from St Clements. I appreciated their comments and prayers when the going was getting tough.

Thank you to Christine, Steve, and Tina, who provided me with a writing retreat in northern NSW, where I could get lost in my craft.

I have appreciated the efforts of those who edited my wordy tome.

Thanks to David, who saved a file when I really needed it.

And to three Bible Study groups over the years, thanks for adding my writing to your prayer list. We made it!!

Thanks to Lyndall for her keen eye.

"I've come to a frightening conclusion

that **I am** the decisive element in the classroom.

It's my **personal approach** that creates the climate.

It's my **daily mood** that makes the weather.

As a **teacher**, I possess a tremendous power to make a child's life miserable or **joyous**.

I can be a tool of torture or an instrument of **inspiration**.

I can humiliate or **heal**.

In all situations, it is **my response** that decides whether a crisis will be escalated or de-escalated and a **child humanized** or dehumanized."

Hain G. Ginott

Contents

Introduction

It was the end of a busy week at Pennant Hills High (Sydney, Australia), as I headed across the main quad to my Year 10 lesson. I was prepared and practised, having taught this lesson already this week. But I always approached Year 10 classes with caution, as they were the hardest group to teach and inspire. Ian and I were working with material that was less than ideal and trying to motivate the Year 10s nonetheless. Students reluctantly filed into the room.

"Year 10 didn't have to do Christian Studies last year," I had been told the first lesson, "They got to go home early! Why can't we go home?"

Because I am being paid to teach you, I thought to myself.

There are people in our community who think this lesson is important for you, I could have added.

After a few weeks this reluctant assembly of students had settled into a Friday afternoon routine. The girls sitting in the front had been the hardest to crack. They were cheekily full of attitude, always talking and making distracting comments that I didn't appreciate. On this particular Friday the attitude started as soon as they were seated. One of them was holding something.

"I got a letter from Mr Rowe," one girl excitedly shared with her friends, as she unfolded small hand-written pages on her lap. "It's for all of us," she told them.

It was thoughtful of the previous teacher to write to the girls, I thought to myself. They must have really enjoyed *his* lessons. The letter was now being passed from one girl to another as they talked among themselves. The letter made it to the top of their desks. I moved to another desk at the side and tried to command the rest of the class. Their conversation centred on Laura Palmer, who had been 'wrapped in plastic'.

I started the lesson, trying to rise above the scene in front of me, with their longing for the past. This was hard. If these girls could have wished me away they would have. They wished Mr Rowe was still their teacher; but he wasn't. It was me! This was *really* hard. I wondered if others in the class could tell that I was struggling? I could have been invisible and it wouldn't have mattered for all the interest students were showing. But somehow a lesson struggled on for those 40 minutes, with me wounded by the comments and behaviour of the girls in the front row. They had meant to hurt, and they had succeeded. The lesson went for far too long.

The bell rang. It was over. And to think I had to do it all again next week.

All through my next class, Year 7, the feeling remained – of being unwanted and rejected. It was a tough afternoon. When the final bell rang, I packed up, collected my briefcase and headed for the car park, fighting back tears.

Peter Kneale, an English teacher and supporter of the Christian Studies program, caught up with me, just past A block.

"How's it all going?" Peter called from behind me. I slowed down to walk with him.

I could have told him.

I should have told him.

But I didn't.

"Yeah, fine!" I said, as I caught myself, holding my voice under control.

I answered his other questions, pleased of the distraction. But I thought later, that I should have told him how I was really feeling. He would have understood. If Peter had seen my tears I would have appeared very real. He could have been an encouragement to me right then, when I needed it most. But I wasn't prepared for that moment; I wasn't prepared to be that honest.

Where does this story *Teach Pray Love* begin? Maybe it starts here, in the emailed words of a friend. Tues 26/2/2008

Dear Helen,

I am sorry that it has taken me so long to write you back. You have been heavy on my heart recently. I know that things are tough for you right now. I wish you and I could get together for a cup of coffee and talk.

I know that things seem uncertain now. Things are not turning out like we all hoped. I am sorry for that. I was excited with you. Now, I am sad with you.

Although, your story has taken an unexpected turn, it is still your story. It is also still very much a love story. The beauty of your love story was never about a man. Your story is about your First Love. That is the story you should write, and that is the story people would be blessed to read. Players in the story enter and exit, but the Hero never leaves. Your Lover knows your heart. He has not forgotten nor has He over looked all of its desires and all of its needs.

Act III is underway. It has all the twists and turns of a good drama.

It is hard to see how it is going to turn out. However, we can be sure of one thing: Our Hero always prevails. The Bridegroom wins His bride in the end. We anxiously wait, through all the twists and turns, to see how He will accomplish all that He has promised.

I am on my knees as well as on the edge of my seat.

With Love,

Doug

PART ONE

1990-1994

Chapter 1

The Beginning

In the beginning was The Committee,

And the Committee was with God,

And the Committee was like God.

Through The Committee all things were decided.

Nothing was decided without The Committee.

In The Committee was new Hope

Hope for Scripture in the local community.

That Hope shines in the darkness of unbelief;

And the Hope of The Committee has not been extinguished.

(Reworked John 1:1-4)

Before the Beginning was **Joost Gemeren**.

Joost was an evangelical Dutchman who lived in West Pennant Hills, a leafy suburb in north-western Sydney, with his wife Margaret and their two teenage daughters. Joost was a nurseryman with a large parcel of land, a simple lifestyle and a big faith. As a family they attended their local Anglican church.

"At the time, our two daughters, Roslyn and Meredith, were attending Pennant Hills High," Joost explained. "What I heard from them about their Scripture lessons made me think these lessons were probably more counter-productive than helpful. That does not mean I had a low opinion of the teachers who conducted these lessons, but it was just beyond most of them. Roslyn, my eldest, said that she dreaded Scripture lessons as it used to be utter chaos. She had an old lady as a teacher and the kids just mucked up and she was not able to control the class. Meredith's Year 7 teacher, a local minister, had reasonable control, but there was obviously utter disinterest in the class to what he had to say."

Joost heard from his friend Wally Bower, of a Christian Studies program that had been successfully established in Galston High School. It had the **support of all the local churches** in having one salaried **trained teacher** to teach Scripture lessons as **part of the school's timetabled lessons**. (These three factors were important aspects of this new approach to Scripture).

"What I heard from Wally spurred me to action."

That was May, 1984.

By December that year there was The Committee, and . . .

- a constitution

- a budget of $27,000

- a curriculum

- a teacher

That's what I call progress! Father Denis Callahan, of St Agatha's Catholic Church, said he would "put $1,000 on the table" on behalf of his church, to get the program going.

Preparation

Changing jobs can be life changing. But you don't necessarily recognise that at the time. It's when you put away something you know well, something you are good at, something you can do almost without thinking, and step into the unknown that change happens. You leave behind all that is familiar and embark on a course that is uncharted. So it was for me at the end of 1989.

I had been teaching at Auburn Girls High for five years. I had arrived as a 33yr old and was departing as a 38yr old. I really enjoyed the cultural diversity this school had offered me, over that time, with students from over sixty different countries. During my time at Auburn Girls I had grown as a teacher. In Year 12 Home Science, I had taught a 3unit extension class for the first time. I had undertaken my first senior class in Textiles and Design, taking them through the Higher School Certificate. For the last three years, I had been a HSC marker in Home Science. But I knew it was time to move on. Five years was the longest I had been at any school. I knew I didn't want more of the same. It was time for a change. If I stayed at Auburn Girls I would be encouraged to go for a promotion's position. I would be 'inspected'. I wasn't overly ambitious, and I had seen how much energy this inspection process extracted and how much time these promotions' positions demanded, with all the ensuing administrative work. I didn't think that was for me, or where my heart lay.

Up until now I had mostly worked in government schools, in city and country NSW. This time, for some reason, I wondered if I might find a Home Economics teaching position in a private school. So, for the first time in my life, I looked in the Careers section of *The Sydney Morning Herald*. This was quite different to applying for a transfer within the Department of Education. I remember buying the *SMH* that Saturday and taking it home. I remember sitting at my kitchen table, opening up to the Education pages and skimming the columns of advertisements.

Only private schools advertised in *The Herald* in those days. I was looking for the right subject heading: *Home Economics*. Then I saw it. The advertisement jumped off the page at me.

CHRISTIAN STUDIES TEACHER

Pennant Hills High School

Full time & part time position

I read the details and I knew. I knew right then that this was my new job! My heart had leapt as I read the job title and the school name. But why would a job I wasn't looking for excite me so much? As I think about it now, I realise that there must have been a deep, unexpressed longing in me for an integration of my two passions: one teaching; the other, God.

I had been teaching now for fifteen years in a variety of city and country high schools. I'd had one year off for good behaviour, when I travelled extensively and lived, for a time, in England. Now, eleven years later, I was still enjoying teaching. It was my other passion that may have had the biggest pull. It definitely coloured what I did – both at school and away from it. For as long as I could remember, my consciousness had been full of the reality of God. I had become a Christian at high school and many of the decisions I had made in life were influenced by that first loyalty.

At every school I had taught in I had been involved in ministry to students, through the Inter School Christian Fellowship. I loved interacting with young people in this less formal arena, dealing with content that held eternal significance. While at Auburn Girls High I had been active in the ISCF Regional Committee as well. I enjoyed the extra-curricular events that brought the girls in my small ISCF into contact with other schools. These events included early morning breakfasts, training days, conferences and inter-school camps. The advertisement in my hands spoke of a teaching position that attracted my very core. I would be in a **classroom**, but I would work for local churches. I would teach, but I would teach teenagers about **God**. I knew something of Pennant Hills High too, having visited the school a number of times a decade before. This was the dream job I hadn't even dreamt of!

I had heard something of people being employed as Scripture teachers in high schools over the past few years. The role had been pioneered by people such as Ed Vaughn and Fran Penny. But I had also heard that one of them had been given an office, in an old store room, under a stair well! This seemed like the lowest position you could have in a school. It hadn't appealed to me one bit. But this job was for a '**Christian Studies Teacher**'. It was all in the title. That alone had made a world of difference to my inner response. I could already tell that this teaching position held a significant place within the school.

I knew I was well qualified; 15 years teaching experience spoke for itself! My ongoing involvement in ISCF demonstrated my ability to communicate spiritual matters. That I had been a Director on ISCF Leadership Conferences would demonstrate my leadership and organisational skills. I had a theological diploma. Yes, the qualifications were right. I had only one question, just one: What was the salary? I had recently bought a house in Western Sydney and I couldn't afford a big drop in pay. I knew that in some of these Scripture positions teachers were classified as youth workers, attracting a salary that was less than half a teacher's wage. I knew I wouldn't apply, couldn't apply, if the pay was too low.

Process

A name and phone number were given for enquiries. I rang Warwick Wilson. His voice was friendly. Warwick quickly established that the salary was based on the same salary structure as the Department of Education. Teachers would be paid according to their training and experience. It couldn't have been any better! My salary would be the same as it was now. Warwick also gave me a brief overview of the job and its history. Two teachers were needed, one full time, the other part time. I was excited all over again. I could afford to make the change. This **was** my new job. I knew it. I couldn't wait for it to happen.

But why was I so ready to jump into the employ of a group of churches I knew so little about? I probably need to go back another ten years, to when I returned home from England at the end of 1978. I didn't go back to the classroom that next year; well, not in a teachers' role. In 1979 and 1980 I worked for Scripture Union as an ISCF staff worker. I visited many schools over those two years, encouraging Christian teachers and training and disciplining young people. Pennant Hills had been one of those schools. It had been a joy to combine my two passions then, and I knew it would be again. This new role was still in a classroom, but in one school, not many. That was even better. So, having made a similar life-changing journey into full-time Christian ministry ten years before, it was easy for me to do it again.

I cut the advertisement out of the paper and showed it to some friends, and to my family. I listened to the feedback. It was all very positive. All I had to do now was apply. I hadn't done that before —write up a resume and sit in front of an interview panel. That seemed scary. I needed three references too. I would ask my minister, Simon Manchester. Simon had known me for almost three years as a member of his congregation since I had moved to the west. I would ask Ken Fenton, a minister in Tamworth, NSW. I had worked with Ken on ISCF Leadership Conferences in the north-west. He was the Scripture Union staff worker for the northwest region. And I would ask Rick Allen-Jordan. He had been the ISCF staff worker with whom I had worked most closely with while at Auburn Girls High. Rick was about to take up a new position with Scripture Union in New Zealand.

There are words that people say that you never forget. Sometimes the words are spoken, and you catch them in your mind as they pass. Sometimes the words are written down and you can keep them – in substance and in form. The kept words can speak again, every time you read them. I still have the references that these three men wrote for me. I can't say that I have looked at them very often, as they have been filed away in a grey folder of personal documents. But as I reread them now, the words make me smile on the inside. They do their work again. Not for an interview panel this time, but for me. I am pleased that I kept these words, because now, 28 years later, they speak to me of relationships and the words hold a sense of history; the history of a time and a place that these men were part of; the history of me, as I embarked on a journey into the Christian Studies classroom.

The references that arrived gave me courage. All I had to do now was compile a resume. This has never been an easy task for me. The facts about training and experience are straight forward, but putting my talents and skills on paper, highlighting my successes, I always find difficult. It's hard to applaud your own accomplishments. But write a resume I did. I remember showing it to my friends to get some feedback. Steve was an engineer with the DMR and had been in management for a few years. I thought he would know about such things. After reading my resume Steve said it was too short; I hadn't explained what was involved in some of the ministry roles I had mentioned; I needed to explain it in more depth. That made sense, I realised, as the people who would read these pages would not know me at all, and may not be familiar with the ministries and organisations I had made reference to. It needed more detail. So my two pages became four pages, with more specific detail this time. Finally, there it was, a summary of my training, working life and church involvement on four pages!

In time, I received a phone call to inform me that I would be required for an interview; I had made the short list of candidates! Did I mention that I was excited? The interview was to take place in the home of the Rev.

Neil Flower, at Thornleigh. Neil was the Chairman of the Christian Education Committee. My interview was at 5.00pm, after a couple of other applicants.

With no preparation other than choosing a suitable outfit, I was ready.

Rev Neil Flower began,

"If you were to die after you leave here tonight, and stand before God, on what basis would God let you into heaven?"

This first question surprised me and I was amused. I had done the evangelism course that used this question as a stimulus! I felt like saying just that, but I realised they actually wanted me to answer the question. Neil Flower was checking to see that I really was a Christian. This was a necessary place to start.

Five people sat opposite me; five - four men, one woman. This could have been a job interview for a corporate manager. I was also asked how I would explain the gospel to a teenager. Nobody had asked me that recently. I searched my mind and carefully chose my words. Questions were asked about how I would handle matters of discipline with students. Joost asked me if I was happy to continue the Camping Program initiated by the current teacher. I spoke of the weeks and weekends that I had spent, with teams and students, at ISCF Conferences and camps over the years. Yes, that would come quite naturally.

The panel asked me a question about my devotional life. I told them that I used Scripture Union notes daily, as I knew they would want to hear this. Or maybe I just said that I used SU notes, which implied daily, but in reality it was sometimes less than daily; sometimes with big gaps. But I wasn't quite ready to be that honest with my devotional habits. Someone asked if it would be too far to travel from Blacktown. It wasn't. And I doubted if any of the interview panel had been out my way recently.. Just that the interview went for a long time.

I don't remember too much more, the sun was fading by the time I left. There were three more people to be interviewed the next day and I would be informed of the outcome after that weekend. It would be a long wait.

The Committee must have been influenced by Simon's advice, "*I urge you to nab McNab!*" because they did!

I was so excited. I rang Mum first, then others. This was news worth sharing. A letter of appointment was sent out covering some of the areas that were discussed in the interview. It contained details of salary and the role expectations of each teacher. It was here that I first experienced the grace that would characterise this Committee. My theological training was counted along with my educational training. For the first time I would be paid as a four-year-trained teacher.

People

At my end, I began the bitter-sweet task of telling people that I was leaving Auburn Girls High. It was important to get the order right: first the Principal, then the Home Economics Mistress, Margaret, my colleagues, and finally my students. It was October so I was able to give the school plenty of notice to find a replacement. Colleagues said they would miss me. So did my students. (Yr 12 had already left to do exams, and they didn't know that theirs would be the last senior Home Science class I would ever teach.) My Year 11 Textiles class had assumed that I would take them through to the HSC exams in 1990. They wanted to know who would teach them. It would probably be a younger teacher, Miss Spring, who had not yet had a senior class. That satisfied them and I knew they would like her.

It's only when you leave a job that you hear some of the nicest things people will ever say about you. It had happened when I left Gunnedah High, my first teaching appointment, after three years. Now again, at

Auburn, some lovely, lovely words from the Principal, and from my Head Teacher. Margaret, had taught me as a senior student at North Ryde High School, so we went back a long way. And words from my students; those dear girls that made Auburn Girls High the incredible place that it was in the '80s; girls of varied ethnic background, of varying ability; girls with a generous spirit.

Some Year 9 students organised a class card that they all signed. It was a large red card, one of those jumbo cards produced at farewells. But it was the very SIZE of the card that was a measure of the girls' generous hearts. The words on this card might be the oldest of any that I have kept from students. The words I read in that red card speak of this enjoyment.

"It has been a pleasure to have you for Textiles this year, and it will be very sad to see you go." And, "I hope you will miss us as much as I will miss you."

But it was a much smaller card that surprised and touched me the most. It was a card from just one student in Year 8, with a gift. Some of the students in that class had been argumentative, but her words spoke of a different experience. Her words were very special and unexpected.

"Roses are red, violets are blue"…

I can't remember the gift. But I have kept her words and by them I remember; I remember Dania.

At the end of the Committee meetings Neil Flower organised for me to meet the current teacher, Marty Rowe, before the end of the school year, and also the principal of Pennant Hills High. Marty phoned and invited me to his home one evening. This would be a great opportunity to find out so much more about the Christian Studies position from the inside, and about Marty himself. He lived near Pennant Hills Oval. It was an old brick house. I remember being impressed, and commenting on the new pine kitchen. Marty, a former carpenter had built it for his wife, Helen. No wonder it had the distinct feel of being handcrafted. Marty had a gentle presence. He was young, with two small children and a baby. Marty had a close-cropped beard. He had been the pioneer teacher of Christian Studies at Pennant Hills since 1985, a hard role to forge. It was now time for Marty to step away from a job that had consumed him, and do something different. He was going back to building and construction. The Rowe family were packing up and moving to the Northern Territory, to work with an Aboriginal community. This would be a big move with a wife and young family.

Marty had been trained by Fusion and had worked as a youth worker with Fusion at their Drop-in Centre in Hornsby. He and Helen knew my good friends, Janet and Winston Westcott, who had also done ministry training with Fusion, a para-church organisation, specialising in ministry to youth and families. It was nice to have this one link. Marty asked me what I had 'done'. This was a hard question. I didn't have the youth worker credentials that he had. I was a teacher. So I mentioned my various ISCF activities, and that I had worked for Scripture Union for two years. I also added that I had been to Moore College. We really did have very different starting points!

Marty spoke about the impact of the Christian Studies program he had witnessed in the school. Over five years it had been tangible. Teachers had remarked to him that the students were less aggressive towards each other since his classes had started, and that the school had a new tone. Marty spoke particularly of the class of '87. They had been one of those special year groups. Both the school captains in 1987 were Christians, as were many of the prefects. Their results in the HSC exams were far above the norm. There were so many outstanding results that somebody from the Department of Education came out to the school to see what might have produced this outstanding result.

The only thing they all had in common was that they were all Christians. I smiled. I knew personally of the great students at Pennant Hills High. When I was an ISCF staff worker, I visited Pennant Hills ISCF on a number of occasions. I had been the Bible speaker at their weekend camp and had visited a planning meeting, in the home of their ISCF teacher, Sandy. The Pennant Hills High kids I had met then impressed me too. It seemed that God had been smiling on Pennant Hills High for many years.

Marty told me briefly about the Camps he had run in the school. There was one for each year group 7-9. He also ran ISCF Camps on top of all the classes he had taught each week. Life must have been more than full for Marty Rowe. I expected it would for me too! He invited me to a Leaders' Weekend that he was running in the Southern Highlands for senior students. It would be a good place for me to meet some of the students.

And so, a few weeks later I spent a Saturday at Marty's camp. I watched and I listened. He had such a natural, gentle rapport with his students. Marty had known these young people for five years. Some of them had become Christians over this time. He held a very special place in their lives. I was starting to feel slightly overwhelmed at the size of the task and the shoes I had to fill. It would be hard to walk into a school where Marty was known and loved, and into a classroom where he had put his personal stamp.

It was a relaxed day, as Marty taught these young people from the Bible, shared an informal meal, and sat in the afternoon sun, encouraging discussion and sharing faith ideas. I had much to think about on the return journey.

In 1990, the teaching of Christian Studies classes would now be extended to include Year 10 as well. The Committee had taken the big step of expanding the work and trusted God that the finances for a second teacher would come. The position had been advertised along with mine, and a young man had been appointed. I knew it would be good to have someone to work with in this new role. I always enjoyed a task more when I worked with others. It was nice to know I didn't have to go it alone at Pennant Hills High School. I didn't realise then what an amazing blessing this colleague would be to me, and a number of people, over the coming years.

I met Ian Nisbet for the first time at a special gathering of the Committee. This meeting was convened as a supper, as an introduction to the new teachers. I remember being nervous. Ian seemed friendly and keen to be working at PHHS. He would be working with me for two days a week. Ian was completing his Education Diploma at university as part of a psychology degree on the other days. The other young man present was Geoff Broughton, with whom Ian shared a house. Geoff was the youth worker at St Matthew's Anglican Church. Geoff would also be coming into the school to help teach some classes with us.

We had supper, after which the curriculum was discussed. The Curriculum Sub-Committee had been working on the new course for Year 10 classes. These people were highly qualified: a university lecturer in Education, a former principal, a lecturer at TAFE, a teacher of RE in a Catholic School. They had consulted with people in other states where Religious Education was taught. It seemed well researched and compiled. Ian and I were given a copy. I cast my eye over it, *'Thanking, Caring, Serving, Forgiving, Belonging, Remembering,'* and wondered how I could make that interesting and engaging? But these were only my first thoughts. I knew Year 10 would definitely be a challenge. I agreed with Ian that it would be good to get together and discuss the Year 10 lessons.

During the school holidays, I looked again at the Year 10 curriculum document. There were 20 pages of it, divided into columns. I looked more closely at the content on the early pages.

There was very little here for me to get my teeth into. I flipped through the rest of the document.

Content included:

Understanding our Australian identity, What is gratitude? Lack of caring, Institutions and people who care, Beliefs about caring, Hopes and ideals, Decision making in society, Moral codes, Moral principles, The structure of society, Life and Living, The search for meaning, In touch with God.

Hmm?

The resources listed included:

Red Cross, Bible verses, Animal Farm, Hamlet, Henry VIII, Joni film, pamphlets from government departments, and some Christian biographies.

Hmm?

This was awful, just awful. This might have been what they taught in Christian/church schools, but it seemed to me these people hadn't talked to a 16yr old in a while! I was unable to prepare anything for Year 10. What would I do? The junior course was more straightforward, and Marty had left plenty of resources for us to use for these classes. At least this didn't seem so daunting. The Committee had been very active in securing two new teachers. Their efforts and zeal were apparent. But when it came to stepping into a classroom, here the Committee's influence waned. That's when they handed responsibility over to us, the teachers, their chosen representatives. And it was in the classroom that Ian and I who would try to wrestle that difficult curriculum into submission.

A Present

I realised I needed to create a good impression at Pennant Hills High right from the beginning- particularly with the staff. I wanted them to think I knew what I was doing. So when Mum had asked me what I wanted for Christmas I answered readily,

"A briefcase."

I hadn't owned a briefcase since I left high school. As a Home Economics teacher I had carried a basket, a large blue, plastic basket with a collapsible handle. The open, rigid shape was perfect for all manner of resources that I needed to take to class: food, table settings, flowers, fabrics, cardboard charts, books, and occasionally my camera. I thought my new role would be more about books and folders than food and fabric. A briefcase would definitely create a smoke screen until I really did know what I was doing! Mum told me to choose what I wanted. I found a briefcase, made of leather-look black vinyl, that I was happy to own. It had a modern look about it, being rectangular with solid square corners and opening like a suitcase. It closed with two gold clasps and had a combination lock. Very impressive indeed!

Soon the end of January was rolling around. The school holidays were over (and with little in my hands to teach Year 10) my new career had begun.

1990

Chapter 2

I walked into Pennant Hills High School that first day carrying my black briefcase. It would leave with me ten years later; but I wasn't to know that at the time. I was just worried about surviving my first week! Day one was a Pupil Free Day (as they were called then), so I had a chance to get my bearings before students arrived at my classroom door the following day.

Pennant Hills High School was a familiar place to me. Having visited the school before on behalf of Scripture Union helped me to visualise the new environment I would work in- the only sure thing in my new venture.

A friendly buzz could be heard as I approached the library door, with staff of almost ninety, assembling in the library and exchanging stories of holidays. I caught Nikky Vanderhout's eye and said hello. Nikky was a member of a local church, and she knew I was coming. She had been teaching Maths at Pennant Hills High for many years now, the only person I thought I would know. The meeting began with the Principal welcoming everybody back to a new school year. He welcomed over a dozen new teachers including two Mr Wilsons, both Head Teachers. I recognised Ian Wilson as a Science teacher I had worked with at Seven Hills High in 1977.

Peter Noble went on to relate the successes of Year 12 students in the HSC exam from 1989. There were many students to be proud of, and specific teachers were named and encouraged to share in the achievement. This had the first difference I noticed to Auburn Girls, which was not a school of numerous academic achievers. The principal spoke until recess, without notes or prompts. He only stopped when the bell rang.

"Is it recess already?" he asked.

This was my introduction to Peter Noble's oratory prowess.

Having been introduced to the staff at the beginning of the meeting, a couple of Christian teachers came across and said hello. Peter Kneale was an English teacher, and Gordon taught Industrial Arts. I also spied, and said hello to John Fowler, whom I had known as an ISCF teacher at Chatswood High School.

I was very keen to receive a copy of my timetable that first day. I was told it would change within a few weeks, however, the final format looked like this:

- Yr 7 x 8

- Yr 8 x 5

- Yr 9 x 5

- Yr 10 x 4

Mondays and Thursdays were very full, and Thursday was sports afternoon. I taught all the Year 7 classes, which I was pleased with. I had three Year 10 classes, Ian had five. I had 25 lessons to teach each week, and Ian had 15 lessons over three days. This timetable would keep us both very busy.

Ian asked me the first day,

"What do you think of the Year 10 curriculum?"

"It's hard. I don't know how I'm going to use it!"

"I'm so pleased to hear that," said Ian, laughing. I could hear his relief. "I thought that you would have been the sort of person to have all your lessons organised," he continued. "I was feeling very underprepared!"

I smiled at the thought that Ian assumed I would be super-organised, and I was amused to think we already had something in common – fear and dread of the Year 10 curriculum! I knew then that despite the age difference, (early twenties and late thirties), we were on the same wavelength about communicating with young people.

At the first opportunity we went to visit the Christian Studies classroom, a portable room next to the canteen. There were four portable classrooms in this area, positioned between a few tall gum trees near and the basketball courts. Our room was 3P4. It was very bare and carried none of what Marty may have used to decorate the walls, maybe all tidied up at the end of the 1989. I wanted to make the room inviting and give it a new personality. I asked Ian to help me move all the desks into a U shape, so there was space in the middle of the room. This way the second row was also the back row; a more interactive shape than four rows of tables facing the front. The room needed some strong visuals on the walls. Posters were the first option. Ian agreed. That day I went to Koorong, a local Christian bookstore, to find suitable posters. I told Ian I wanted to avoid the ones that said:

"*There's nothing God and I can't do today,*" with the picture of a cute little kitten; or "*Smile, God loves me,*" with a picture of a chimpanzee.

There were a lot of these images around at the time. They had never appealed to me, and I thought they would detract from the reasoned, relevant approach to faith that I wanted to foster. But at Koorong I was disappointed with the range available. I left with just two small posters with nature scenes on them.

The next day Year 7 arrived, along with senior students. After an assembly and a Peer Support session, the first Year 7 class lined up at my classroom door. Little did these youngest students know that I too was somewhat overwhelmed by this big new school and all it would demand of me.

I did survive my first week, one lesson at a time. With every new day new classes would arrive outside 3P4. Every lesson, 30 more students would line up, all of whom I had to get to know. After a full week they numbered close to 700 names and faces. The faces were easy to remember, the names much harder. With each class I put a course summary on the board, and asked them to copy it into their books as a title page.

This activity kept students busy, and some were creative with their bookwork. I also played a name game with Year 7s and Year 8s, to begin to imprint their names on my brain. This certainly helped.

With two new teachers employed the Committee wanted to introduce Ian and I to the wider Pennant Hills church community – this included churches in Thornleigh, Beecroft, Cherrybrook, Pennant Hills and West Pennant Hills. Within that first week we were asked for photos, and also a brief description of each of our backgrounds. And so, our first photo shoot took place, in Ian's front yard. The house Ian shared with Geoff Broughton was an old cottage on New Line Road, in the grounds of St Matthews. I would get to know both Ian and Geoff better in that house, as we would sit drinking coffee in the lounge room, planning and praying for the work, on many a school afternoon.

We had been asked to compile our own biography to go in the brochure. We both commented that it was hard to write about yourself in third person; about your background and why you were suitable to hold such a position. So Ian suggested that we write each other's background story! He wrote one for me. It was hilarious. And I just happen to have kept his amusing words, my first souvenir from Pennant Hills High. Ian starts with an obvious correction of my name, which the school was already spelling wrong.

"Helen McNabb is a teacher of wide experience. She comes to us after spending the last six years teaching Peace Studies on a commune in Nimbin, NSW. Prior to this she spent five years as a guest of the Department of Corrective Services after she applied her calligraphy skills to manufacturing her own money. Helen's interests are astrology and crystals, the Gay and Lesbian Liberation front and also religion. She is looking forward to meeting your children at Pennant Hills High and would gratefully accept any donations towards her ministry."

"Ian Nisbet and I were going to have fun working, and laughing, together!"

CHRISTIAN STUDIES NEWSLETTERS

As teachers employed by PHCEC, we were required to give regular feedback to the churches that financially contributed to the work. (Geoff Broughton called this group the way it sounds phonetically, *fekek*, and that's how we always referred to it.) I always enjoyed the process of putting onto paper all that had happened at school. It was a joy to tell the stories I was seeing played out in class, at ISCF, or on a Camp. The newsletters varied in size and style over the years, growing from an A4 folded page to an A3 folded page; from using an electronic typewriter to pages that were computer generated. I was not familiar with Microsoft Publisher at this time, and my 'cut and paste' was always done with scissors and glue. The newsletters were always printed in black and white, and while I didn't keep copies of all of them, I still have a few in my possession. I hope you will enjoy reading these little fragments of history, when they turn up from time to time in this story, as they appeared back then. The newsletters will help to tell the story.

Differences

It didn't take long for me to notice some obvious differences between Auburn Girls and Pennant Hills High. One of the first and very obvious occurred because of the staffroom I shared with the Music staff. Students who were signing up for Concert Band and Stage Band had to come to see the Music teachers and be given an instrument from the storeroom, just near the staffroom. Auburn Girls High operated under The Disadvantaged Schools Program. There the small Music Department operated out of one room, using only recorders, a guitar or two, and newly aquired keyboards and some percussion. That's all! A small community band had some students from the high school in it, but also adults from the Auburn community who played all the instruments needed to develop a full sound. At Pennant Hills High, instruments were stacked floor to ceiling on the shelved storeroom: trombomes, saxaphones, clarinets, flutes, violins, guitars and trumpets; not including drum kits and percussion, stored in the classrooms. The difference between the 'haves' and the 'have nots' was glaringly obvious to me. The disparity of resources between state high schools made me angry, and it took some time to get used to this new abundance.

Another difference, that had nothing to do with social class, was also immediately obvious, on a rainy day. At Auburn Girls, the old, double brick buildings had been built with **corridors** going down the middle of each school block. You were sheltered from winds and rain when inclement weather arrived. In heavy rain, you might not need to put your face outside into the rain until it was time to go home. At Pennant Hills High there were no corridors. Every classroom, and staffroom, opened staight outside onto a quad or walkway, straight into the prevailing conditions. Everytime you had to change rooms you were 'in the elements', and when it rained, dodging rain and wind gusts, keeping out of puddles and overflows from the walkways on the upper levels, with all your teaching resources and an umbrella, was quite a feat. The first term of teaching was a particularly rainy one in 1990, and I had a long walk from the staffroom to 3P4 on the other side of the Main Quad. I missed those corridors!

If anything it was a very wet introduction to this new decade. So much so, it made for a photo of a drenched main quad in the 1990 Yearbook.

And then there were the boys! I hadn't had a class with boys in it for over five years. It was an interesting exercise to get them into lines outside 3P4.

"Line up please, two lines. I said two lines."

They pushed and shoved. Walking through two doorways to enter the classroom without coming into contact with someone else could be their first accomplishment of the lesson.

"Adam, don't shove. Slow down."

Some boys were big. They took up a lot of space. Most of the Year 10 boys were tall and well developed and presented a very different presence in the room to the young Year 7's.

"Can you pull your chair in? I need to get past."

The boys were noisy. They did everything loudly. Their vocal interactions often needed subduing.

"Karl and Michael, quiet please, and face the front."

The boys were active. They liked to move, in any direction; on the desk, under the desk, over the desk, around the desk! They fidgeted with pencil cases, pens, rubbers or toy figures. They liked to throw things, mostly paper. Crumpled missiles sometimes made their way into the bin at the front of the room. Cheering erupted if the paper plane made its desired landing! If it failed,

"Please pick it up!"

The boys were smelly! Hot sweaty bodies tumbled into 3P4 after the end of lunchtime on hot summer days; physically spent, it was time to engage their brain, if possible. Note to self,

"Open the windows, and don't get too close!"

The boys could be disorganised. To help with this, I kept some sets of books in the cupboard, to make sure they would arrive onto their desks at the right time.

"Marcus, can you hand out the books please?"

The boys got bored easily. If a lesson succeeded, it was a measure of how well the boys had been engaged.

"Well done today. See you next week."

The boys were curious. They had lots of questions; zany questions; good questions.

"Miss, if there is life on other planets, does God love them too?"

I liked the boys.

Swimming Carnival

During Term 1, it is always nice to stop lessons for the day and enjoy the school Swimming Carnival. Teachers as well as students look forward to this relaxed, yet full day of competition. I realised as I cast my eye around the grandstand and across the swimming blocks, that I knew many of these young faces from class. It was the pupils in the youngest years who were happy to talk and claim me as their teacher. I too enjoyed the interaction, especially seeing who among each year group were the best swimmers. It's not something you readily know about students, as they sit before you; what their talents are or what area they excel in.

Here was something that I could talk to students about, away from the swimming arena.

Three short words

Working at Pennant Hills meant I was now closer to Mum and Dad, and I could visit them more easily after school. A couple of times in the staffroom, Ian heard me say, "I'm going to visit my Dad, then have dinner with Mum."

It was always hard to know how to broach the fact of my parents. One day Ian asked, "Are your parents divorced?"

"No. My father had a stroke."

At least that got that out of the way.

My father had *'had a stroke'* at the end of 1987; a debilitating stroke. After his initial recovery, he was sent from Concord Hospital to Lady Davidson Rehabilitation Centre where he underwent rehabilitation on his speech, his right arm and right leg. Improvements would be slow in coming, we were told. As a family we had held out hope that Dad would eventually be able to come home, and be cared for by Mum. We held our breath for this outcome.

I remember the afternoon Mum shared the therapist's report with me. All that day it was an agonising wait for this vital news. As I hung on her every word, I heard from Mum that the medical team considered it too much for her to care for Dad; he would be cared for elsewhere; he would not be coming home. The knife of grief instantly pierced my heart. But this *is his home*! Tears welled up. I was inconsolable.

"I've already done my crying," said Mum. "Don't cry, love." But cry I did.

A whole new way of living began for us all that day. For my brother and I, we now related to Mum in one place, and Dad in another. For Mum it must have felt like her marriage was, in some ways, over; but in other ways it had only just begun. Her vow to love *in sickness and in health*' was to take on new proportions. Mum would need all that she was made of to endure the next who-knew-how-many years? But she is made of strong stuff, my Mum, and she drew on the deep resources within, and found in her faith, real sustenance to keep her going.

After Mum's lengthy search to find accommodation for him, Dad was finally settled into a nursing facility in Marsfield, just one suburb away. St Catherine's Villa was run by the Sisters of Charity. Dad's Catholic faith had been what had opened the door to this local health care institution. He was accommodated in the wing known as Bethany. Bethany is the biblical town where Jesus' good friends lived. In the form of nursing nuns and staff, those friends of Jesus live there still.

Mum had been given a book to read over this time of transition, *When Half Is Whole*, and she was encouraged to let us read it too. The title of the book was a powerful one, and well described the situation in which family members of stroke victims find themselves. Half of Dad was gone – the half that had led an independent life at home; the half that walked and talked, climbed ladders, painted houses, caught buses into the city for business; the half that had put petrol in the car, gone on picnics and holidays, tended his garden beds and pruned the roses, and went to church; the half that spoke with his wife and children. The half of Dad that we now had couldn't speak or use the right side of his body, and he now spent his days in a wheelchair. But he understood our conversation and the things that were going on. Dad was better off than some at Bethany, being mobile in his wheelchair. He could wheel himself to his room, out into the well-kept garden, into the dining room and to chapel - which he attended every day.

Dad's therapy continued on his right leg and arm, but not on his speech. He had given up in frustration in the early months, resenting the seemingly childish action of blowing into party whistles and seeing no result. We had a variety of ways to talk to Dad, but it was always hard when we needed to ask him a question. Dad had just one perfectly formed word, which he would use to get our attention. When used over and over we knew he was agitated about something, and we gave him our full attention. When I hear myself use that single word, as an exclamation, even now, I can hear Dad's voice in it!

It had taken me over twelve months to be able to leave Bethany after a visit, to say goodbye to Dad there, without tears in my eyes. When I walked away, down the long corridor and out into the car park, the knife in my heart was twisted each time. But it's amazing what awful things you can get used to, when 'awful' becomes your reality; when awful provides the shape of your weekly, and for Mum, her daily, routine. By 1990 we were used to this dreadful reality that had settled on our family.

I didn't say all this to Ian Nisbit that day in the staff room, just that Dad had '*had a stroke*'. Those three short words conveyed so much.

The introductory lesson for each class, kept me going for a whole week, whereby it was time to start thinking about, and teaching the curriculum. One of the maxims I had come across in my teaching career while at Auburn Girls High was:

I HEAR, I FORGET

I SEE, I REMEMBER

I DO IT, I UNDERSTAND

This had made a big impact on me, as had the accompanying statistics. I had been stunned to hear that people remember only 10% of anything they read once; 20% of what they see; and 30% of what they hear.

Memory of content increases as these approaches are combined. If I hear and see content I can remember 50% of it. And *doing* something associated with learning raises the percentage of recall to 80%. These were astounding figures to encounter well into my teaching career. So *hearing, seeing* and *doing* must go together. Students need to hear content, they need something to look at, and they need something to do. Teaching a practical subject like Home Economics, these insights made great sense to me. We did a lot of 'doing' in my old classroom.

It was those three lines of wisdom above that would drive my methodology in my Christian Studies classroom, at Pennant Hills High. It was only the content that would be different in this new classroom of mine. The lessons needed to be varied and very 'hands on', with things to hear, see and do. A Christian Studies exercise book would be an important resource to record, in a variety of ways, the content covered in class over a year.

So, **how to teach** was not a problem for me. But **how to teach Biblical material** - this I had to think through. I had learnt good Bible content in every church I had attended over three decades, as well as at L'Abri and Moore College. But I had learnt *how to handle the Bible creatively* from Scripture Union. Within SU ranks, I had seen modelled, again and again, interactive methods of communicating Bible truth; on Beach Missions, at Camps and through ISCF I had experienced methods of Bible teaching that made the Bible come alive, for young and old alike. I knew I would employ these methods in my new classroom. These methods included hearing, seeing and doing. With their emphasis on creative Bible teaching, Scripture Union was on the forefront of educational practise, and had been for years.

Both Ian and I had to teach each of our lessons multiple times. When you repeat a lesson, you soon know if a lesson is working or not. If it feels slow or ordinary the first time, it feels that way **every** time. I realised, very quickly, that I now had the rare opportunity to fine tune a lesson after the first one, so that it would finally 'hum', and the content could have maximum impact. This was the very great benefit of teaching Christian Studies. Most teachers never have this luxury, and make changes, where necessary, in lessons for the following year. I, on the other hand, could make changes in a lesson for the following day. I often did this in that first year .

There was a curriculum document for Year 7-9, but this was now five years old, and Marty had made great progress with it, adapting the lessons to his own style. I really just followed Marty's overview of the year, term by term. He had left a whole year full of lesson outlines, with student worksheets. It was that filing cabinet drawer full of lessons that was my place to start (not the curriculum). I would read over each lesson, see how Marty had done it and then maybe adapt it. I liked to create my own worksheets. Doing this I was grappling with every lesson myself, and every new topic, while still having Marty's wealth of resources at my fingertips.

The **Yrs 7 and 8 syllabus** proved easy to get my head around. The curriculum contained a lot of concrete learning, with stories from both the Old and New Testaments. Genesis 1-3, Jesus' life, work and teaching, Noah, the Ten Commandments. I knew the content, I just had to work out *how* to present it. I was pleased to be teaching all the Year 7 classes. I would get to know this whole Year 7 cohort, and these students would begin their Christian Studies lessons having the same experience and foundation.

One of the most enjoyable units of work I did with **Year 7** was looking at the story contained in Genesis 1-3. This Creation story produced innumerable questions, some of which I could answer; some I couldn't. *"But what about the dinosaurs?"*

I invited the Christian science teachers, Ian Wilson and Jeff Cox, to visit 3P4 for a lesson. They gave their understanding of Genesis 1-3, and how they understood science fitted in with the first chapters of the Bible. They attempted to answer the questions that had stumped me. My scientific colleagues weren't able to come to every class, but those students who heard them speak had their world expanded. I hoped that would have given the Bible a credible face.

"But what about the dinosaurs?" It was one of those questions that just wouldn't lie down!

It only takes three chapters for this world, which God created and gave to men and women to populate and enjoy, to be ruined. The Year 7s were drawn to the story line; to the simple beauty of Genesis 1; to the wonder of the creation of people in Genesis 2; and to the excitement in Genesis 3, with God's enemy arriving on the scene. Students understood the tension it describes and the blaming that occurs after Eve and Adam listen to the snake and disobeyed God.

"What would have happened if they didn't disobey? Would we still be in the garden?" I'd be asked.

"Well if that hadn't happened, do you think their children might have disobeyed, or their children… ? I don't think it would have taken long at all. But it did all start with Adam and Eve, both held accountable and punished by God, and having to leave the Garden as a result."

Theologians call this understanding of paradise lost, of living outside the Garden, the *fallen world*. That was the main thing I wanted the Year 7s to understand. This world is not the way God made it. He didn't create the world with sickness and pain and death. It's an understanding about our world you could miss if you didn't read the first three chapters of the Bible. This understanding becomes a foundation to build on when talking about the bad things we experience in this world, especially with Year 9. It's not the way God planned it and he didn't create these things to hurt us. Don't blame him. But the term *fallen world* is a complex term. Fallen from what? So I simplified it – '**God's world- spoilt**'. That captured it all. That was the concept I wanted Year 7 to go away with.

It was time to finish with the talking and the questions and 'do' something.

For our 'hands - on' activity we would need paper and scissors, coloured pages and glue, and a sense of fun. Year 7 and I would create a **banner**, as a visual memory of those chapters of Genesis they had studied. I bought a roll of brown paper and carefully drew up the large letters. I tore coloured pages from magazines and grouped them into colours. GOD'S WORLD would be done in vibrant colours; SPOILT was completed in black, white and grey.

Over a week all of the Year 7 classes participated in creating a giant collage - in reality a mosaic of coloured paper. Where one class would finish, another class would take over making each letter a different colour.

Finally it was finished and ready to become the banner across the back wall of 3P4. My room was taking on its own personality and speaking of the topics we had covered every time the students entered the room. It was becoming an attractive space for the other classes to learn in as well. I enjoyed this colourful activity, and I enjoyed seeing the Year 7 classes enjoying themselves.

The teaching over, it was time to see how much the students had learnt; again, they had to *do something*. I proposed to give assignments to every grade, with the exception of Year 10. In doing this, I always gave students a wide variety of options to choose from which made the completion more enjoyable.

In the final lesson we had fun watching the movie, 'The God's Must be Crazy'. Marty had this among his lesson plans, and it was a good way to finish the unit of work on Genesis, and talk about when a coke bottle, sent by the 'gods', invades their world, and spoils it. I got some brownie points from the students for this lesson!

This unit of work came after an introductory unit of lessons I put together myself. It was a 'getting to know you' unit before we got into the heavy Bible stuff. The first one was finding out the meaning of everyone's name (from a baby naming book). I loved this lesson as every student got some direct interaction with me. I found out my name means, *Light*. I liked that - *Light*. We looked at what **Jesus**' name means too: *God will save his people*.

I also put together a quiz, 'about me, your Christian Studies teacher'. Students were surprised, and didn't get many answers right, but we had some fun in the process.

"How would you find out those answers if I'd given you those questions as homework? School records, your passport, teachers, friends." They had some good answers. *"We are going to check out things about Jesus using a variety of ways to do that."* So, Year 7 and I had plenty to keep us busy for the year.

Year 8 began with a unit of work on Heroes. It included Noah and Daniel and Joseph. I was already starting to think that these people weren't the heroes of Year 8 students. I remember wrestling with the content about Noah's Ark, to work out what stance I would take here. I decided to have a lessons outside. That would be different. We would examine the dimensions of the ark, to make it more real. So, weather permitting, we all traipsed out to the school oval and stepped out the converted measurement for 100 cubits. This boat was as big as a football field. (Not having seen any cruise liners of recent vintage, these proportions seemed huge!) I started to rethink the whole Heroes unit for next year

I had a new flatmate sharing my home in 1990. Lyndal had been a friend of Rosemary and Karl from church. She had recently been to Moore College, doing the same course of study that I had. Lyndal was looking to go overseas fulltime in the near future. When I was preparing this new content, and I got stuck, I would knock on her door and ask her some deep theological questions: do you believe in a figurative Adam and Eve? Do you understand the Ark was a world-wide event? Some nights we would talk for ages as I sorted these things out in my mind. They were good times.

Discipline

The success of the whole Christian Studies program depended on how well we individual teachers could manage 30 lively students for 40 minutes at a time. It also depended on the support we got from the school. It wasn't long before Ian and I needed help with classroom discipline. It would only take two or three in a class, or even one for that matter, who wanted to sabotage a lesson, to take all the attention and derail the lesson. This could make a class nothing but a chore.

- there was the noisy class, with many students constantly talking;

- there was the rude person; just one or two students with a big personality who would want to derail the lesson, maybe with the use of humour;

- there was the defiant student, who would arrive angry and then try to start an argument;

- and, there was the student who just didn't want to take the Christian Studies lessons seriously.

All of these students could leave us feeling angry or frustrated, deflated or disappointed, or, all of the above!

But we had a great champion in Lyn M, the head-teacher who was assigned to Christian Studies (from Languages area). If we referred a student to Lyn because of their poor behaviour, she would act promptly on it. If it was an afternoon incident, Lyn would deal with the person/s involved the first thing the next morning. From this clear pattern of cause and effect, students knew there were clear consequences for poor behaviour in Christian Studies classes. Lyn M was our supporter at the beginning, in the middle, and at the end of my time at PHHS. As teachers in 1990, Ian and I felt well supported, and without her strong backup and her continuing hands-on discipline the Christian Studies program would not have been as strong as it was over the years.

The **Yr 9 syllabus** was more conceptual, to reflect the bigger things that these teens were thinking about. From just looking at the topic headings, I knew the Year 9 program would be interesting and also a challenge, for me and the students. It started with a unit called *Barriers to Belief*, looking at the reasons why many people don't/can't believe in God. Then there was a unit on Self Esteem.

The Yr 9 unit on *Self Esteem* was something I would have to get my head around. I had never needed to address that issue head on before.

And then there was the **Year 10 syllabus**! What to do? I think Ian and I found a starting point, amongst the very bulky syllabus, that might work. But it proved very hard going. We had a few weeks of 'pulling teeth' with these young people who had known and loved Marty, and who weren't responding well to our attempts to get them thinking. It was awful. Just awful!

So began the journey, but more so a routine. Every week, for the next 40 weeks of the school year, I sat in my study at night and prepared lessons. I pooled the resources I had at my disposal, though sometimes I started from scratch. First I had to get my head around the content, then choose ways to communicate that content with young minds. This usually involved preparing lesson aids, for example worksheets, overhead summaries, finding a video clip, magazine or newspaper article, creating a script to be acted out, finding a poem, or developing props whereby I would entertain the troops!

Four lessons a week, only four, but they needed to be so very well planned and prepared for. I wrote a lesson plan for each of the four lessons. I gave a copy to Ian, for him to use and to make it his own. Ian ended up teaching one lesson behind me, so we could share resources, like the portable TV and videos. That pretty much consumed my spare time throughout that first year.

Year 9

All the while Ian and I made progress with the junior classes, we were always struggling with the Yr 10 lessons. Sometimes it was a win; sometimes it was a loss. We were blessed to have Geoff B as a colleague with some year 9 classes.

Geoff Broughton, as a church youth worker, was keen to come into the school and help us. Geoff, during his first year at St Matts, had taught some Christian Studies classes under Marty's direction. Geoff was a member of PHCEC and could contribute in that forum in a unique way, with his first hand classroom experience. In our first year Ian and I had five and three classes between us, on a Tuesday afternoon, over two periods. Geoff turned up the second Tuesday of Term 1, with an offer we couldn't refuse.

"Choose the six worst kids in your Year 9 classes, and I will make a third class out of them."

Geoff was committing to come in every Tuesday afternoon for the whole year, to share some of the burden with us. I probably shouldn't say 'the worst' students. But there were those who had already showed themselves as wanting a bit more attention, or having a loud approach to classroom communication, as well as those who were just plain ready to derail the lesson. Geoff knew some of these students already, and was quick to make the choice himself,

"You, you and you are coming with me."

These students were quite pleased to be made an exception of, leaving readily with Geoff, whom they knew, to one of the Music rooms or a nearby portable classroom. Six less students in the class did make a big difference. Now we were able to get to know a smaller class more quickly and class discussions became more manageable. Thanks Geoff.

The first Year 9 unit, **Barriers to Belief**, was an opportunity to find out what faith questions the students had. I was keen to do some surveys and gather a list of questions the students were actually asking. It was no good to just assume what they were thinking. I asked for responses under the headings;

WHAT DO YOU THINK GOD IS LIKE?

WHAT DO YOU FIND HARD TO BELIEVE ABOUT GOD?

I WISH GOD COULD SAY SOMETHING ABOUT . . .

I'D LIKE TO ASK GOD THESE QUESTIONS . . .

When all the response sheets were collected in class, I read out the questions that had been asked, just before the lesson finished – not hiding the bold or daring questions either. Some were humorous; some were very serious. This helped students to know some people asked serious questions and others had asked silly questions. They also learnt that I had a sense of humour!

Below are a selection of comments and questions from those first Year 9 classes.

WHAT DO YOU THINK GOD IS LIKE?

I don't have a clue

He is a kind person

He is loving and caring

He always forgives you

God isn't there

God is someone with a grey beard & he is big and strong

I've never seen him

WHAT DO YOU FIND HARD TO BELIEVE ABOUT GOD?

A lot of things

That he created the world

I have not seen him

He never says anything or shows himself

Nothing, because I believe and I want to

There is no real proof that he exists

I'm not sure. I'd like to believe but some things make it hard

He is a mythical creature

I WISH GOD COULD SAY SOMETHING ABOUT . . .

Can you stop war and famine?

Why can't we see you?

How he made the universe

Why do we have AIDS?

Could you help us stop the world's problems?

Why is my family the way it is?

Why do you punish some people and let others live with all the luxuries?

What should I do to trust you more?

I'D LIKE TO ASK GOD THESE QUESTIONS . . .

When will the world end?

Why are there hungry people?

Why do I have trouble with my parents?

Why do we have to die?

Why did he let his own creation go bad?

Why can't you fix the problem?

What is heaven like?

Why do we have war?

Why didn't he give us proof that he existed?

I CAN/CAN'T BELIEVE IN GOD BECAUSE . . .

- *because of Noah's ark, Moses and all those bedtime stories*
- *I don't believe in rubbish (bullcrap)*
- *I've read the Bible and I believe that Jesus is the only way to eternal life*
- *I have not seen him*
- *He's not true*
- *Otherwise how would the world have got there*

Year 9 sure had a lot of questions!

Every class contained some similar faith questions, and then some unique, questions. At the end of this survey I read all the students responses aloud in class, answering some questions quickly on the spot.

I explained that I would answer the most frequently asked questions in class, over the next weeks. For my five Year 9 classes, there were different issues that I had to research and prepare for each class. This got me digging into reference books, concordances and the Bible. I certainly had my work cut out for me with Year 9.

YEAR 7 BIOGRAPHIES

One of the things Christians do well is to tell the stories of other Christians who have lived remarkable lives. These stories serve as encouragements to us, whatever age we live in. Three names had been included in the Year 7 program: Nicky Cruz, Corrie Ten Boom and Brother Andrew. Marty had been in the habit of reading the story of Nicky Cruz, **Run Baby Run** to his Year 7 classes. A well-thumbed copy of this book, with places marked and notes made, was among the books I had inherited.

I had not read a book aloud to an audience for a long time – if ever! This took a little while to get used to, but I got plenty of practice, reading this story to all my eight classes. This certainly reduced the relentless preparing of new lessons for year 7 in Term 4. But much more was happening than a few early nights for me. The story of Nicky Cruz is as life-transforming as you will ever get, and each week students were transported out of safe and comfortable Pennant Hills, with themes of witchcraft, family breakdown, teenage rebellion, gang violence, good versus evil, and finally redemption.

Nicky was born and raised in Puerto Rico by witchcraft-practicing parents. Bloodshed, occult practise and fear were common elements in his young life. Nicky suffered severe mental and physical abuse from his parents, once being declared by his mother, " **You are the Son of Satan.**" At the age of 15, his father sent Nicky to live with his older brother in New York, to give him a fresh start. Instead, full of anger and rage, Nicky chose to make it on his own.

Nicky's loneliness was not disguised by the toughness he showed on New York streets. At the age of 16, Nicky joined one of the toughest street gangs in the city – the Mau Maus (named after a bloodthirsty African tribe). These gang members and their girls became his family. His life with the gang became an endless account of drugs, alcohol, sex and violence. But late at night Nicky would go back to his room and to a loneliness that made his heart ache.

This storyline kept Year 7 enthralled as I read an account of a boy/youth who was encountering life as far from life in Pennant Hills life as they could imagine. This book was probably not written for a 12-13 year old audience, but I think my students appreciated the brutal reality I was exposing them to, knowing this was a true story. There was only one part of the storyline I watered down for their ears, details of a sexual encounter.

Reading this story, page after page, lesson after lesson, I became very familiar with the text, and with where to place emphasis or use my voice with added expression. I could hear the improvement myself, and enjoyed reading out loud. I was learning to read ahead, to use a couple of seconds to look up and observe the students' faces. They were listening intently, even those with their heads on the desk. Most students watched me as I formed every word. Their eyes told me they were living the story; a story that had grabbed them and carried them along. A question would come as students walked in the door,

"Are we reading more of the story today?"

I usually began reading standing up, walking across the room for variation, and eventually, in almost fluid motion, so as not to be a distraction, I would sit on a chair or the teacher's desk.

The action in New York continued. Within six months Nicky Cruz became president of the Mau Maus. He was arrested many times by the police, but never made it to gaol, despite one court-ordered psychiatrist pronouncing Nicky's fate as, **"headed to prison, the electric chair, and hell."**

Nicky's life was interrupted when he met a street-preacher named David Wilkerson. No matter what he received from Nicky, the preacher showed Nicky unconditional love. No matter what he received at Nicky's hand, David Wilkerson left Nicky with one truth; "Nicky, Jesus loves you."

After verbal abuse and humiliation; "I just wanted to tell you, Jesus loves you."

After threats of physical violence; "You could cut me into a thousand pieces, and every piece would cry out, 'Jesus loves you'."

Year 7 were hearing these words, from the mouth of David Wilkerson, and maybe for many, for the first time; **"Jesus loves you."** It was a powerful and moving narrative to read.

Eventually this message did penetrate Nicky's heart. If you haven't read this autobiography I will allow you the experience of reading how God pursues Nicky, with the relentless passion and purpose that love stories are made of. Nicky's transformation is obvious as he in turn pursues the God who softened his hard heart. Nicky went from gang-leader to evangelist in just four years, returning to the streets of New York where he had once been feared. Nicky Cruz's message of God's unconditional love has been transforming the hearts and lives of people since then; from New York to all parts of the world; from the 1960s and into the third millennium. My students recall this story, long after many other lessons have been forgotten.

"I remember a few things from high school. I wish I could remember more. I loved metal work and drama but the other classes were a bit boring. One thing I do remember was Christian Studies. Even though I wasn't the most well behaved boy I was always curious about God and never dismissed Him. Most of the CS classes were a bit lame but one story has never left me.

Run Baby Run was a story that any boy could fall into. The detail of a guy who was on the wrong side of the law was exciting. To hear how he came to the Lord was amazing. I like it how even though he was a bit of a trouble-maker and did some terrible things to people, he still wasn't afraid to listen to someone who wanted to help him. One of the key points of Nicky coming to a faith in God was the witness given by the pastor, (whatever his name was).

Even though Nicky gave him a real hard time he didn't give up on him nor give up on faith. I think it will be a book that I will read to my kids one day. I got to hear Nicky Cruz speak a few years ago."

Brett Taylor, Year 7 1991 written for the author in 2013

Yr 10 – a new beginning

As you already know the Year 10 classes were not easy! Some lessons had a good energy about them, which produced discussion; others didn't. A phone call I received at school one day, after that Year 10 lesson that almost reduced me to tears, would change all that. Anne Yarham introduced herself as a Christian Studies teacher from Barker College. Anne and a couple of other teachers, Gai and Andrew Grant had been meeting with Marty to share ideas and encourage each other in their work. An invitation was extended to Ian and me to join them for a meal one Friday night. How wonderful! These teachers all worked on Sydney's northside, with Anne at Barker College, Hornsby, and Gai and Andrew Grant, working respectively at Mackellar Girls and Manly Boys High Schools. We discovered that they had each written, and published a book for the teaching of Christian Studies in schools. How very impressive! We were learning from the experts! And so began a couple of years of getting to know, and learn from, these three inspiring Christian Studies teachers.

Anne Yarham's large, thick, red spiral backed book was titled *The Great Australian Scripture Book*. She had found time, along with motherhood and working fulltime, to write down all of her lessons, from Year7-10, and have them published. What a great resource this was. There was so little material for youth work that had been written by Australians at this time. So many resource books were American, and often just not relevant for our context. I too would dip into American books from time to time, but to have a home grown book on teaching Christian Studies was fantastic. This was a great resource, and I referred to it often in 1990.

The Grant's book was something quite different, as was their approach. It was interesting to see different peoples' approaches to the same topics. There was certainly no 'right way' of teaching Bible knowledge and concepts. Andrew and Gai had written a book specifically for teaching Yr 9-10 students. It was called *In Search of Meaning*. This included a Teacher's Guide and a Student's Workbook. Wow! The front cover was immediately of interest. They had used a Leunig cartoon. Michael Leunig is a local cartoonist whose popular comments on life have been regularly published in Australian newspapers since the 1970s. Because of his quirky take on social issues, Leunig has been refered to as a prophet of our times.

> *"Leunig identifies our plight. His solitary human, an Everyperson travelling on foot, peers forward into the landscape"* in search of heart and soul.

> *"Leunig's genius is to leapfrog over the carping protests of narrow rational mind by using images that speak directly to the soul, the spirit the psyche and the heart – all those wider capacities we are missing like homesick children."*
> An Authentic Life, *Caroline Jones, p95.*

This cover cartoon was an impressive beginning; a solitary individual searching beyond himself, and into the heavens to find some meaning in life.

The Grant's approach was to examine the many areas teens look to find meaning in their lives, and highlight the outcomes of this search. Eventually the book takes you to God and His offer of forgiveness and fullness of life in Jesus. As well as the continuing Leunig commentary on life, many images were used in the book from teenage culture. Songs, celebrities and popular TV shows and movies were refered to that all echoed a search for something more in life. The workbook was very visually attractive. Gai and Andrew rightly understood what young people were thinking about, and knew how to engage teenagers' minds by understanding, and using, the images from their culture. As Ian and I sat in the Yarham's Roseville flat that first Friday night, hearing about the way the Grants connected with teens, we just knew we wanted to use *In Search of Meaning* with our Yr 10 classes. The title was even one of the headings in our Yr 10 syllabus.

I took a copy of the workbook to our first meeting of PHCEC for the year. We both tried to **sell** this workbook to the Committee in a big way; one, because it was a dynamic way to teach the things 16 year olds were thinking about; and two, because there would be a financial cost involved, a big cost. Every student in Yr 10 would need their own copy of the *In Search of Meaning* workbook, at $5 each. And that was the discount price. We were asking the committee to fund these books for all the Yr 10 classes. We tried to show them how close it was to the Year 10 syllabus.

Ian and I suggested that this material could be trialed for the year. The request was tossed around, talked about and evaluated by the Committee. But we got our answer that night - we could buy our 250 workbooks! That was one thing I really appreciated about PHCEC. They could make decisions quickly, so you weren't left holding your breath, not knowing the outcome until the next meeting , one term later.

Ian and I were relieved and excited at the same time. Here was something that would finally engage our Year 10 classes. I had bought a copy of the

Teacher's Guide that first Friday night and had read and absorbed the philosophy behind the workbook, so we were able to use the concepts in our classes straight away, before the workbooks arrived. And so Ian and I started our journey with Yr 10 into a search for meaning in life.

In the first lesson of our new beginning we got students to draw their own cartoon posters of '*Life is like…*,' prompted by a number of Leunig cartoons on the topic. The students' responses were insightful, original and sometimes quite profound. I included some of these comments in the first Christian Studies Newsletter that we put together in Term 1. Many students enjoyed the opportunity of reading their philosophy out to the class. The workbooks and content were readily accepted by our 15yr olds. We teachers, and our Year 10 classes, never looked back!

Life is like …

A brand new baby – my niece!

Heather Lorraine Blue Sky McNab was born on a sunny Good Friday, after two weeks of rain. This baby girl was a gift that only my brother could give me. Thank you is not enough!

Mum and Dad became grandparents for the first time.

There was much excitement in the wider family too, as the McNab's and the Jone's, and the Kerslake's welcomed this new family member. A baptism was held at Christ Church, Gladesville where Geoff and Megan were married. A wide selection of family gathered at North Ryde after the event for a celebration.

We looked forward to seeing our new baby girl often. When Megan went back to work part-time, it was arranged for Mum to mind little

Heather a couple of days a week. Mum thrived on this connection with her grandaughter and they developed a special relationship. Mum would regularly take Heather up to Bethany to visit her grandfather. As Heather grew, and walked, she was well known for going up to all the residents in the loungeroom and greeting them. She was a happy and friendly little girl.

I would often visit North Ryde after school on those days and spend some time with my niece. Heather was enough to bring a smile to my day.

An opportunity came for me towards the end of Term 1 to reflect on my work. Ellie, a Science teacher, caught up with me one afternoon as I was walking to my car. She asked me about the new teaching role I had undetaken at PHHS.

"Do you miss your Home Ec. classroom?"

This question took me by surprise. No one else had asked me this. I had to think for a moment, and was surprised at the response I gave her,

"No."

I don't think Ellie realised how her simple question made me reflect on that first term. The fact was, I was thoroughly enjoying my new classroom and all that went on it. It was as simple as that. I had started something new, and even though I compared the two schools in the first instance, I did not miss my Home Ec days at all; I was enjoying my new role too much. Every day I had young people asking questions of faith that stirred my heart. My job satisfaction was on the up and up.

The **Year 8's** were a great bunch of students. Nikky Vanderhout was their Year Advisor. She had a wonderful way with the students, mothering and befriending them, helping them on their journey through high school. Nikky had already indicated she would be willing to help out on the Year 8 Camp later in the year. She had participated the previous year on their Year 7 Camp with Marty. Plans for that Year 8 camp were well under way.

Construction

Many trees and shrubs stand as a greeting at every entrance to Pennant Hills High. The foliage buffers the harsh angles and surfaces of man-made structures that confront you once inside the buildings: concrete, steel, pebbled-cement and glass. Pennant Hills High School was built in the 1960s using a new cost-effective building style, as compared to the brick construction of the previous era. Cement slabs were poured off-site, to precise measurements, faced with pebblecrete and then assembled by the use of cranes, between steel uprights. Each cavernous space was identical to the next; every hard angle at 90 degrees; all large windows facing away from the quadrangle. A large, flat metal roof crowns this functional design, but lends nothing to its aesthetic appeal.

This new building on the Pennant Hills landscape in 1965 stood in stark contrast to the old primary school a couple of kilometres away. The primary school, constructed in 1850, had a double-brick construction, 15ft ceilings, large paned windows and a high-pitched gabled roof. With the arrival of the secondary school on the scene, the local community gained a new high school building of financially expedient modernism. The high school buildings have stood the test of time, and when I'd walk through the empty Main Quad at the end of a school day, I often noticed its ugly, cold exterior.

It's a good thing schools aren't empty places. Each morning, when students and teachers fill the grounds, mostly centred around and in the buildings, a life is engendered that is as organic and changing as each new day. Then the buildings fall into secondary significance, as teachers and students alike take on the larger landscape that is a school community. And so it is at Pennant Hills High.

The fabric sea of navy, sky blue and white that filled the Main Quad at every assembly stood in stark contrast to the surrounding pebblecrete walls, the weathered cement, and the grey metal lockers of 25 years. The young tanned faces and limbs, consistently uniformed; blondes, brunettes and redheads; the healthy bodies that filled the Main Quad every morning spoke of the affluence in the surrounding suburbs. This was a very different neighbourhood to downtown Auburn.

I learnt very early not to give tests. I think the only one I gave was in Term 1. I realised that a test just highlighted what students already knew about themselves from their academic classes - who was clever (good at remembering) and who wasn't. I didn't want to reinforce these stereotypes, so I started to use the Christian Studies assignments as my measure for how much a student understood, and how motivated they were. The assignments highlighted different intelligences, and it soon became the measure for determining a grade for student reports. I didn't use a numerical mark, but a grade like: A+, A, A-, B+, B, etc. This was combined with a book grade to give students a general idea of how they were going, some being more interested in written work than others.

The next unit of work for Year 8 was on the **Parables**. These stories that Jesus told I found fun to work with, yet each profound in their message. Here we were touching the heart of the gospel. I approached each parable differently.

THE PARABLE OF THE SOWER

Matthew 13.1-9,18-23

A farmer went out to sow his seed. As he scattered the seed . .

some fell along the **path**; it was trampled on, and the birds of the air ate it up.

Some seed fell on **rock**, and when it came up, the plants withered because they had no moisture,

Other seed fell among **thorns**, which grew up with it and choked the plants.

Still other seeds fell on **good soil**. It came up and yielded a crop, 100 times more than was sown.

"He who has ears to hear, let him hear."

Jesus' disciples asked him what the parable meant. He said, 'This is the meaning of the parable:

The seed is the word of God. Those along the path are ones who hear, and the devil comes and takes away the word from their hearts, so that they may not believe and be saved.

Those on the rock are ones who receive the word with joy when they hear it, but they have no root. They believe for a while, but in the time of testing they fall away.

The seed that fell among thorns stands for those who hear, but as they go on their way they are choked by life's worries, riches and pleasures, and they do not mature.

But the seed on good soil stands for those with a noble and good heart, who hear the word, retain it, and by persevering produce a crop.

I chose a variety of parables and presented them in different ways. I had fun with the Parable of the Soils/Sower, and took my Yr 8 classes outside. The high school grounds had all the environments I needed.

- Plenty of bitumen/playground for the path

- There were garden beds with huge stones and sparce planting, for rocky soil

- There was a very overgrown/blackberry section of vegetation at the back of one of the portables

- And on the border of the school property, backing onto New Line Rd, there was a magnificent vegetable garden to represent good soil. I showed pictures of this in the local churches, and was told that the home belonged to one of the members of the Uniting Church!

Then I gave out an assignment; simple, and with loads of choice.

> Yr 8 Assignment
>
> Update one of Jesus' parables that we have covered in class:
>
> 1.   Write a story   or
>
> 2.   Draw a cartoon or
>
> 3.   Present a skit   or
>
> 4.   Create a poem

I gave students some time in class to begin, and two weeks to complete this assignment.

Bryce, the narrator, and Simon got roped into Sandra's play! Sandra's group presented the Parable of the Unforgiving Boss. I remember being impressed by their preparedness when I saw a big bag of props arriving with Sandra a couple of lessons later.

The following story was written by a Year 8 student, after a couple of lessons on Outcasts.

JESUS AND THE MIGRANT OUTCAST

Jesus had just fed 5,000 people in the Domain by the miracle of the Big Mac and the Super Fries. He and his disciples were walking through Hyde Park when they saw a group of men bashing up a migrant. Jesus was very angry and chased them away.

Then Jesus went to the man and helped him up. He took the man to his house, made him comfortable on the lounge and gave him a meal. This black man became one of Jesus good friends.

(This story was written by an Asian student.)

It seems our migrant friends had trouble being accepted 25 years ago, as now.

Reports

Well into the first semester it was time to write student reports; lots and lots of them; 700 of them! The due dates were staggered, so they didn't all need to be ready at once, but it was still all a bit of a marking marathon and report writing wrestle. I used school time as well as nights to complete some, as well as needing to use both Saturday and Sunday to keep on top of the deadlines. Report writing usually rolled into a second weekend. But there was a deadline waiting, and I would endeavour to keep it. My reports were always handed in on time. My best reward from this labour of love was getting some feedback from the students,

"Thanks Miss McNab, Christian Studies was my best report!"

"Thanks for the good report, Miss."

"Thanks Miss, you said really nice things on my report."

And that was that for reports, until the end of the next semester.

PHHS Camping program 1990

It was well into the Term 2 before I had the energy to organise the Christian Studies camps for the year. The venues were varied;

- **Yr 7 Camp** went lakeside,

- **Yr 8 Camp** went mountainside,

- **Yr 9 Camp** went beachside.

- There was no Yr 10 camp; only a hand-full of students were interested.

It's hard to know how to record all these camps. There would be between 30-40 of them. I have many camp photos of students with fresh, happy faces. They are taken in a variety of environments, over a ten-year period. With them many stories could be retold; many experiences relived.

But if you are quiet enough, you might hear the excitement of getting ready for Camp on these pages. There was train travel, and bus travel, and on a couple of weekends, 4-wheel drives. There was canoeing, sailing, and water sliding on the lake.

At **Kiwi Ranch**, on Lake Munmorah.

There was volleyball, a couple of trampolines and a games room. There was camp food, healthy appetites and hamburgers on the wharf. There was a water slide for eager bodies, some in wetsuits. There was a horizon of manmade silhouettes, as local pelicans sailed past. A morning to think about good news from the Bible's pages. Nights of concert fun and musical items. Of mad times in messy bunk rooms; laughter and fun could be heard everywhere. Of more water sliding the following day, this time head first! Lots of merriment and fun could be heard, on the shore and on the water.

There was a train to **Gerringong**, and a good walk, as the cars carried heavy bags.

There was beach and sun, waves and surfing. There was salty air in our lungs as our group swarmed over the rock platform. There were games on the beach as adult eyes watched the water babes. There were walks and swims, good food and long talks. There was sand modelling, and talks on life modelling. The parachute appeared and kept a circle of students challenged for a morning, and laughter continued to be the flavour of the day.

The **mountains** beckoned us in the cold months;

A theme of **Christmas in Winter** proved a suitable subject and we all brought a present. Jesus was the best present, and lots of discussion was had with these keen young minds. A walk to **Ruined Castle** almost proved too much; for some, this was their first bush walk. Rock falls were scrambled over, ascents conquered. A great sight was had from the top; refreshing, heady views of the National Park. Baked Dinner and gifts exchanged; some laughs, and the simple pleasure of a Christmas tree. Teens thrive in free time fresh air, as friendships are fostered and forged. Student leaders share meals, games, rooms and talks with junior.

This group thrived on each other. Laughter and fun was everywhere.

PHCEC

The Committee continued to be an encouragement to us. I looked forward to meetings when I could tell these men and women the stories from the camps and the classroom. One Committee member said this was his favourite church committee that he was a part of it – because it was about lives being changed.

They wrestled with issues of money, fund-raising and paying the teacher's salary. It wasn't always smooth sailing. When times got tough and funds were low a special appeal might be launched to make up the shortfall.

And the generous people in the Pennant Hills and Cherrybrook churches would make up the funds needed.

PACIFIC HILLS VISIT 1990 – I call this my **3D classroom**

Something happened at the end of Term 3, quite independent of me, which took my classroom to a new level of interaction. A friend from my church, St Clements Lalor Park, a friend from St Clement's approached me at church about the possibility of bringing a group of students from his school, Pacific Hills Christian School, to Pennant Hills during their Year 10 Service Week. I warmed to the idea straight away. Andrew had an affinity with our school, having grown up in West Pennant Hills, and with his parents still attending St Matthew's Anglican Church. But an even stronger tie stemmed from the hands-on job - Andrew had been working as a labourer on our new school site. This was his casual job in uni holidays. During this time the two courtyards at the back of the high school were under construction,

Andrew's concept was to train up a team of Year 10 students to give their testimony, to play some Christian music and answer questions that might be thrown at them from my Christian Studies students. The Team would be available for every lesson, both with Ian and me. I was hooked on the idea from the beginning. Andrew, as a Music teacher, was ideal to bring these young people to a place where they could perform some recent Christian music, and also to be ready to share their fledgling faith in my high school, with teens very close to their own age. I cleared this activity with the principal and the Committee. It was going to happen.

There was much preparation at the Pacific Hills end as I briefed Andrew on where each of my classes were up to and what content we had covered over the year. At my end there was much anticipation by me, and preparation of my classes to receive guests into the school, and into our classroom. Finally the week was upon us. It was almost a holiday for me because, for the first time all year, I didn't have to prepare any lessons! Andrew brought a team of 12 kids with him. The idea was to use three students in each lesson, rotating students so that the same people weren't always giving out every lesson. These students came with a variety of backgrounds and skills, and personal apprehension.

The Pacific Hills' team arrived early that first Monday to set up the room with musical instruments and sound equipment, sporting casual clothes and carrying a bundle of nervous energy. The classroom was set up in a less formal arrangement, in a semi-circle, without desks. The format followed a similar pattern for each class:

- some popular Christian **music** was played, with vocalists, guitars and keyboard

- one or two Pacific Hills students would **talk about how God** had become a big part of their life

- students could **ask questions**

This format worked well for each class, from Year 7-10. I remember how scared the PHCS students were when questions from the Year 10 classes got a bit negative. They were experiencing the heat of opposition to their beliefs, not something they would likely experience in a Christian school. Andrew was able to 'rescue' the situation if needed as he carefully monitored the classes for serious hustlers. And so this pattern was repeated every day, with every class.

This team started with a sense of fear and trepidation, and progressed to a sense of confidence with telling their story - except for Year 10 classes.

Our Christian students were thrilled to have these new faces in the school, those who were stepping up and putting their faith on the line. Some of our students quite soon came to 3P4 at recess and lunch to hang out with these new friends. This was quite a lovely flow-on to watch, Christian community at work.

The Pacific Hills' team came to ISCF too and enjoyed the fellowship with other Christian teens. John Fowler suggested that we have a barbeque at the end of the week to wrap up their time with us. What a great idea! The Friday lunchtime bar-b-q was well attended and spirits were high. These young people had been stretched in their faith as they stood up for Jesus and gave voice to their beliefs. But they had also served me, the fulltime Christian Studies teacher, as they joined me in the proclamation that was Christian Studies in a public school. Thanks Andrew, thanks PHCS team!

December 1990

As December arrived, at the end of my first year, report writing for 25 classes was in full swing. After many nights of writing and two full weekends, my reports were ready and handed in on time. What a relief! The mood in the staffroom got decidedly lighter as the last couple of weeks arrived. It was a fun time. It was an important time with classes too, to 'finish well'. I never really did Christmas lessons, as most units of work lasted till the end of the term. Most classes asked if they could have a party - an end of year treat. Chips, lollies, drinks, maybe some cake; I was all partied out by the end of the year!

As well as joining the students in a celebratory mood, I reflected on what I had achieved in this, my first year at Pennant Hills High. How could I measure the success of my teaching year? As I thought about it I realised that I couldn't answer that question. I didn't know what impact the content had made on the students. Had any of them moved along in their thinking about faith? Had any of them moved along in their beliefs and embraced a faith in God? I had no idea! I realised that I needed to make some changes here. I needed to keep my finger on the pulse of how students were reacting to the themes that were being taught. I would do this the following year, by asking students to evaluate the lesson, and comment on the topics when a unit of work was finished. Evaluation had been a big focus in education, in the late 80s, while I was teaching at Auburn Girls High. I needed to implement some of those techniques in this new environment. I guess you could call that my resolution for 1991, which was only a six-week holiday away.

Chapter 3

As I look back on the year that was 1991, I am reminded by the photos I have that it was a year of relationships; building on those begun when Ian and I took over from Marty Rowe. Those relationships were with staff, with the Committee and of course with students.

One photo was taken at our Commissioning Service in February 1991. Ian and I were being commissioned, along with Geoff B. Jenny Robinson, from our staffroom, had come to join us that evening, which was an encouragement to us. When you get four people together who share a keen sense of humour, you are bound to get a good photo. It looks like we are still laughing at the joke from just before the shutter was pressed. I like this photo.

The next photos were taken on the day of official school photos. As well as individual photos, Ian and I made sure we had a photo taken together that could be used with promotional material the Committee would produce for 1991. When we went on deputation we often saw this photo displayed, along with the church's missionaries. I think it's the nicest photo Ian and I had together.

I organised for us to have a **MUSIC Staffroom photo**. Other teachers were keen for this to happen too. We knew the head teacher of Music would not be in any such photo (He hated photos with a passion, and usually got out of being in the Staff Photo by hiding).

I quietly brought his mug, with his name on it from the staffroom sink. The others were amused when I gave the KEVIN mug its own chair, and in so doing he took his rightful place next to the Music staff.

The shape of year 7 was different in 1991. A new high school in the area, Cherrybrook Technology High School, had been formed and was in the planning stage. The first year 7 classes, three of them, were formed and borded at Pennant Hills High. That meant 11 Year 7 classes this year. Ian took the three classes from Cherrybrook and I had all the PHHS Year 7 classes. That was a lot of repetition! The new high school would be ready for the school year of 1992.

I used to smile to myself, in those first years, when I got up very early to go to an **ISCF breakfast at St Paul's Carlingford**. You see, I had invented these breakfasts when I worked as an ISCF staff worker in 1979-80. The concept was a way to get ISCF students together from nearby schools for food, fun and fellowship, very early in the morning. They started at 7ish and concluded at 8ish. Many keen young people had been gathering together now for over a decade.

"If you make the toast, they will come." And come they did.

The ISCF Breakfast became one of the first school outings of the year. The senior students had done a fantastic job of letting all of Year 7 know about ISCF. They had run a special meeting for them with lots of games and information about what was planned for ISCF in Term 1. When the breakfast was advertised, a good few students had indicated they were interested in going. We just needed to organise how everyone was going to get there and back to school on time. Were there enough teachers going to drive all the kids back?

There is an ISCF photo from a **breakfast in 1991**. The school captain, Brad, is amongst our senior students, those tireless Yr 12s who worked to produce an interesting ISCF meeting each week. He is right at the back with Mr Fowler and Mr Cox. Other seniors are in the front row with Miss V. I can also see a very young Julia, Naomi, Sarah Piper, Paul Williams and Marcus. Marcus has reminded me that I used to pick him up in Castle Hill, so he could get to the breakfast. That wouldn't be allowed today.

But mostly as I look at this photo, I can see these juniors who would grow into leadership roles in ISCF, in years to come. Having this positive involvement from a variety of students was a real encouragement to me. Here were some keen young people who were willing to stand up for their faith at high school. Some Christian kids weren't that brave to do this.

The beginning of the teaching year in 1991 saw me trial a new approach to teaching content.

SIX THINKING HATS

I came across this method of **teaching about thinking** in the early 90s. It appealed to me because of its simplicity and because it was, in essence, a visual tool. There were many content areas in the Christian Studies curriculum that promoted fierce debate between students who held diverse opinions, for example, Creation, Jesus moral teaching and abortion. Even the junior students could argue fiercely about something that they saw as important. But I noticed many of them would 'get stuck' in their thinking. Students were very one-eyed and couldn't begin to think about, let alone consider, somebody else's point of view. When I came across this system, devised by Edward de Bono and used extensively in education, business and government, I knew I was onto something good. It was more than just good. It provided a wonderful key to opening discussions up to a healthy coverage of a diversity of opinions.

As in any group discussion, when young people air their views, it's normally the most knowledgeable, the most eloquent or the most forthright (loudest!) person who carries the argument. I sometimes found I was very dissatisfied with the result of open student discussions. So much content might be left uncovered, not investigated, ignored. Students may never even think of how somebody else might feel in a certain situation. Or that somebody's feelings about an issue so overwhelms the discussion that many important facts can be missed. Through using the Six Hats method, with a very structured approach to thinking ideas through, our investigation of content and our appreciation of other people's opinion took on new life.

The premise of the method is that the human brain thinks in a number of distinct ways. De Bono identified six ways of thinking, and assigned each a hat, and a colour.

- **White hat:** INFORMATION What are the **facts**? Any questions?

- **Yellow hat:** STRENGTHS What are the **good points**? How will it help?

- **Black hat:** WEAKNESSES What is **wrong** with this? Caution, judgement

- **Red hat:** FEELINGS What are my **feelings** about this? Emotions, intuition

- **Green hat:** NEW IDEAS What is **possible**? Creativity, suggestions

- **Blue hat:** THINKING What **thinking** is needed here? What do we do next?

I searched out and purchased six caps in each of the colours. In explaining to the students each way our mind thinks, I put on the appropriately coloured cap. I detailed how we would restrict our thinking and comments to one area at a time, moving on when our ideas were exhausted. I would mind-map the discussion on the board using the coloured hat headings with coloured chalk. Students took to this readily, and if someone made a comment out of context I'd say, "Hold onto that for now. We are not up to that hat yet" or "That's an emotional response, wait till we get to the red hat!" I used this with Yrs 7, 8 and 9, and needless to say, our discussions took off! Students loved using this guided method of discussion and were more satisfied at the end of one of our topics,

Example:

Topic: **JESUS rose from the dead**

FACTS: this happened during the reign of Herod and Pilate

- many people saw Jesus die, a sword was thrust up through his body

- a few followed and saw his body sealed in a tomb

- Roman guards paid to make up a story that his disciples came and took his body from the tomb

- a variety of people claimed to see him alive after his crucifixtion: 1, 2, 10, 100s

• STRENGTHS: - death doesn't have to be the end

- it's not just the story of one or two people, many people saw Jesus alive

- Jesus was fulfilling prophecy about himself

WEAKNESSES: - this is not humanly possible, nobody else has done it

- Is this part of a hoax from people who would like Jesus back from death?

- It all happened so long ago – it can't be proved

NEW IDEAS: - that a human being can have life after dying

- that it's all true!

- That Jesus had the power to beat death!

- Jesus' claim that he really was God

FEELINGS: - this is very surprising

- I am relieved that death can be escaped by someone

- It's just too unbelievable

THINKING: - how do we go about checking the truths of this incident?

- Where would we go for more information?

Now this may not be completely thorough, but it sure allowed us to cover more ground than when everybody was just calling out ideas, or jumping from one point to somewhere else completely different. With the use of our Thinking Hats, I think my students, as well as myself, left the classroom feeling that we had achieved something. I kept the various caps in the deep drawer of my desk in the classroom, ready to tackle narrow thinking with six easy colours!

PERSONALITY PROFILE... and it's effect

I first heard of Myers-Briggs through my involvement with Scripture Union. SU Council members were targeted as a group of volunteers who could benefit from understanding how we worked individually, and together, as a decision-making body. The M-B Type Indicator offered a way of determining where an individual gets their energy from and where they like to focus their attention. Adele Smith, an SUFM staff worker, was our enthusiastic practitioner and trainer. Adele had completed the M-B training course and was keen to open the world of 'type' to those of us who gathered on the first Monday of the month.

We each had to fill out numerous pages of questions where we chose the most preferred way of working out a number of options. These pages were then sent away for analysis. Our assessments came back, and were explained to us the next month. We were each given four letters that explained our Type.

My Type was described as **ESFJ**.

I quickly learnt what these letters stood for.

E- extravert (*No surprise*!) :you prefer to focus on the outer world of people and xx things

S- sensate :you tend to focus on the present and on concrete information gained from your senses (*Doesn't everyone?*)

F- feelings :you tend to base your decisions primarily on values and on a subjective evaluation of person-centred concerns (*Well, of course!*)

J- judgement :you like a planned and organised approach to life and prefer to have things settled (*Exactly!)*

This was all very interesting. A folder of information was supplied which I took home and devoured with interest. I could see why Adele was excited by this. I was too. This information was showing me who I am! Mostly, you just get on with doing what we have to do, without too much thought about it all. But this was like having a huge mirror that had followed me around. It not only accurately highlighted my actions and responses but it gave a reason for them as well.

Characteristics frequently associated with ESFJ made interesting reading:

I also found it interesting to read about the other types as well. An **INTP** was the complete opposite to my way of gathering information and making decisions. Reading about my opposite helped me to understand myself more.

As I read again now over pages of **ESFJ** analysis, I am reminded of strengths **and** weaknesses that were highlighted for me back then. This was altogether interesting, and also a bit scary.

- **ESFJs** can have a hard time understanding those who do not look at the world in the same way as they do. Those who do not share their views can find **ESFJ** judgements confining and sometimes sharply critical

- have a high need for affirmation from others

- because of their tendency to make quick judgements, they often seem sure that the worst will happen

Reading about these weaknesses was quite sobering, but rang true. I enjoyed trying to work out what 'type' other people I interacted with were. This was fun.

Movies and TV clips

Ian and Geoff were savvy with modern media, and with their influence, I found myself, from time to time, dipping into movies that were popular with youth culture. These helped to begin the discussion on a number of topics. More often we used video clips from the evening news, or current affair programs. The Grants told us they had a video cassette ready in the video player all the time, ready to hit PLAY if programs like Current Affair were of particular interest. I started to do the same thing, keeping a note on the side of the video of its latest recorded contents. Students really enjoyed the use of video clips, as either motivation or content, in a lesson.

Sometimes we showed a whole TV program. **The Simpsons** cartoon had just started in 1989 and it was showing weekly on TV. I had heard about this irreverent cartoon but had barely watched an episode. It was Ian and Geoff again, who alerted me to the positive themes this show carried. I needed to be convinced that this was a good idea. Marty had left a video with a couple of Simpsons episodes on it, so I took it home as 'required viewing'. I was quite delighted in what I found in The Simpsons.

Back in the early 90s was a controversial figure back in 1990, especially among Christians. Many saw Bart as a loud-mouthed character who disrespected his parents, teachers and other adults. The fact that Homer Simpson was a less-than-perfect father in a dysfunctional family did not help either. As a result some Christian parents did not let their children watch The Simpsons at home. The fact that Marty had used some episodes in the curriculum, we as new teachers didn't see the need to run extra episodes by the Committee. In Year 7 the students, fairly early in the year, get to watch *Homer meets God*, with God getting a pretty good wrap from the writers of the show. He was all- powerful (takes the roof of Homer's house) as well as being immanent and personal (he talks to Homer and his pets - Homer's cat). God was so big you never saw his face, just his body and long beard. There was much to be drawn out of this episode on the nature of God. I secretly think some young teens were pleased to be watching this 'banned' show in Christian Studies, knowing it would be unpacked by the teachers. Over the years another popular episode was when Bart prays for a miracle- and gets one. That was a good place to talk about prayer.

The first movie the lads introduced me to was *The Breakfast Club*. They were keen for us to use it in the Self-Esteem unit with Year 9. I watched the movie at home, and understood why Ian and Geoff were passionate about the movie and its themes. The movie revolves around five students who have to spend a Saturday school detention together. They arrive wearing their stereotypes the school has given them: the jock, the brain, the hopeless, the princess and the basket case. Over the course of the day these roles are examined and broken down, as they get to know each other and their individual family circumstances. Life was not perfect for any of them.

This movie had a lot of 'language' in it, with the 'f' word being used a few times. It also highlighted the use of recreational drugs. I couldn't see the Committee warming to that! At a Committee meeting I explained our desire to use this movie, and asked that the members of the Committee watch the movie. An evening was set for Committee members to gather and see The Breakfast Club. I wondered how it would be received. We got an answer fairly quickly. The members were a bit cautious about the language used, and some of the themes (smoking of dope in the school library). Len Russo was worried about the negative picture that was painted of the teacher concerned, being useless and arrogant. Geoff and Ian went into bat and explained that the language is not foreign to many of the students who would watch the movie. He explained that to have a movie that started in youth culture, embracing relevant themes, was a hard thing to come across. They listened, and to their credit gave us permission to use *The Breakfast Club*. Geoff saw this as a watershed in the thinking of the Committee. Christian Studies wasn't just for the children of Committee members, and Christian parents in the area, but Christian Studies was the one place where every young person in the school would come, and we had a chance to influence them, variously, with the gospel.

The suggestion by Len Russo to use *Dead Poets Society* in the Self Esteem unit was a gift from a wise man. This suggestion would have more impact than I could have imagined in 1991. After a while *Dead Poet's* became the movie of choice, instead of *The Breakfast Club*. I loved showing this boarding school movie as not many of the Year 9 students had seen it (especially as the years ticked by). Viewing it in class with fellow teens, over four lessons, was a significant shared experience and the movie formed the basis for our discussions for many weeks, as a variety of self-esteem issues were raised.

Tell magazine had just done an article on the *Dead Poets* movie, and I used images of Mr Keating and several of the boys to put together a small booklet for use in class. There was a work-as-you-go assignment.

Questions included:

- ❖ Why is Mr Keating regarded as a hero?

- ❖ How could he be regarded as a 'Christ-figure'?

- ❖ For each of the boys - the problem they faced - how they overcame it

- ❖ Suggest an alternative for Neil besides suicide

- ❖ State a problem you face.

- ❖ List alternative courses of action you could take

- ❖ Find words from a song (poem) that express your view of life

- ❖ Choose one boy from the film and explain how his life might be different if he had a relationship with God

Something seems to happen when you discuss candidly some of the 'hot potato' issues, such as suicide. Students are seeing that they can talk to the Christian Studies teachers about anything. *Dead Poets Society* was a cinema journey worth taking, this year, and every year. Responses to these questions were an enjoyable read, as students spoke honestly and openly on things they held dear.

Pretty Woman was a new release in 1990. This movie about a prostitute falling in love with her client had themes of love and lust that I could use with Year10, as part of *The Search for Meaning* theme. I used the fast-forward to speed through unsuitable scenes or conversation. I used relevant scenes, and didn't use the whole movie. Year 10 students were very pleased to have this contemporary movie used in class. I made sure class finished with the shopping scene with the Roy Orbison soundtrack playing in the background. 'Big mistake! BIG! HUGE!' And so we finished on a pretty note. That we were using current movies gave us merit in the eyes of the students.

The grass is greener, and I was on the right side

As expected, PHHS proved to be a good school; better than good – an outstanding school. Across the academic year, students performed at the top of their game in many fields, not the least in academic progress. It was here that HSC honours continued to impress.

Sporting achievements were numerous; in cross-country, football, volleyball, netball, swimming and more.

Music performances were many, both at school and also other events that took them away: the Stage Band, the Concert Band and the choir.

The **Debating teams** attracted a strong reputation. Some well-spoken, fast speaking, intelligent students won awards, and brought home a group prize.

School musicals were now a reality with the new school hall: music staff, and English/Drama staff united to put on a 'gala event' each year.

Drama performances alone, it took months to prepare a dramatic rendition of a newly created or familiar production.

Some students, perhaps many, were all-rounders and performed seamlessly across all areas of activity. I hadn't seen this type of ability for a long time. At the end of the school year I would see names on the Speech Day program for academic achievement, knowing they had also been in the debating team, in the cast of the musical and the winning netball team. Impressive stuff!

In the 1990s PHHS won its reputation as being one of the top comprehensive, co-educational high schools in Sydney.

ISCF was a joy for me to be a part of, and I looked forward to it. I could see a joy reflected in the faces of the students who came through the door of 3P4 for our weekly ISCF meeting, and a love for each other. There were students from Yr 7 right up to Yr12. Brad Maxwell, our boy school captain, made sure his extra-curricula activities didn't keep him from coming to ISCF, which I noticed and appreciated. Brad was a classic extrovert, and loved nothing better that to play games with the juniors. We had many prefects who regularly came to our group, who were great role models to the younger students. We often played a game or two, had a devotion time and then a short prayer. (I would miss them at the end of the year when they did their HSC exams and left the school.) Peter Kneale, from English, had agreed to lead the PHHS group. I turned up every week too, but with these capable seniors, we didn't have much work to do!

Classes were learning about creation and Jesus' life; about heroes and parables; about life and why people suffer; looking at the mountain we climb to find higher love. There were many classes to teach every week. It was a blessing to me from the senior students to lead ISCF themselves.

And then there were the CAMPS! I was more organised with booking sites this year and soon many fun weekends were planned. There are many more photos from these camps; too many to reproduce here. Stay tuned!

Romance 1

The social scene of a 30+, female, who is also single and Christian

I was lucky to still have many single friends to spend time with and carve out a social life. Together with these friends, we had become a part of a Christian singles group called CS&A (Christian Sports and Activities).

This group served single Christians (from 25-50yrs) from all over Sydney, and put on all manner of events. There were bush walks and balls, tennis nights and bush dances. We were reminded that the group wasn't a lonely hearts club, but we were also pleased to hear, from time time, that two of our members had become a couple; and maybe just a little jealous too!

I'd had my heart broken some years before, and I had steeled myself to keep going with this social scene, and to be hopeful for a romantic interest again.

Romance 2

A new beginning

It was through a friend at my previous school that I found out he was back; back from overseas. I didn't think I wanted to see him; to see him and possibly pick up where we had left off. No thank you! It had been too painful saying goodbye. My heart had been broken and it had taken a long time to get over the hurt and disappointment. I didn't want to go there again. No, I would keep my distance deliberately, and wait and see if we just 'bumped into each other'.

Sometime later that same friend invited me to her church – and he was there! What would I say?

"Hi, I heard you were back."

"Yes, since Christmas."

"So where are you living?"

In a friend's flat, and closer to me than last time! He was still looking for a teaching job. He was settling back in. I didn't ask him to dinner, which would have been a natural thing for me to do; but that wouldn't have been wise.

Just a, "Goodbye Rohan. It was nice to see you."

That was enough for now.

Oh dear!

Year 9 Big Issues - Abortion

(I record at length how I approached the big issue of abortion, to help Year 9 do some critical thinking on an issue. They were ready for an in-depth study now. I didn't realise that it would get me into trouble!)

The lot had fallen to me to prepare work around the big issue of **abortion**. Generally speaking, the number of abortions had increased dramatically from the 1970s when **'Abortion On Demand' reform** was instituted across the nation. In 1991, abortion law in Australia was determined by each state.

Abortion law in New South Wales is primarily based upon the *Levine ruling* of 1971 which declared abortion to be legal if a doctor found 'any economic, social or medical ground or reason' that an abortion was required to avoid a 'serious danger to the pregnant woman's life or to her physical or mental health' at any point during pregnancy. *Wikipedia*

I needed to do some extensive research here. I already had some books on this topic. The first two were written by people I had met when I was a student at L'Abri in **England**. Susan Schaeffer-Macaulay's book explained the reality of pregnancy and the wonder of a developing child to a young mind. The book deals with the issue *'when something goes wrong'*, and gives case studies of a number of disabled children. The photos of inter-uterine life were stunning.

I had purchased Richard Winter's book, *Choose Life*, a few years before. I was keen to see in print the issue of abortion tackled from the L'Abri perspective; that life is precious – all human life. The abortion issue had been fiercely championed by Francis Schaeffer, the founder of L'Abri, in the last decade of his life, and is addressed dramatically in his film series *Whatever Happened To The Human Race*. His teaching had certainly shaped my own views on this issue.

As I needed some facts that were **Australian**, I went looking for some local publications and came across, *Abortion in Australia* on Koorong's shelves in early 1990. This publication gave me up-to-date statistics and information for the local scene. The first two books had amazing coloured photos of a developing embryo at various stages of life, from five weeks to six months; the human form in its journey into the world. Modern medical photography was giving us images that previous generations never imagined. Richard's book also contained graphic images of aborted foetuses in various forms that were harrowing to look at because their very humanity screamed out from the pages. They were brave photos indeed to harness the mind of the thinking individual who might finally need an image of mutilation and death to instruct his/her senses. These **were not** images I would use in class, but they certainly informed my own mind. My aim was not to shock and confront, but to give Year 9 students **some information to help them think through t**his controversial issue for themselves. Geoff Broughton made the comment that some of the girls may have had abortions and the issue needed to be treated carefully. That wasn't something I was initially thinking about and his comment shocked me into the probability of having girls in our Year 9 classes who had had an abortion. This was reality indeed.

The abortion issue was not just black and white, and I wanted my students to understand that. There are so many reasons why a woman may come to want/need an abortion that I knew it would open up a very wide discussion indeed. But a teacher can't address an issue like this unless she has really thought through her own personal situation; this can't just be a theoretical discussion.

I reflected on my own situation. If I had become **pregnant** when I was at school, what would my parents' reaction have been? I couldn't really imagine that happening to me in the 60s, as I hadn't been in a relationship that produced that amount of passion! But what if I had? I tried to envisage my parents' response. I know they would have been shocked and disappointed to begin with. It was the 1960s, and I was a good girl who went to church. But my mother loved babies to bits. She wouldn't have liked the way I had made her a grandmother, but her love for a baby of mine would not be diminished because it was conceived out of wedlock. I did know that about her. Dad would also have supported me no matter what too. I could see myself living at home with them and a new baby. And I realised that this was quite different to the actual experience of a family known to us, where the daughter was sent away when she became pregnant, as an unmarried teen, in the late 60s. She gave birth to the baby and was forced to give it up for adoption. This family were church-goers too. I knew my parents would not, could not, have imitated them.

And I reflected on the big issue of **being raped**. What would I do if that happened to me and I got pregnant- now? I was 38 and unmarried. I would still love to be a mother. I knew that, but this way? Imagine that. What if it really happened? The Christian Studies teacher gets pregnant! I wonder how long I would be able to continue my job. There would be nobody to support me. I would have to live on social services and I probably wouldn't be able to pay my mortgage. My life as I knew it, would end. But I would have a precious new life to look after. Mum would still love a baby of mine to bits. It would be hard, but I would continue with the pregnancy. I could never have an abortion.

In my research I learnt much I hadn't known before, especially about abortion practise in Australia. I read extensively and became quite informed on the topic. I developed a series of lessons that would deal with the issue of abortion, and included what I understood was God's perspective. I didn't want to 'shove it down their throats' at all. This topic needed time to raise the issue, to generate questions, to supply information and details for sound discussion and to finally speak from a Christian perspective. This unit of work would take four weeks.

WEEK 1

Students were asked to choose **where they stood** on the issue of abortion. A statement is written on the board, one opinion.

THE PRODUCT OF ABORTION IS JUST A PART OF UNWANTED TISSUE FROM THE WOMAN'S BODY

And then another opinion,

HUMAN LIFE BEGINS AT CONCEPTION.
ABORTION IS THE TAKING OF A HUMAN LIFE

I drew an imaginary continuum across the room and put a question on the board,

Is abortion OK?

I AGREE   NOT SURE   I DON'T AGREE

I then asked students to take a position on that line that represented their point of view. I asked students to justify their position on the line. Here was the beginning of our discussion. It was very interesting to see where students stood. Some students would notice they were the only one standing at "I don't agree" and move away quickly. Others would stand confidently with their view. Some said life stars when you are born! What a contrast.

It was time for a quiz! I devised this quiz from the facts I gained from *Abortion in Australia*. Let's see what we are dealing with here. The quiz was aimed to show the high and increasing number of abortions performed every year in Australia; in 1988 80,000 abortions a year. Most students were surprised, even shocked, at these statistics. This all generated a host of questions to which I would give short answers. And I explained that abortion was **an issue that Christians had different opinions about**. At the end of giving the answers to the quiz and answering some questions, 40 minutes was well and truly up. For the many questions that were already raised the answer was often "Well, it all depends on when life begins." I hadn't made my opinion known as yet, and would defer questions about that till another lesson. I wanted these young people to think this issue through for themselves, and not just automatically adopt my view (especially the churched kids).

WEEK 2

This week we looked at the facts needed to inform the discussion on abortion.

- **Why might a woman want an abortion?**
- **How are abortions performed?**
- **What are the alternatives to abortion?"** (especially for a teenage girl)
- **What if you know the baby will be born deformed in some way?**

One of the biggest areas of discussion, for the girls, was about the instance of being raped, and becoming pregnant. I had found the reading I had done helped discussion here.

The area of **being born deformed** was fiercely debated, and it seemed that everyone had an opinion.

Firstly, what defines disability: deafness, blindness, malformed limbs, ability to walk, ability to talk, and mental disability? Who decides these important guidelines?

"They need to be able to contribute to society," was offered by students as a guideline.

Their answer disturbed me, so I asked them, "By your definition a human being is reduced to a dollars and cents contribution to the national economy?" The answer disturbs me still, and upon reflection, based on some of my 15 year old's definitions in these 1990s abortion lessons, our Australian Paralympics champion Kurt Fearnly would not have had the right to be born. And Australia would be the lesser for it, as Kurt continues to push his own physical boundaries, like completing the Kokoda Track – not walking but crawling!

I remember one student who told the class her mother was advised to have an abortion because her baby would be born disabled, but her parents decided to continue with the pregnancy. When the baby was born, he was absolutely perfect. Doctors can get it wrong!

I would make a reference that some young women have no choice in the decision to have an abortion. If they are young and unmarried, the girl's parents can step in and force an abortion upon her. The girl may have to agree but may also later regret the choice made for her. I wanted students to be aware of the range of dynamics that come into play in such a situation, and not to see pregnant teens as someone who has done something 'wrong'. There were times when **they were greatly wronged.**

I would later find out that there would have been **much discussion** between Year 9 students about this issue over the next few days.

WEEK 3

This week the philosophical debate would begin – if it hadn't begun already.

- **When does life begin?**

There is no better way to answer this question than to watch the miracle of life take place in a film. I had one such video that begins in a hospital delivery room where all the excitement of full term labour is taking place. Then the storyline goes right back to the beginning as a sperm fertilises an egg, and the cell divides. The inter-uterine filming that follows the development of these cells has to be some of the most breathtaking images ever captured on film. This continues for some twenty minutes, describing in great detail, every new development in this tiny human being, until the baby is six-seven months old and accumulating fat and growing stronger.

And then the film takes us back to the delivery room of a French hospital. The strenuous activity of the mother is obvious as the father stands by encouraging her. The crowning of the baby's head is seen. The students realise that they are going to see the actual birth of a baby and a reticent excitement begins. Wide eyes don't leave the screen. Smiles creep across young faces. More strenuous pushing and a tear occurs in the woman's vagina, with some blood, as the baby's head pushes through. Squeals from many! The father, who can see his baby, is quite overwhelmed. The doctors assist the safe delivery of a dark haired child into the world and place it in its mother's waiting arms. Quite simply the parents are overjoyed. The father wipes away tears. A new life has begun its journey into our seen world, after nine months of development and existence in the unseen world. We had been witness to the miracle of life, from conception to birth. There are lots of comments as I turn the video off.

"*Miss, you should have warned us,*" said a boy.

"*I'm never having a baby!*" exclaimed a girl or two.

I smiled. It was quite a precious moment, every time, to watch the miracle of birth with a class, and I realise that most of them had not had this experience before.

At each stage of development I asked the class, "Is that baby alive?" Finally I ask one last time -

"*When does life begin?*"

"*At conception,*" volunteered a brave voice.

"*When it was born,*" echoed a stubborn one.

"*When the heart started beating,*" came another response.

"*When it could live outside the mother's body,*" replies another.

As the bell rang and students left my classroom, they continued to talk about what they had experienced. Forty minutes had elapsed, and in that time we had taken a most amazing journey; teens had been transfixed by the miracle of birth, faces had held the wonder of individual development and minds had been expanded. I loved my job!

"Miss, are we going to watch that birth film?" asked the first students from the next Year 9 class who arrived at the door of 3P4.

The news was spreading.

WEEK 4

The final week focussed on the Bible, and in the end, the student's informed opinion.

- **What does the Bible say about abortion?**

- **Where do you stand?**

My comments in this lesson included the following;

The Bible says nothing about abortion – it is silent on the topic. Why? The birth of children was seen as an enormous blessing to the people of the Bible times. The more children you had the more you were blessed by God. How much has society changed since those days! Now some people see children as an inconvenience or a nuisance. Now 'things' are more important than children. Even though the Bible doesn't mention abortion it does say a lot about the value of human life.

I had prepared some Bible verses for students to consider. I used three from Richard Winter's book.

The Bible is **pro-life**. The opening pages of the Bible tell us that humans have been created in the image of God. This is what gives our individual lives value and purpose. We are not just like the animals. We have been made like the God who created us, and we have been made for a relationship with Him. God values all human life, no matter what you look like, how old you are or how smart you might be, or how able you are, because all humans reflect God's image.

"The whole weight of Scripture seems to point to the fact that the unborn child, the developing foetus, is known, loved and valued by God, even if the tiny child is not yet able to reciprocate the relationship."[1]

With many relevant Bible verses I showed how Christians use the whole Bible to piece together theological points of view on various issues.

Many students found these verses shed light on the position they were taking. Others were hearing for the first time that God saw them, knew them, before they were even born. At this point I made the comment that **all churches** take the stand for the **sanctity of human life**, all of life, born and unborn. And that all churches have written into their statement of faith the right to life of the unborn baby. *If* there is a choice

1 P63 Choose Life, Dr Richard Winter M1988

to be made here -*Choose Life*. It was in this context that I finally told students (if they asked) where I stood on the abortion issue.

In conclusion, it was important to place this issue in the big picture of God's redemptive love.

"We all do things that are wrong in life. For some women or girls, they might feel that having had an abortion was wrong and feel guilty about it now. The God who made us in His own image, who values and loves us, can forgive us for the wrong things we do in life, including having an abortion. His love can bring healing and peace in your life."

(I would meet a woman in my school a few years later, who would testify to the peace of God, to a small class of my students, after having an abortion in her past. It was a bold and brave testimony.)

After four weeks it was time for some **evaluation**. I drew the imaginary line across the classroom again.

Our question remains: **Is abortion OK**?

I AGREE   NOT SURE   I DON'T AGREE

I asked each student to stand along this continuum again. Where did their opinion lay? Much movement took place as students jostled for position. And I watched quietly. I noticed that some students had changed their positions from Week 1. The 'NOT SURE's had moved closer to a point of view. There were more people at the 'I DISAGREE' end. Others stood boldly still at 'I AGREE'. I again asked individuals why they were standing where they were. This activity was my evaluation too, a visual one, to see that with information and discussion, some students had taken a decisive stand against abortion, or were happy to own their own opinion about it, wherever they stood. It was a satisfying moment. I told them that, in years to come, they would probably know of people, friends, who would contemplate and even have an abortion. You may be in a position to offer support and even advice into that situation, I told them, and it will need gentleness and great wisdom.

I felt my students had 'grown up' during the weeks of our discussions. Their minds had been stretched and their hearts had been touched. It was often at this point that students would stay behind to talk, to tell me they now understood that abortion, in most cases, was wrong. Some picked up the books I had on my table and would see the images I had not shown to the class – the results of abortion; of tiny human bodies in plastic bags or metal dishes. Students' faces were shocked and their hearts understood.

It had been quite a marathon, four weeks, and nothing promoted the same heated debate in class than this topic did. I hoped I had modelled **how to approach controversial topics.**

1. Be informed
2. Listen
3. Try to understand the other side
4. Look for biblical input

Ian and Geoff may have used a similar approach when discussing the Big Issue topics they were presenting to Year 9.

In this first year of working together, Ian and Geoff said they didn't really want to teach the unit on abortion, not knowing a lot about it, or feeling uncomfortable as a man presenting the information. I understood. I suggested that I teach all the classes on abortion, and that they teach every class the Big Issue they had each prepared. This was a great idea and allowed for the person with a passion for that particular issue to deal with the topic. I'm pretty sure the students enjoyed swapping teachers for a whole month too!

But I haven't mentioned what would always happen after Lesson 1 or 2. I would get a phone call from the Principal; could I come to his office. I had no idea what this was about the first time.

"I had a phone call from a parent about the lesson you gave on abortion yesterday."

I was somewhat stunned.

"Their daughter told them you said in class that having an abortion was wrong."

Now I was completely stunned! "No. I didn't say that," I tried to explain. "I wouldn't say that."

The Principal repeated another pronouncement I had reportedly delivered.

"No. I didn't say that either," I defended. "They may have interpreted what I said in that way, but I didn't say that."

This was definitely a case of communication breakdown. I tried to tell the Principal the structure of my lessons and how I was trying to generate debate. I think I was understood by the end of our conversation, but it made me very aware that students could misinterpret the things I was saying and presenting. And maybe I wasn't being as neutral as I had planned to be! It made me very aware that our classroom discussions were prompting discussion at home, and confirmed my understanding that this topic was a very unsettling one.

Then one year I had double trouble. There were twin girls in Year 9. They were in different classes, but after our lessons they were quite sure I had said abortion was wrong. There had been great discussion about this at home. I got the familiar phone call, this time from Lyn M. I told her again what I said and didn't say. Lyn told me of the girl's objection to what was being discussed and that they were being withdrawn from Christian Studies classes. I was sad about this outcome, but it was something I couldn't change. The decisions had been made. It made me quite reflective. Was it worth losing students from every other Christian Studies class over the next years? The answer was No! These girls would now not have the opportunity to hear about God's love for them. They would not hear, again, of the death of Jesus to save needy people. And in not hearing this they really would be missing out. A big shift took place in my thinking. If I was going to continue to put people off, such that they might leave my class, I was making bad choices. My new choice was to not do the topic of abortion over the next few years. When the topic did resurface, because students were asking questions, I re-presented the issue in a very pared back form. I used stimulus pictures of non-threatening images and asked some open questions. This then was the basis of our discussion. I didn't want to 'lose' anyone else.

I had the opportunity in October 2007 to attend a L'Abri Conference in St Louis, at Covenant Seminary. There I had the privilege of catching up with Richard and Jane Winter. Richard was at the time the Professor in Practical Theology and the Director of the Counselling Program at Covenant. Richard was most surprised to see his book in my hands (now out of print and out-of-date in our rapidly changing social and medical environments).

He exclaimed when he saw the book in my hand, "Where did you get that from?"

"It's mine, I bought it with me – for you to sign," I said smiling.

Over Sunday lunch in their back garden, I told Richard of my work as a Christian Studies teacher, and how his book had 'got me into trouble!' He was delighted to hear my story.

> *To Helen,*
>
> *With good memories of your visit to English L'Abri and thankfulness for your work in spreading the good news.*
>
> *Richard Winter*

As I write this I can overhear the news bulletin on ABC Sydney radio. The Australian parliament is to take a vote on changes to abortion and euthanasia laws. Individual politicians want the right to vote with their conscience, and not necessarily with their party, on this controversial issue. The battle continues, as politicians try to legislate for those in our society who don't have any power or a voice. The facts and statistics may have changed since Richard wrote his book in 1988, but the Bible's statement of the value of all human life, born and unborn, young and old, able and disabled has not.

Yr 8 Christian Studies Camp

More than the year before, we could call 1991 'The Year of the Camp'. Year 8 Camp saw a trip to Rathane, in The Royal National Park. Many of the students who had been to Kiwi Ranch the year before returned for some more adventures, often with a friend. Some new faces were included too, (after all the stories that filled classes since last Camp.)

With its location on Port Hacking, the drawcard of sailing was a big one. All who wanted a go on the river were rewarded by their patience. Others spent the morning in simple pursuits around the coastline. There was nothing simple about the abseiling event in the afternoon. The view of the river from a high vantage point was quite spectacular. The Yr 8s threw themselves into learning new things, and we developed a nice relationship with this group of young people. These photos found their way to the noticeboard onto the walls of 3P4, and into the shared history I was developing. After each camp I made up a poster of photos and displayed them on the walls of my classroom. These were a highlight long after camp was over.

Yr 9 Christian Studies Camp

Some of these students had been asking all year about the Christian Studies Camp. There were lots of questions about dates and the new site, especially as it involved the beach, and were very pleased the lesson. When I arrived in class with camp brochures in my hand. If I had been more organised we may have had a date that was actually in summer! But thankfully the weather hung around for our April adventure in Gerringong.

I was impressed with this site when we came with Yr 9 the preceding year. There was lots of room for beach adventures and many of the photos are in the sand or on the rock platform, (before the days of swimming restrictions). The only rule we had was that you couldn't go swimming without a teacher present. The students stuck to that, and with Jeff Cox, Ian, Jenny and Steve Robinson, with young Sam, and myself, there was a good pool of teachers to ask.

Some Yr 9 boys had a special request, "If a teacher could come with us, could we have a swim before breakfast?" Bless them! Jeff Cox obliged, and I must have too! I have some dawn photos to prove it!

Ian was the MC at the Saturday Night event, with Rev Stephen Robinson sitting at the side - in a dress, for a skit. The look on the campers' faces when they saw it, was just delightful. So ministers can have fun too!

Romance 3 October, 1991

My bedroom was a large room at the front of my house with windows to the northern sun letting in large amounts of light. In 1991 one wall held a feature wallpaper of large dusty pink flowers. And one wall was a dark stained built-in wardrobe. After three years the built in wardrobe was still stained dark brown. I still hadn't got around to changing it. It was time for a change; a full renovation was in order. All in all, it could have looked better. I knew I wanted an *olde worlde* look. I could see it in my mind; more wallpaper, but this time with a small all-over print, just part way up the wall, and a frieze. I learnt this was called a dado line. I returned to the Auburn area to a specialist wallpaper shop I knew of. There were so many to choose from. I settled for a soft apple green paper with a tiny cream flower. I chose paint to match the wallpaper print, and it all toned in with the patchwork quilt I had finally finished.

It's the one renovating skill I have, painting. I can't build, or do plumbing or electrical work, but I can paint. I needed to borrow a ladder from Mum's garage, Dad's painting ladder. I always think of my Dad when I paint. He painted like a professional. I had seen him do it many times over decades at Farrington Parade; meticulous preparation; careful cutting in; two coats, maybe three; soaking brushes in turps. It's like Dad is there when I have a brush in my hand. I always buy the best paint, just like he did-*Dulux*. Dad's painting days finished before the advent of water-based paints and he never knew the ease of a water clean up. This apprentice was pursuing more modern ways. I wonder if he would agree.

I was ready to go. I started with the timber wardrobe, and painted the four large doors a light cream colour. The difference was amazing. The solid dark wall of wood was gone and the room already looked much bigger. It took till the October long weekend to get organised to paint the other three walls, a big job.

"What are you doing on the long weekend?" he had asked me the next time I saw him.

"I am painting my room."

"Would you like some help?"

It was a nice offer. It was a loose arrangement for the Monday, and that was all that was said. I wondered if he would come. I had hired a steamer for the day to get the old wallpaper off. I had filled the steamer with water and it needed to heat up. There was a knock at the door. He had come! There were smiles all around and then explanations of how the steamer worked. 'I' had become 'we', and we were soon ready to go. The wallpaper was vinyl and needed extra time to get the steam to work through the top layer. Eventually the vinyl just peeled off, all in one piece.

However, the backing paper layer was still firmly attached to the wall. More steaming was needed. We refilled the tank many times. When it was thoroughly saturated the backing paper could be easily removed with a metal scraper. Soon the whole wall was free of its coloured paper decoration. But I was somewhat shocked at what lay beneath. The wall was quite rough and bumpy, unlike the other painted walls. Is this why it had been papered over? What would this look like just painted? We were about to find out.

The paint went on easily with a roller. I had used them when painting the outside of the house, and I had been won over. Dad had only ever used a paint-brush. I wondered if Dad could see how easy it was, if he would give his nod of approval. One wall held the large windows and it was painted relatively quickly. It was nice to work together, and so close. I avoided long glances and kept things friendly.

It was time to let the first coat dry, as a late lunch rolled around. I made some sandwiches. By late afternoon we had covered the walls, from ceiling to hip height, in two coats of paint. The bumpy wall was now well disguised. We had done well. He was in no hurry to go anywhere, and I had nothing to make for dinner. I extended an invitation,

"Do you want to get take-away dinner?"

That was agreed on as a good plan. We drove to Kings Langley and ordered some Chinese food. It was good to still be together. I served up the meal onto plates. Dinner for two, how very nice!

The evening lingered until it was time for him to go. I stood at the front door as he descended the front steps. He turned and smiled; a long, charming smile; too long. And in those moments something occurred. I felt it happen! During his long gaze my heart had escaped. I was falling in love with him all over again. I hadn't meant for that to happen.

Darn! I flopped onto my bed and stared at the ceiling, reliving the day. That's what you do when you fall in love. But I knew this was dangerous territory.

I was inspired by the difference the painting had made to my bedroom walls, and the problem wall now disguised with two good coats. Next I needed to tackle the wallpaper. After my Mother's and aunt's immersion in the world of ready-pasted wallpaper in the 60s and 70s, I felt quite at home here too. 34 Farrington Pde still had wallpaper in most rooms. This was familiar territory. With only short pieces of classic paper to hang, it wouldn't take too long. I worked on it during the next week. The next time He came to visit I showed him the results of my work. I think he was suitably impressed!

My *olde worlde* room renovation was done. It was just me that was undone!

What we learnt at St John's

One of the distinctive marks of St John's, North Ryde congregation was the passionate faith of its women. These women had mostly moved to North Ryde in the 50s and 60s with their husbands, to create families and make their homes. Most of them saw the little parish of St John's become independent from St Anne's Ryde, and have Rev Arthur Kimmorley appointed as the first fulltime minister. Arthur had encouraged his congregation to trust God in all areas of life. Teaching was his biggest gift, with many of his sermons being like lectures at a Bible College. I'm sure the Prayer Chain would have readily grown out of that Sunday teaching and the women's own Bible Study Group.

The Prayer Chain had an order for phoning each other with a prayer request, coming right back to the first caller so she would know the message had made it right around to everybody. Once someone received a call they had to pray for the person in need before the next phone number in the chain was called. The Prayer Chain had been operating for years. Men, women and children made the list; health was prayed for regularly, as well as other difficulties that life threw up. I was always hearing from Mum about church news, and sometimes what had been put on the Prayer Chain recently.

Monday 7ᵗʰ October, 1991

Mum rang me at home with the most disturbing news. It had come to her on the Prayer Chain that Brad Smith was missing, just off Narrabeen, feared drowned in a diving accident. Brad had been one of the young adults who had moved away, and who had most recently joined the Air Force. It seems Brad had been with a friend on a dive and they were both missing. This news was almost too awful to imagine. Across North Ryde, the Prayer Chain was at work letting the ladies, and families, know what had happened to one of their young people, our Brad. In North Ryde, in the mid Blue Mountains, out at Alectown, across Sydney, prayers were said for Brad Smith and his friend; prayers, and waiting. The waiting was not so hard for those of us who had work to be immersed in over those days; such information can be moved away from, so that routines can be continued. How hard for the family to wait - to hope and to wait, and to pray.

And that's what they did.

Janet Smith told me, "I just didn't give up hope, even after a few days had gone by. We thought Brad could have been washed further down the coast. It was possible he was still alive."

Wednesday 9th

Then the terrible news came through; Brad's body had been located, and that of his friend Rick. He was found in the deepest part of the submerged boat they had set out to explore in, which also contained much silt. If this silt had been disturbed by the two men they may not have been able to find their way out.

The St John's Prayer Chain, as well as the grape vine, went to work to tell us all the sad news. It was on TV. We could read about it in the papers. This wasn't just a news story; this was Brad's life, cut so tragically short. And there was Fran, Rick's girlfriend of a few months. She too, was one of ours. What a sad time it would be for all concerned. We kept our eyes on the SMH for details of the funeral.

My thoughts kept coming back to Brad. He was six years younger than me. I'd seen him grow up, with his two other brothers, and a sister (also Janet),in our midst at St John's. These guys were more my brother's age and over the years the three Smith boys were always coming in and out of our house; having Bible Study, or a meeting, or supper after church on our back verandah, with the rest of the Fellowship. Brad, and his brothers, had been an active part in the youth group and in church life. I trust that Brad had known the saving grace of the Lord Jesus.

He had grown up and then, like others, he had moved away. Over those years Brad had moved away from the church too. The silent question in everyone's mind was,

"Where did Brad stand with God now?" It was a haunting question.

I realised how hard it had made this time for Brad's family and the friends who loved him. If it had been a few years ago… If he had been going to church …

But I didn't entertain these doubts for too long. As I read the stark reality of the newspaper reports I understood that Brad would have known what was in store for him. He had been an experienced diver, and he would have fully understood his situation that Monday afternoon; he couldn't see his way out; he was not attached to an anchor line; there was no way out. It was just a matter of time. I can only imagine the Bradley Smith I knew, calling out to the God of his youth – his First Love.

The conversation in his head would not have been long on words, but full of fear and deepest faith. The kind of faith you pull out of your duffle bag when you are at the bottom of the ocean with only a little oxygen left - face to face with death. This is what Arthur Kimmorley had prepared Brad for, these final moments. Brad knew what he needed to do to get right with his God. All he had to do was call out to Him. I know Brad did that. I just know. And the Jesus who had walked on water, and calmed a storm at sea, was there for him. Before anyone knew Brad was even missing, he had taken the hand of Jesus and walked right through Heaven's gate – in his wetsuit!

With this view of events, it made the funeral easier, for me at least. I had asked for time off school to attend the funeral, and was pleased to have Neil Flower cover my lessons. I would go back to school as soon as the service was finished. No memory of the casual fun-loving Brad today. It was a full military funeral, the likes of which St John's and North Ryde had not seen. Brad's coffin was draped in the Australian flag, his cap stark against the red, white and blue flag. That solemn mood that descends on a church when someone too young has died had arrived before I did. All the church people were there - so many of them. This was huge for the families who had known and loved Brad; the Krenmar and their boys; the Condons; the Waterhouses; the Bliss's; Cansdells; the Bliss family. Some of the young people arrived separate from their parents, some together. All the ladies were there Mum, Dorothy Kenning, Dot Thornthwaite, June Jones, Joy McLeod, Elsie Henze. Also Stephen Kimmorley arrived with his Mum Elsa, from the Central Coast. And Robert Taylor was there. He would have known all of the Smith boys from Sunday school classes.

Janet had come down from Parkes, with baby Claudia. I sat next to them. A new baby for the St John's family to meet and love! My brother Geoff arrived from work at Concord Hospital, and sat next to Janet. He was delighted to cuddle little Claudia,

"You forget how small they are," he said, with Heather now 18 months.

More of the young people started to arrive; John Small, Tim Durbidge, Dale Condon, Peter Karp. It was some years since I had seen some of these younger St John's friends. Nice to see them, but it was for such a sad occasion. I saw Julie Worsley across a few rows. Julie was closer to my age, and still a local. We had a quick chat later.

It was hard watching the family arrive; Mr and Mrs Smith, and Matthew and Janet. Mr Smith was not well, and the two brothers had a big load to carry today. Mark Smith arrived with his Janet and their young boys, to say goodbye to a brother and a favourite uncle.

Then Fran arrived, physically supported by her family. She was wearing sun-glasses, but they did not hide her grief. Today she would say goodbye to her long-time friend and new boyfriend. This was so very sad.

Janet Smith said she was shocked to see an aunt arrive at the funeral with a camera. But now these photos of the military procession, taken on the day, are very precious to them. They are a tangible memory of the day the family and friends of Bradley David Smith said goodbye to a son, a brother, a brother-in-law, a nephew, an uncle, a cousin, and a friend. It was also the day the army said goodbye to one of their men! They, on the other hand, had known the fighting-fit Brad Smith who had signed up in 1985 to serve his country.

The cortege made its way down Cox's Rd. Airmen in pristine military uniforms formed a guard of honour in front of the hearse, marching ahead of it, past the shops in Cox's Rd; left onto Wicks Rd; onto Epping Hwy and all the way to the Northern Suburbs Crematorium. A military funeral the like of which North Ryde has ever seen before – and most probably will never see again.

The prayer chain went back to being available to any who had a need.

It was later that year that Janet phoned me. Little Claudia was being baptised, and they wanted me to be the godmother! How nice. What an easy answer that was. I already was godmother to little Nicole Hogan, to young Heather and now to Claudia Ellyn Westcott. I'm told she carries a link to me in her middle name.

I drove out to Alectown that weekend. The service on the Sunday was in the Uniting Church in Parkes. Everyone was in their best clothes. It is a big thing to stand out the front of a church and make some promises on behalf of a little child. A great responsibility.

All done, we were back to the old farmhouse the Westcotts called home, and back into casual clothes and a filling lunch for family and friends.

So I now had three goddaughters. And I thought that would be all!

The cost

There was sometimes an interesting cost to pay for this job that I loved. When I met people for the first time they would naturally ask me, 'What do you do?'

'I teach Christian Studies at a state high school,' was my reply. At this point the conversation would die a quick death, or, on the other hand move onto new places.

'Now there's a gutsy woman,' remarked an old acquaintance.

'That must be a challenge.'

'Good on you.'

Those outside the field of education saw my job as scary. Those inside the school walls saw it as remarkable that things sailed along smoothly.

There was the time I received a wedding invitation from my cousin's son, Graham. How nice. It would be a late Spring wedding on the north shore. Our family had been invited., but there was just one problem. I had already booked, planned and invited Year 8 to a Christian Studies Camp on that weekend. We were going to Gerringong. It was a long way from Roseville. Could I possibly make it?

The main obstacle was that I was the only teacher on the camp. The rest were youth workers and parents. I didn't think I could leave my responsibilities on the Saturday. There seemed no way forward. Mind you I didn't take this problem to the Committee, as I was sure there was no solution to my dilemma,

Occasionally I see the wedding photos from that day with the family in their wedding best and I am sorry again that I missed this family gathering.

I did miss the occasional social event, but when at the camp I was fully present and made the most of the time away to encourage and equip young lives.

At the end of the year I penned with calligraphy a verse from Isaiah to use in a Christmas Newsletter. The following quote is from that term 4 Newsletter

"As we approach this Christmas season we have much to thank God for. Especially at this time we thank Him for the gift of his Son. We thank God that He broke into history to bring us to Himself. Our task this year has been to bring students to an understanding of this God and of his love for them. We have had the joy and privilege of seeing young people letting God into their lives, and becoming Christians.

Ian has met regularly with the boys who made a commitment to Christ at our April camp. We have both spent time with the new Year 7 Christians from our October camp, to teach and encourage them, and we have enjoyed the freshness of their new faith.

We have covered many areas and issues in class to help students see God's perspective on life. In a small way this is where the truth of the gospel touches lives, through Self-Esteem, Relationships, and Search for Happiness.

We have enjoyed our second year in the school, feeling very much at home. We have lots of laughs in our staffroom and appreciate the good friendships God has provided there. We are thankful for Peter Noble and Lyn M for their continued support.

We would like to thank *you* for your continued support of this work. Your prayers encourage us and your donations enable us to be in the school. Thank you. It is nice to know we are part of a big team.

May we wish you the blessings of the season as we celebrate the birth of the Prince of Peace."

Helen and Ian

1992

Chapter 4

It was in late January that I met my new colleague. Chris O'Flaherty. He had been appointed the first Christian Studies teacher for the brand new Cherrybrook Technology High School. Chris and his wife Peta, lived in a house on the grounds of Christian Literature Crusade in West Pennant Hills. They had recently settled there with their two young children, after leaving their mission agency WEC (World Evangelisation Crusade) to seek this school employment. Chris had a primary teaching background, which would stand him in good stead in a creative classroom. He had spent time on the outreach ship Doulos, on one of its teams. There he prepared for and encountered international evangelism in ports around the world. This was awesome and a huge step away from my background. Chris and I would end up making a good team; no, the best team!

Chris's lessons at CTHS, for Year 8 and the new Year 7, were rostered over two days, on the new site, all 15 of them. He then had more lessons with me over a three-day period at PHHS. It was a very full load. Chris was interested in my tried and true lessons, and where able, used these very ones for his own Year 7s and 8s. With a wife, a toddler and a baby at home he didn't need to reinvent the wheel here.

Chris had a keen sense of humour so we got on very well. He also got on well with the teachers in the MUSIC staffroom, especially Ian Barker. If those two had their Myers-Briggs personality done, I'm sure they would come out the same. Both were admired and loved by their students; both had a laid back, creative approach to teaching. But I'm getting ahead of myself on this.

Chris would always wait for me, at the end of a busy day, and walk out to our cars together. I appreciated this brief time of debriefing and touching base before the day was over. Sometimes we would stand and talk at a car for a while. Other times, Chris would invite me home for coffee. I don't think I ever needed to say no. This was a lovely way to get to know three year old Ben and toddler Kate.

Peta was a lovely, fresh, outgoing wife and mother. We would often talk deeply and became good friends too. It was inspiring to hear of their mission goals for the future put on hold while the kids were small. And Peta had quite different ideas about the need to have a big house full of new furniture. I liked listening to what seemed like radical ideas and watching the O'Flahertys live simply. It helped me to examine some areas of my own life with new eyes.

Chris was soon on the church visit circuit; we mostly visited separate churches. I remember one church that invited both of us to its early morning service. We both left warm beds to be there on time. We were welcomed at the door, and the minister found us as we sat together at the front of the church. It was a short chat. He told us when we were on, and that we had five minutes to speak; the two of us! As the minister turned and left Chris looked at me and we both wanted to laugh out loud.

"You have the three minutes slot," said Chris, "you can say more. I'll take the two minutes."

Chris said this with a smile on his face and disbelief in his voice. How could someone invite a man in fulltime Christian service to speak for two minutes! It was almost an insult. Some of the ministers we interacted with were very jealous of their time in church - they didn't give it away easily. At the end of the day the feedback we got from parishioners to the news we shared was that they enjoyed every second!

Year 8 and the **SUPERMAN COMIC 1992**

Sometimes the best lessons 'just happen'. Geoff Broughton was following my development of the Heroes theme with Year 8, and the study of Superman. One day he asked me,

"Did you know that in the comic book series they have just killed Superman?"

I was astounded! The man of steel – dead?

"How will they sell the comic anymore?" he asked, obviously himself surprised by this turn of story.

Not a good story line for business, I reflected. Geoff told me of a comic book shop in Parramatta where I could get copies of this Superman comic. I pursued the comic that very afternoon and found myself in a shop filled with comic books, both recent and vintage. My brother would have loved this store! I flipped through the Superman comics and found the relevant ones where Superman dies. Also available was the following edition where all the superheroes and the people of Metropolis held a funeral for their Hero. I flipped through its pages. Again I was astounded. After the funeral when Lois Lane and her Editor visit Superman's tomb in the centre of the city, they found it . . . empty! The cartooning at this point takes my breath away. It looks exactly like a scene inside Jesus' empty tomb; two friends who have come; an empty coffin; and questions.

This **IS** the Jesus story - death and resurrection. Superman had been modelled on the real hero, Jesus, only he didn't just save a city but the whole world from the consequences of sin.

For class I reproduced the comic story of Superman's death on overhead transparencies. I read the cells with dramatic effect. The students were glued to the images they have not seen before, some reading ahead quickly. I came to a gripping end, as Superman lay dying in the arms of Lois Lane. He had just stopped his fatally wounded enemy from destroying Metropolis.

Lois Lane, 'HE'S GONE!'

Henderson, 'NOT REALLY. I'D SAY FROM THE LOOK OF THINGS HE'S BACK! SUPERMAN IS BACK.'

Students are as surprised as I had been at this turn in the story. Superman is dead! They leave the room somewhat subdued.

I began the next lesson by saying, "Can you believe that Superman is dead? Well it seems that he is. This next comic even has the story of his funeral." Students are surprised again.

And I read the story again, showing the pages of one comic briefly around the class. Students were engrossed. Then I came to the scene where Lois Lane and the editor visited Superman's tomb, unnerved by reports that people had seen Superman alive.

This image also surprised the students.

"Who does this remind you of?" I asked.

And somebody always replied, "Jesus."

"But the one difference," I continued, "is that Jesus wasn't a fictional character. He lived and died and rose again two thousand years ago in Palestine. His life is the model for all other hero figures that we have invented to make us feel good. Jesus laid down his life to save each of us from the consequences of our own wrongdoing. And to demonstrate that he **was** God he didn't stay dead. Jesus beat death, the last enemy of mankind, and he now lives with God always, calling us into relationship with himself."

It was time for the students to have their own paper images of this superhero event!

The bell goes. Bags and bodies move. Minds are still at work. There was much life in my classroom today. Sometimes the best lessons 'just happen'.

I had asked the students who their heroes were. Often it was a sportsman, sometimes a great world leader. Othertimes it was their parents. I would sometimes mention my hero, who at the time was Ethna Gallagher, an English calligrapher who lived and taught in Sydney. I had been to one of her summer schools and to a workshop in her Studio. I admired her work and lifestyle. I didn't mention my other heroes – people who left home and went overseas in the service of the living God. I made friends with some of these people when I was at Moore College. Soon I would have a few more of these heroes up close and personal.

'Would I become a missionary?', still loomed in the back of my mind.

THE CASE OF THE VANISHING CORPSE[2]

It was on one of my frequent trips to Koorong that I came across this interesting book. I had in my hand a small paperback. It was written by an Australian author, Kel Richards. The title was curious- *The Case of the Vanishing Corpse*. I read the book blurb on the back, and I was sold.

I looked forward to reading this contemporary old tale, and it made it to the top of my reading list. Each chapter left me curious for more. In a clever way Kel Richards had brought the first century into the twentieth century. There were phones and fax machines; cars and camels; sandals and secretaries; vans and vandals. This tale was one of mystery and

---

2 The world of Ben Bartholomew ... a world of stand over gangs and armed terrorists, a world of religious fanatics, petty tyrants, spies and nightmares, which explodes with intrigue and danger when a corpse disappears from a sealed tomb. The Case of the Vanishing Corpse is the ultimate locked-room mystery

intrigue. I knew this story would work well with Year 7, and through its use, focus on the person of Jesus. It seemed that in class I would read two chapters each week. All the wonder and interest of reading a book to students was experienced again, and enjoyed.

Year 7 and I had a delightful time romping through Jerusalem with our main character, Ben Bartholomew. Ben was a private detective based in Jerusalem, in 33AD. As the book opens Ben has just been hired by the high priest Caiaphas to investigate the missing body of Jesus Davidson. (On the personal front he has just bumped into Rachel, his old girlfriend.)

The High Priest in Jerusalem employs Ben Bartholomew.

"There is a missing person ... he is also dead."

Ben is bemused by this request. He has never heard anything like it!

"Bring me the body of Jesus the Nazarene."

Ben is reluctant to be involved with this powerful Jerusalem figure, but the strength of Caiaphas's bodyguard, Shagmar, convinces him it would be in his best interest.

This body had been missing from its tomb for a few days. Ben accepted the case, the most curious he had ever been on - a *missing person* who happens to be dead. In so doing Ben finds himself mixed up with the Jewish underground, the RIA. And so the investigation begins. Ben gets taken blindfolded to an unknown destination, threatened and told that he will also report his findings to the Roman Investigation Authority. The local underground boss wants all the information that Ben finds out about the missing body case.

Ben systematically locates and interviews all the people involved in the Jesus Davidson case:

- **Guards** on duty on the day of Jesus crucifixion
- **Doctor** who signed the death certificate

- **Lawyer**, Nicodemus, who offered his tomb to place Jesus' body in
- **Pilate,** the governor
- **Jesus' disciples**
- Mary **Magdalene**

Rachel, Ben's ex-girlfriend, gets mixed up in the Davidson case as well. She was befriended by some of the women disciples. Rachel pursues her interest in Jesus' way of life by following the disciples to Galilee, and the gathering of Jesus' followers who meet there. Ben is getting close to the truth in Galilee when Rachel is kidnapped by the mob, and taken back to Jerusalem. Ben now takes on the hero role and pursues her, doing what it takes to set her free.

Finally Ben makes his finding to Caiaphas. He presents all the possibilities, and comes to the only conclusion that fits the evidence, but you'll have to read Kel Richard's book for that!

As the book closes, Ben and Rachael were last seen catching a bus to Caesarea.

The Case of The Vanishing Corpse is used with permission by the author, **Kel Richards**

Cough, cough, cough

Things were progressing well before ISCF CONFERENCE, with plenty to organise and lots to do, until I got a cold, a bad one. I usually get one bout of flu each winter; in a bad year, maybe two. Not the fever-hurting-muscles-aching type of flu, but the weeping-eyes-running-nose-coughing type of flu, which is really just a **very bad** cold. I think this particular health risk comes with my profession. My last couple of colds had been nasty, settling on my chest, and staying for a while. I would usually need three days off school to feel on top of such a cough/cold. The coughing alone just wore me out. As well as being very untimely this current cold was heavy and chesty.

At school on these days, whenever I needed to talk over student noise, my involuntary coughing would start, and not stop. Communication seemed to almost stop. It became difficult when a glob of phlegm sealed across my throat, and airways. My body worked hard to clear the blockage in my lungs; I knew I needed to cough the phlegm up, so it did not settle again. This was hard when I was with other people, so sometimes I had to just cough and swallow it. A few times I needed to leave the classroom when the coughing became extreme. I would cough and cough and cough, my eyes would water, until I could bring up the phlegm and breathe naturally again. This ailment seemed to wreck havoc with me.

It was Tuesday in the last week of term. I was commanding my classes the best I could this day. I'd had a coughing session during the morning, mid-lesson, that had really rattled me, and I had spent time outside the classroom coughing, coughing coughing. I felt like I was wearing out. I now had two lessons until the end of the school day. While teaching Year 8 I started to get a pain in my chest, a significant pain. And when I coughed slightly it hurt. I continued teaching; more pain. I was trying to work out what was going on. I stilled myself and noticed that when I breathed it hurt, and hurt bad, and only when I breathed. But breathing wasn't optional, and so the pain continued and intensified. Soon it was excruciating. I knew I couldn't teach my last class. I couldn't go on. I needed to sit down, to lie down. I knew I needed some help. The next Year 7 bounded into the classroom.

"Just sit quietly for a minute," I said and left the room.

But I also needed to tell someone about my abandoned class first. There was no one around. The Head-Teacher Administration was on Level 4. I climbed the stairs; slowly, very slowly. I walked into the office and found Kevin.

"I have just left Year 7 in 3P4, (breathe, hurt), I'm not well (breathe, hurt), my chest hurts (breathe, hurt). I need to go back to the staffroom and lie down." It was obvious to Kevin that I was in pain.

The walk back to my staffroom seemed a long way. Once there, I cleared accumulated junk from the yellow vinyl chairs under the window and lay across them. I was going nowhere fast. It didn't take long for Nila, our deputy, to arrive at the staffroom.

"What's wrong?" Nila asked anxiously, as she entered.

"It just hurts when I breathe," I replied feeling the pain with every gasp.

"I called an ambulance," said Kevin as he also arrived.

An ambulance! I didn't think I needed an ambulance! I understood they had stopped what they were doing to focus on my health crisis. They stayed with me until the paramedics arrived, who asked a lot of questions.

"Have you got any pain in your arm?"

"No."

"What is the pain like on a scale of 1-10?"

"Six-seven."

"Is your chest tight?"

I then realised they thought I was having a heart attack.

"No, no. It just hurts when I breathe." I knew it was somehow related to my coughing.

My blood pressure was taken. They attached me to the oxygen tank they had wheeled in. By now Chris had come off class to see what was happening. Kevin was covering his lesson. Chris walked in to see me attached to an oxygen machine. I smiled.

"A bit of a dramatic way to get time off class!" I said.

Chris smiled back. I think he was relieved that I could still make a joke.

"We'll need to take you to Hornsby Hospital. They will do some tests on you," said the ambulance officer.

Not yet, I thought to myself. I was conscious of the time. It was so close to the end of the school day. I didn't want to be wheeled out in front of departing students. Not if I could help it! But I wasn't in any position to negotiate this. Chris said apologetically that he couldn't come with me, as he had to pick up the kids and mind them this afternoon.

"That's OK."

"I'll ring Neil Flower," he said.

Just after they assisted me to lie on the stretcher the bell rang! Those students who were quick to leave class saw ambulance officers wheeling Miss McNab across the Quad and assisting her into the back of an ambulance! They looked quite concerned. It was this departing news that students carried home that afternoon.

I repeated my story to the nurse in Emergency. "It just hurts when I breathe," I said, breathing and hurting.

A hospital gown was put on me and I was attached to a few machines. Tests were done; lots of tests to eliminate a heart attack. Now the pain seemed to have localised to one spot in my chest, and I felt sore on the inside. I may need to have an x-ray. Neil Flower arrived, and waited outside until he was allowed in. I repeated my story to him, "It just hurts when I breathe."

"He asked, "Is there someone we can call?"

"Yes, my brother. He works at Concord Hospital."

The staff helped find the number, and dialed it for me. I just had to ask for 'Geoff McNab' at reception. I told him what had happened.

"I'm in Hornsby Hospital. Can you pick me up later?"

It appeared that he couldn't. Geoff had his counselling class on tonight. He was towards the end of the training. If he missed any more lectures he wouldn't be able to finish the course.

"OK." I was disappointed.

What would I do? Would I need a taxi?

After watching the monitor over a period of hours, the medical team decided that I hadn't had a heart attack. I had torn the lining of my lung. This was from excessive coughing. Yes that made sense; very good sense. The very first intense pain I felt was some of the tissue around my lungs tearing away. Rest was the suggested medicine. Neil called Geoff Broughton and arranged for Geoff to meet him at the hospital. I felt bad that I was putting so many people out. By now I was feeling better. By the time I was finally released it was well into the evening, and dark outside. I gave Geoff Broughton my car keys for his trip from Pennant Hills to Blacktown with my car. I travelled home, a passenger in Neil Flower's land rover, and was very thankful when we arrived home. It was obvious I wouldn't be at school for the rest of the week.

"I'll organise cover for your classes tomorrow," said Neil. "I may be able to do some lessons myself in the morning."

"He enquired, "What do you have planned for the holidays?"

"I'm going to Leadership CONFERENCE," I said.

"Well you aren't now," he recommended.

"But I have to. I'm the Director!" I said, thinking of all the tasks I still had to do.

"You aren't in a fit state to go away. You need to rest," Neil insisted.

I knew he was right. My mind was working on this.

"Maybe I could just go part-time," I said imploringly. "I will help get things going and come home after a few days."

This seemed to Neil to be a suitable option. He and Geoff B left, to pick up Geoff's car from the high school car park. I was very grateful for the care of these two Committee members, brothers in Christ, and their mercy dash to Hornsby, and then all the way to Blacktown. I rang Chris to let him know how I was. He said they had received many calls about my departure from school in an ambulance. It seems phones of Christians scattered through Pennant Hills, and beyond, rang hot that evening, with the news that Miss McNab had suffered a heart attack at school! No, it was just a torn lung!

I rested and felt better with every new day. My lung was healing as the torn tissue repaired itself. At this time Mum was away on a holiday with Aunty Bet. I wouldn't tell her about this little hospital episode, as she would only worry after the event. By the time Mum did come back from Queensland, and I came back from CONFERENCE, my cold had all cleared up. She would never know.

I did go to ISCF CONFERENCE, as the Director, on Day One. I didn't come home on Day Three. But that may not surprise you!

When innocence left us

For most of us it was just an ordinary Wednesday night. But arriving at school the next day I became aware the previous night had been far from ordinary for one of our school families. I could sense something was wrong when I walked through the first garden quad. Students were in tears. Girls stood with their arms around a friend who was weeping. What had happened? A note on the Sign-On book would give meaning to what I had witnessed. One of our girls in Year 8, Chloe, had died the night before from an asthma attack.

This was a great shock, magnified today because Chloe was a twin. I had taught both Chloe and Lisa. They were both attractive, sporty girls, with a great outlook on life and lots of friends. As I walked to the staffroom I realised that those most affected were many of the Year 8 students who had been on both the Year 7 and Year 8 Christian Studies Camp, and whom I had got to know well. This loss had come right into the heart of their peer group. This would be huge for all of them.

I made my way back out to the students. Could I be of any assistance? It would be hard to know what to say. But today they didn't need words just a hug and a listening. Some of these friends spoke out their thoughts; others were quiet, wiping away tears. It seemed easier for the girls to cry. The boys, also in a state of shock, didn't know what to do, didn't know what to say. They just stood together and gave concerned looks towards the girls, who gathered in small groups.

At a brief staff meeting the Principal explained what had happened. The asthma attack came suddenly; the ambulance didn't get there in time. A mantle of sadness seemed to visibly settle on the staff assembled. My Year 8 classes wanted to talk about Chloe's death. They were more subdued than normal, and looked to me for some answers. Discussion about death was not on the Year 8 curriculum, but this is where life had led them today, far too early. So we talked. The other Year Groups, 7, 9 & 10, were not as affected by this and for the good of all I continued normal lessons.

The ongoing drama that is associated with the unexpected death of someone so young continued over the following days. Staff were told of funeral arrangements and encouraged to attend if they knew the family. A Year 8 assembly was held. Lisa hadn't returned to school, and her absence at this assembly made the double sadness of Chloe's untimely death even more apparent. Students were missing both their friends.

Year 8 students were given the funeral details. Friends of Chloe and Lisa were encouraged to go to the funeral with their parents. It was to be held at the local Catholic Church. The Principal asked me if I would speak at the funeral. It seemed a fitting thing for the Christian Studies teacher to have something to say, and I agreed. But I had no idea what I could say. I did know the girls to be active Catholics from discussions in class, and that gave me a place to start.

I was very moved to have a Year 8 student show me a poem she had written as a response to Chloe's death. Her beautiful words made me aware of how losing a friend was affecting these young people. The unimagined loss; the tears; days of unanswered questions; wishing it hadn't happened; lonely, sleepless nights; thoughts turning to God. This grief remained like a visible stamp on all the students concerned, for days; grief that would find its full expression on the day of the funeral. And as I searched for the right words to say, I decided to use that poem.

Students arrived for the funeral of Chloe at St Agatha's Catholic Church, Pennant Hills, with their parents. This was very likely the first funeral the Year 8s had ever been to. They entered the large, pale-brick church in family groups. Students weren't dressed in school uniform, but in clothes of their choice. There was no thought that these sad young people would be going back to school today.

This was a moving thing to witness, and I reflected on the big role parents would have played this week in the lives of their children, as they struggled to come to grips with the reality of the death of a friend. Parents were there to support their children, but also to give their respects and support to the twin's parents, whom they would have known through a variety of community organisations. That it was an asthma attack that took young Chloe was in itself a reason for parents to hold their children tightly. This could happen to anyone.

I hadn't met Chloe and Lisa's parents before, and observing their very public face today was a moving thing. They were immaculately dressed, and stood with the quiet dignity of successful migrants, now bearing the weight of unfathomable loss. They carried their own grief of the loss of a daughter, but their biggest role today was to support Lisa, as she attempted to say goodbye to her beloved sister. It was sad to see Lisa's young face with the trauma of the last week engraved upon it.

We were welcomed by the parish priest and the farewells began. The Principal spoke on behalf of the school, of Chloe's character and achievements, and the great loss of a fine young PHHS student. He spoke very personally about the untimely nature of Chloe's death, having two school-aged children of his own. Two of Chloe's friends read out their combined tribute to their dear friend. It was a brave thing to be able to do, and no one minded their tears. Then it was my turn.

"A girl in Year 8 wrote a poem to express her feelings about Chloe's death. I will read just one verse.

> *I shed a tear, each night I lay*
>
> *I hope and wish and cry and pray*

Here are four responses to death, "I HOPE and WISH and CRY and PRAY,"

- We can **WISH** . . .

- We can wish that things were different.

- We can wish we could go back.

- We can wish that we could make it better.

But we know that these wishes can't come true.

So we **CRY** . . .

This is the most human of all responses to death. Our grief is real and it hurts. Jesus had a friend who died. His Name was Lazarus. Jesus was very close to him and went to visit Lazarus's sisters, Mary and Martha, to comfort them. We are told that when Jesus arrived at Lazarus' tomb he was so deeply moved that he cried. Jesus grief was real and it hurt.

And we can **PRAY** . . .

This is a very appropriate response to death.

We reach out to God in moments of great need, to tell him that we hurt to ask for his help and to acknowledge the hope he alone can give us.

And so we have **HOPE** . . . when we believe in God.

We have hope in the Person who was a friend of Lazarus. Jesus said to Martha, outside her brother's tomb,

"I am the resurrection and the life. He who believes in me will live, even though he dies. And whoever lives and believes in me will never die."

Then Jesus proved that what he said was true. Firstly, by bringing Lazarus back to life; then by beating death himself and coming back from the grave, having conquered death forever and for everyone who trusts in him.

A great HOPE, our only HOPE.

At the end I concluded with a prayer.

The most moving part of the service was Lisa's goodbye. She had chosen a song, made popluar in recent years, as a tribute to her sister. The words of *Wind Beneath My Wings* filled the church as a lone sister owned the words,

'Did you ever know that you're my hero?'

TEACH PRAY LOVE

Young and old alike listened, through tears, to the familiar words, today given a new meaning. As the service ended, grieving youth, parents and High School staff alike moved out of the building into the morning light.

I had struggled that day to find the right words for that final prayer I offered. I still have the handwritten page of notes I read from at the funeral. The prayer I read is on the back of these pages. I can see my first attempt,

"that through Chloe's death many would be drawn to the God who has power over death."

But I had thought twice about it, and crossed it out. Chloe's funeral may not be the appropriate place to speak of any good outcomes of her death; it may not be fitting. So I crossed those words out and wrote others that I read as a prayer.

It would be three years later, when I had the opportunity to hear the Christian testimony of some of the very students who sat in that funeral service, that I would realise my unspoken prayer had been answered. By then some of these Year 8 students were in Year 11, living Christian lives and having student leadership positions in ISCF. As training for an evangelistic event I had encouraged a small group of them to put their own Christian story into words, using a simple outline. It was time for me to hear these young leaders' voice, and their testimony. I didn't quite know how they would speak about the growing faith that I had seen in them, over the last few years.

"My name is ... and I grew up in a Christian/non-Christian family. When I was in Year 8 one of our good friends died. Her death really made me think about God. Was I ready to die? What would happen to me? It was then ..."

Each of the Year 11 students began their stories the same way! They all came back to that sad week, and the death of Chloe, as the time they decided they needed to take God seriously. I was quite taken aback when I listened. Their words were like music for my soul. I understood afresh that even in the darkest times of our lives God is present, quietly bringing about his good purpose. The prayer I wasn't game to pray out loud that day had been heard by God even so. It was the same prayer that adults around the Pennant Hills area prayed in their churches, in their small groups, in their homes; that through the death of this young PHHS student, other students might become aware of the things of eternity and that they may reach out to the God who loves them.

These few Year 11 students seated before me, in 1995, had looked death in the face that week in 1992, and chose Life.

Thank you to the many unseen faces who prayed for Lisa, her family, and her friends. Most prayer is silent and unseen. But the Father takes notice of his weak ones when it's almost too hard to pray; and He takes action, in His own time.

Broken

It was a sad story; a chapter in our family history that changed it forever. In 1967 Mum's sister June, and her husband Jimmy, were killed in a car accident, involving a truck running a red light in Parramatta, one Saturday night. Their three boys were left as orphans. Various family members stepped up, including my Mum and Dad, and Aunty Bet and Uncle George, to take the boys into their home and care for them. In the 60s there was no help, no services, no extra money. There was no counselling for these boys 13, 10 and 8 who acted out this trauma in their lives in various ways. As hard as the relatives tried not one of these new home situations worked out, and eventually our cousins all went into foster care. In time a court case awarded each of the boys the grand sum of $2,000 for the loss of both parents. Over the years, from time to time, we heard what each one was doing. One cousin was in the Blue Mountains;

another had moved to South Australia; another to Queensland. It had now been almost two decades since we had seen them.

I received a phone call one night from my cousin Philip. I was so surprised. He must have just tried the phone book to find me. Philip and his wife, and daughter, were visiting from the Gold Coast for a Sydney holiday with friends. Phillip had had his wallet stolen. Could I lend him $100? At this point my head was racing. I felt like I was being used. Was his story even true? What will I do? What will I say? If there wasn't a young girl involved, my second cousin, I may have reacted differently. I asked him where he was staying. Mt Druitt wasn't too far from me. I arranged to meet up with him in a couple of night's time.

When I went to visit Mum the next day I told her of my surprise phone call.

"You'll never guess who I had a phone call from last night."

"Who?"

"Philip Ware."

Mum's face changed as she took in what I had just told her.

"He's here on holiday with his wife and daughter. His wallet got stolen and he asked if I could lend him $100."

Mum was dumbfounded.

"Those Wares are all the same," she said. "His parents were always getting into financial difficulty and I would bail them out. You're not going to give him the money are you?"

"He's *family* Mum! I can't not do it!"

"I don't think you'll see the $100 again."

"Maybe!"

While I watched TV after dinner Mum was on the phone to my Aunty Bet relaying this family news. These boys - men, were the closest these women had to a sister who had been lost.

"Helen said he's family." I overheard from the back verandah.

I knocked on the door of a small house in Mount Druitt. I had $100 in my bag, in an envelope. The door opened, and there standing before me was the spitting image of my Uncle Jimmy. I hadn't seen Philip since he was a young teen. Now he was a man, and the family resemblance was undeniable. It unnerved me. I met his wife and young daughter, my second cousin. It was pleasant enough getting to know them. Philip asked after the rest of the family, Geoff and our cousins; and especially Joan, his favourite aunty. I handed Phillip the envelope. He was very thankful and said he would reimburse me when he got home. They would be catching the bus on Saturday. I made my move to leave and said my farewells.

I have not heard from Philip again. There is a debt standing between us, and now he probably won't make contact again. But he's still family!

It's still is a sad story.

Baptisms

There were some students who grew to have a special place in my heart. These were those I saw frequently – in class, at ISCF and on camps. One such student was Anita, an Asian student who was going to Pennant Hills Baptist, with her friend Sarah. I was delighted to be invited to her baptism, one Sunday morning. I had only been to the baptism/ christening of babies. This would be different.

The large pool was uncovered at the front of the church , heated over hours and readied for this confession of faith. Anita had friends and family gather to witness this event in her life. She was interviewed by the pastor about what had brought her to this event. At the right time Anita appeared in a white robe (plus shorts and a t-shirt) to join the pastor who was waiting for her. He carefully held her back, carefully until Anita was submereged. It was short and sweet. She arose a new person. She would live for Jesus. This event made me question the baby baptisms we do in the Anglican church.

Then there was Anthony. Many friends arrived to share this night with him. Anthony also was Asian. His parents at this stage were doing business in China. His best friend Tim Kirkegard had friended him into the kingdom. The Kirkegard's hospitality was something that he needed and it warmed his heart. I was grateful to accept Anthony's invitation to his baptism at West Pennant Hills Community Church. He spoke with passion about what had led him to this point in his life. Again, a large fount of water was ready. And so was Anthony in shorts and a white t-shirt. Under the water he went, and arose a new person – he was ready to live for Jesus.

Luke, a friend of Anthony and Tim and Sam, was also baptised that night.

Thankyou Anita and Anthony for inviting me to this special event in your lives. (Years later Anita married an Anglican clergyman and Anthony pastors a church of international students in Sydney's northwest. Well done good and faithful servants).

Romance 4 1992

I wanted to see *Shadowlands*, the stage play of C.S. Lewis's personal life. It was on at the Opera House Drama Theatre. I asked if he wanted to go. He agreed. We drove into the city and parked at The Rocks. It was a mild evening in September, and still light as we walked around to Bennelong Point. We talked freely in the fading light. It was like we were on a date. But no, we were just good friends! We sat at the back of the large tiered theatre and soon became enclosed in darkness as the story played itself out. I had not fully realised the implications of this drama; an older Christian man oblivious to the affections of his lady friend; then a love and passion that was cut too short; and then painful loss; some interesting parallels. (He told me later he'd thought I'd taken him to see the play because of the similarities to our friendship.)

The show over, we walked back besides a sparkling harbour. No vibrant restaurants or bars in 1991. No noisy throng of people enjoying themselves on a spring evening. It seemed like just us. He was so close. How I wished he would hold my hand. It would be so natural; so easy. But no, we were just good friends. Back at home and a goodnight greeting from the car! I wondered when I might see him again? It seemed to be something I never knew, which did not help my 'in love' condition.

Romance 5

Some months later I had dancing on my mind. My friend Kathy was very involved in preparations for the ball to be put on by CS & A. I heard about all the progress from her. Like many other Christian singles, I was looking forward to it. But what would I wear? The ball committee, of Phil, John, Kathy and x, decided we singles might all need to brush up on our dancing skills before the big night. A dance lesson was organised for anyone interested, at the Snowy River Dance Studio in West Ryde.

The room was very full that Saturday afternoon. We would go through all the classic ballroom dances that would be on the dance program. I needed to concentrate! We started with a simple dance, as people were still arriving. I was dancing with someone and looking across the room, when *he* walked in. My heart lept! He was with a group of people. *He* was coming to the ball! This was not something I had anticipated. He had been invited by some other women, who were 'just friends'

I watched from afar, until it was time for a progressive dance. I would soon be in his arms.

Concentrating on both footwork and my conversation was no easy thing! Slide, slide, turn, smile! And then he was gone, on to the next partner. I told Kathy during a break that he was there! Kathy had known about him from the early days. She was surprised too, and could sense my excitement. Or should I say my dilemma. He was going to The Roaring Forties Ball, but not with me. What should have been a night to enjoy became a complicated one. How would this all go?

I was hoping I might end up on a romantic journey with Mr Right, as well!

An opportunity arose that quite took my breath away.

Romance 6 September 1992

The Roaring Forties Ball

It was close to midnight as I sat in my blue satin dress conscious of the hour. The last bracket had just been announced.

"Gentlemen, take your partners for the last dance of the night."

I heard a familiar voice and turned.

"Would you like to dance?"

My heart leapt. He had saved the last dance for me! I was both surprised and overjoyed. I smiled, inside and out, as I rose to my feet and my partner. But too soon that joy would turn to tears. Tears that I feared would spill out of my eyes, down my cheek, exposed – while I was still dancing with him. I had to hold them back; back from the wave of emotion that the music had evoked.

'Should auld acquaintance be forgot, And never brought to mind . . .'

It was the music of goodbye.

It had been a thrill to be getting ready that night. The highlight of a year of singles activities was here, The Roaring Forties Ball. Hair washed and styled; make-up applied; carefully painted toe nails peeping out of high strappy sandals; perfume. It was time for the dress. The electric blue satin fabric had a deep sheen that caught the light. The sound of the satin rustled as I pulled the dress over my body. It was cool and silky to the touch. The ballerina length skirt was full and generous, falling from a shaped, gathered waist. I turned in front of the mirror to adjust the fabric bow that attached at the back. It was a beautiful colour and a beautiful dress. Not mine though, I had borrowed it! My fairy-godmother Kathy had lent it to me. She was helping to organise the Ball and had bought herself a new dress for the occasion. New earrings completed my outfit. I admired my reflection in the mirror. A transformation had taken place in me as I dressed. I felt like a princess.

The anticipation of months had only increased when I knew that he would be there. He was going to the Ball- but with someone else. I would dance with him, if only in a progressive Barn Dance or two. That in itself seemed something that would further our relationship. I had two stops to make before I drove to the Round House at Kensington. I visited Dad in the nursing home on the way. I wanted him to see my outfit tonight. Dusk had fallen as I gained entry through the front security door. All the residents were in bed by now and things were very quiet. I made my way through the empty corridors to Dad's door, wondering if anyone would see me dressed for a night out. The only sound was my high heels on the polished vinyl. Dad's eyes smiled in surprise as I walked into his room. I turned around in my satin dress for his approval. He nodded and smiled in appreciation. I told him where I was going and how Kathy had lent me the dress.

"Mum's minding Heather tonight, so I'll call in to see them too."

It wasn't a long visit that night, I had just wanted Dad to see his little girl all dressed up. As I walked back down the quiet corridor I was warmed by including Dad in this moment of my life, just as I would with Mum. The anticipation was building.

Young Heather greeted me at Mum's door, already dressed for bed. Heather's eyes took in the spectacle that was Aunty Helen dressed for the Ball. It was like something out of a fairy tale, and I was part of it.

"Can you help me practise my dancing?" I asked her.

I twirled her around the lounge room. She too would be a princess one day.

"Can I borrow your pearls?" I asked Mum, heading for her bedroom.

"Yes," came her reply.

"Can you check the bow at the back, and do up the hook and eye?" I said turning away from her.

I stood still as she secured both. I chatted about my visit to see Dad. Mum had enjoyed the news knowing the delight it would have brought to him. Time for a couple of photos before I left; one with my young dance partner, then a more formal one to capture the night Helen went to the Roaring Forties Ball.

Once inside the Round House, I felt familiar with my surroundings, even though it had been 20 years! I was also familiar, too much so, with the uncertainty I felt about interacting with him. I enjoyed the distraction of seeing everyone dressed up. My eye was drawn to what other women had chosen to wear. Some were in smart clothes with hems to the knee; others in long formal gowns. Many of the men were in dinner suits; some in a smart jacket and tie; all a myriad of colours and looking very glamorous.

We were seated in groups, with four men and four women on each table. Conversation seemed easy, but my eyes were quietly searching for him. The first dance bracket came and went. Then I saw him come in with a group, across the other side of the ballroom. I tried not to keep looking, but I would frequently dart a look across the room, between crowds of dancers, searching for him. A tasty meal was served in the middle of the evening, and there was much mingling over the dinner table. But it seemed we were always a ballroom apart. We had danced together a couple of times, during the progressive dances, so at least we had exchanged greetings.

Then I heard a 'Hello'. Rohan had crossed the ballroom to say just that, and to catch up with me. My heart was warm within me. He crouched beside me, as there were no spare chairs. We caught up with each other's news. He was in the throws of deciding to do more study- an English as a Second Language qualification, This would take him to another state. He had dreams of maybe teaching in Europe. This meant he would be going away. The next bracket of dances started and he moved away back to his side of the ballroom.

The last hour of the night went by quickly. I was sitting pretty much by myself, lost in my own world. People around me rose to take their places on the dance floor for the final bracket of dances.

"Would you like to dance?"

My heart leapt. He had saved the last dance for me. Everything in me said "yes." We both smiled.

I was soon in his arms. This was no small thing. He had come with another group, another lady, and he had chosen to dance this one with me. We silently understood that this was a big statement to make. There were a number of different dances, and we stayed together, with a little conversation. He reflected on his leaving; it could be as soon as February. This was getting painful. Then the last dance, Auld Lang Sine! The tears welled up behind my eyes. This was really hard, unbearably hard. I was in his arms, but he was leaving. He didn't notice my tears, and after the last song he escorted me back to my table. He cast his eye across the room and noticed that his group had already left. This was a statement too!

"I think I might be in trouble," he said as we parted company. He made his way out into the night.

A few moments later I walked back to my car veiled in the blackness of the night, only to find my coach had turned into a pumpkin.

Romance 6, November

Sometime after the ball I summoned the courage to address this situation head on. I needed to talk to him about the past, his frequent visits, that last dance. We were going out for coffee. In those days you needed to go all the way to Parramatta to find a coffee shop open on a Saturday night. I knew exactly what I wanted to say, piecing it together and rehearsing it in my mind all day.

It was a pleasant enough evening, but I was seriously distracted about when to ask these questions.

"I want to ask you some questions," was the way I would begin. But I kept missing the opening. Cake and coffee arrived, and left.

"Are you OK?" He asked.

"Yes," I replied, realising I was on edge.

Darn, it was getting late. Dare I start this conversation now? They started to clean up around us. It was time to leave. I had to do this. I just had to. I summoned up all my courage. We got into his car.

"I want to ask you some questions," I began.

So sitting in the shadows of the multi-storied car park we began.

"Yes."

He turned slightly to face me.

"You know how you have been coming around a lot."

He nodded his head.

"Well I'm wondering if you have done that just because I live close by. Would you have done that if you'd been living, say, in the southern suburbs?"

"I think I would."

"Because it seems like you have been fairly attentive, and I don't want to read it the wrong way."

"Well yes, I like your company and it's nice to do things together."

"Is there any more to it than that? I just need to know. We have spent so much time together in the past; holidays etc. When you left for Europe you asked me to help you in that final week. I met all your family. At the airport you gave me that great big hug. Then letters you sent that kept arriving. It was a very natural thing to fall for you along the way."

'I've been such an idiot!'

"Well I just wonder if any of those feelings might ever be returned, or if we will just be friends? You don't need to answer me now. But I need to know."

"OK."

With great relief I said, "Boy that feels better having said all that! That was hard. I bet you weren't expecting that tonight!"

He laughed. "No, I wasn't."

We talked easily now. It was time to start the car for the drive home. I had opened a door, but I felt good about it, sort of. He pulled into my drive way and I said goodnight, and as I did so I leant across and kissed him on the cheek.

"That's just in case you don't come back."

"I think I will."

He came back the very next afternoon. I was surprised, but delighted to see him. We sat on the lounge together. We hadn't been this close before. We talked some more, and held hands. I couldn't quite believe this was happening, but it was. And then he kissed me, or maybe we kissed each other. I was a bit rusty at this. He was quite new to this scene. But it felt good; very good. Before the end of the afternoon we were quite practised. He didn't want to go, but he was on the rosters at church. He was expected.

"Bye."

We were definitely in a different place now. But I wasn't quite sure where. I went into my room and lay on my bed. I stared at the ceiling and relived the evening. I stood in church that night with a light heart with no one knowing that romance had finally made its way to my door.

There were meals at his place, and at mine. Passion was on the menu too. Were we journeying to a new place?

My friends and family continued to fill my life. In October my friends Jenine and Robyn put on a 40th birthday afternoon tea for me, in my back garden. All the kids came too.

Heather Lorraine in the front; Yolanda, little Alice Winter and Amy McKnight; Hayley Stewart next to me; Dunlops – Gill hiding, James and young Kathryn. Together with my church friends and a speech from our friend Robert, it was 'Hip Hip Hooray!'

Thanks friends.

Above: Helen and Ian's first staff photo;

Below: My classroom with Year 7 and Year 10 work.

Above: Three generations of McNabs – with baby Heather;

Below left: Christmas calligraphy 1991;

Below right: Heather Lorraine and Helen Lorrraine ready for summer.

For to us a child is born.
to us a son is given.
And his name shall be called
Wonderful Counsellor
Mighty God, Everlasting
Father, Prince of Peace.

Above: No light food for thought for this young lady;

Below: Yr 7 camp on the Saltshaker, with Rev Andrew Campbell.

Clockwise from top right: My first
dance partner; PHHS assembly
1992; Chris and Ben at sunset, Lake
Munmorah.

Above: SU National Conference, NSW delegates 1993;

Middle: Helen and Chris. I think the joy shows…

Below: 3P4 post-Discovery. The only photo with my famous curtains.

1993

A favourite photo of a young Lachlan Neil Jefferson McNab;

Below left: ISCF Leadership Conference team, Gerringong 1993; Below right: PHHS Music staff/Christian Studies.

Above: Lance Sergeant Neil
McNab, approx. 25 yrs;

Below: Wedding Day of Neil and
Gwen, 18th May, 1951

Clockwise from top left: ANZAC Day, 1994; My friends Janet and Shane on the day of my father's funeral; All that survived the fire; My prayer diary, 1993; The first page of my new journal;

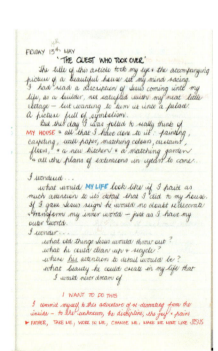

FRIDAY 15th MAY

'THE GUEST WHO TOOK OVER'

The title of this article took my eye + the accompanying picture of a beautiful house set my mind racing. I had read a description of Jesus coming into my life, as a builder, not satisfied with my neat little cottage – but wanting to turn it into a palace. A picture full of symbolism.

But this day I was jolted to really think of MY HOUSE & all that I have done to it : painting, carpeting, wall paper, matching colours, curtains, floors, + a new kitchen + a matching garden + all the plans of extensions in years to come.

I wondered ...
what would MY LIFE look like if I paid as much attention to its detail that I did to my house. If I gave Jesus reign he would no doubt re decorate + transform my inner world – just as I have my outer world.

I wonder ...
what old things Jesus would throw out?
what he could clean up + recycle?
where his attention to detail would be?
what beauty he could create in my life that I would never dream of

I WANT TO DO THIS

I commit myself to this adventure of re-decorating from the inside – to this unknown, the discipline, the joy + pain.
▶ FATHER, TAKE ME, WORK IN ME, CHANGE ME, MAKE ME MORE LIKE JESUS

1993

Chapter 5

" *I have come so that you might have life and have it to the full.* " JESUS

1993 would be a significant, if not pivotal, year for me in many areas. It began as many others have, celebrating at a New Year's Eve party with friends. I had plans to spend a week at CMS Summer School and then I was off on a journey of discovery. . .

It was on afternoon radio that I had first come across something that stirred my curiosity; something that would change everything I did in my classroom. As I drove home from school, I heard a radio interview and stories of how teens were being inspired to enjoy learning and increase their self-esteem at a weeklong leadership course. Amazing stories of transformation were told and I knew I wanted to find out more. This related directly to the Yr 9 lessons I taught on Self Esteem. I sent for an information pack, and that's how I discovered '**Discovery**'.

"Discovery is designed to assist teens to grow both personally and academically, through providing positive foundations for the establishment and nourishment of a positive self-concept. To achieve this, Discovery creates an exciting learning atmosphere over a 7 day program."

A booklet set out the aims, outlined the program and held many testimonies from participants of changed attitudes and improved grades.

I wanted to know how those outcomes were achieved; these radical transformations that were attested to. But I was a bit suspicious as well. Was this something I could get involved with? I wondered if I would agree with the ethics behind a *secular* leadership course. The program ran over ten days for leaders - which included three days of training, before the teens arrived for a week of *Discovery*. Being a leader came at a cost. $500 of cost! This was a lot of money in 1993. But I came to see the $500 as an investment in my teaching career. So, I applied to be a leader on *Discovery*. After an interview, I was accepted. The next course was to be held in the upcoming January holidays. I still wasn't sure what I would discover at *Discovery*, but my intention was to take the good, and leave anything I didn't agree with behind. I did not know at the time that I was heading into a full blown Accelerated Learning Conference, a term I was yet to become familiar with.

A few provisos were placed on participants, both adults and teens. While participating in the *Discovery* program you could not make any contact with family or friends; no phone calls or letters. That seemed an extreme request, especially for married participants and those with families. And you couldn't mention religion. Hhm! But I was willing to follow these rules to be a part of the course. So in mid-January I boarded a chartered bus at Central that would deliver me, and others, to the doors of an educational facility, on the edge of Canberra. Another bus arrived with adult participants from Melbourne. All we were asked to bring was casual clothes, a notebook and a packet of coloured felt pens. When all assembled, we were a group of about 30 trainees. We arrived the first night for a meal, and then an introductory session in a large training room. Quite a few of the group were young adults, some of whom had done the *Discovery* program as students. They had now come back to contribute something to this life affirming approach to learning and living and continue with the positive way of living they had found.

We had small, individual rooms, but the program was so full all we did was fall asleep there, at the end of an emotionally draining and physically demanding day. That first night we met our trainer, or facilitator, Michael Wall, a bearded, floral shirt wearing, 35 year old from Hawaii. He seemed to have only one speed – full on. Over three days of training, our adult team would be introduced to the *Discovery* methods and experience ourselves what the teens would participate in. We soon began to step out of our comfort zone with Michael.

He gave us our first task on **Day 1**- learning to juggle. This was not to be a flashy party trick, but a learning exercise to help us to become aware of our reactions to learning new things. We had to listen to our internal dialogue as we fumbled to keep the balls in the air, and ask the question of ourselves, did this inner voice help us or hinder us?

Over a long morning, we trainees felt what the teens would feel; the frustrations, the failures, the dropped balls, the lack of rhythm. This was hard. Then came some success, in small steps. Michael showed us how to 'chunk it down': how to take a big task and break it up into smaller pieces. This is how you learn everything. This is how we learnt to juggle. We felt very proud of our gradual progress, first two balls, then three, slowly as the rhythm came. Some people took to this skill readily and had four balls in the air by the end of the afternoon. To read, 'these learning principles' would later be applied, by Jo, in the academic arena.

When our juggling task had been mastered, we were encouraged to celebrate our achievement. We celebrated to music and were invited to dance around the room for the length of the song. This felt very weird to me, but many got right into it. And every time we needed to celebrate our successes over the next ten days, the music cue would begin, 'Celebrate good times! Come On!', and everyone would jump up, and dance.

And sometimes this song was just used as a cue . . . for a break between sessions. This felt a lot like Pavlov's dogs to me, but I did get used to it and became very good at dancing and being spontaneous! And in doing this, the idea of celebrating our successes in life, large or small, was repeated, reinforced and enjoyed. How often do we stop to celebrate the achievements in life, especially the many small ones?

There was no time to think at Discovery, as we moved from one activity to another, from one hour to the next. This is typical of the accelerated learning process, where you are constantly confronted with new ideas and experiences. This is quite different to the way we, as adults, learn and experience the world, at our own comfortable pace. There was another teacher at Discovery, Rob from Terrigal High, with whom I would debrief at the end of an exhausting day, maybe over dinner or between dinner and the evening session. This helped both of us to be able to verbalise our observations of the teaching techniques being used. Rob and I were watching with teachers' eyes. We commented on the unhelpful things in the program, as well as the good, and why we thought they were used. I was very grateful to have Rob's company, interaction and critique of what we were both finding very stretching.

Michael used a flip chart to summarise the main points in any session. These were made with huge felt markers, always colourful and clever, using pictures as well as words. They usually challenged some preconceived idea that might be holding us back. These colourful posters would be displayed the very next session, gradually covering the whole front wall. The room was being filled with our learning. It was a constant visual reminder of all that we had learnt. The learning environment was becoming 'ours'. And I was absorbing it all.

The task for **Day 2** was a 500m run, around the college oval. We were told this would be no gentle jog; it must be full steam, as fast as you could! I knew this was not going to be pleasant. I knew I wasn't fit; and I knew a jog all the way around the oval would have been challenge enough for me, let alone a sprint! As you undertook this activity you had to listen again to your internal dialogue. Mine had already started - "I can't do it. I know I can't!" So, on this sunny Canberra morning . . . "On your marks, get set, Go!."

Off we all sprinted. A number of the Training Team stood at intervals around the oval to cheer us on. I sprinted, but it didn't take long for it to feel uncomfortable. people were striding past me. And I was slowing. I knew I couldn't keep up this pace. I slowed to a jog and fell way behind the others. I tried to keep going. I stopped to catch my breath then ran some more. I got to half way around the oval. I was being encouraged to go on by a Trainer near me, but I couldn't. I had a stitch in my side and my head was throbbing. My lungs were already exhausted and everything started to hurt. I had to stop. I had to take huge deep breaths. I was feeling dizzy. I was given some water. I had to sit down.

"No don't sit down!"

But I was beginning to feel sick by now. I lay down on my back, in the grassed lanes, with my hands over my face, my hot head throbbing. I just couldn't do it. I was now the last of all, quite a distance behind any others, and lying down. Some runners had already managed to finish. This was just awful. It took a while but my breathing became less laboured I was encouraged to get back on my feet slowly, and breathe deeply. I thought, "I should just give up now."

This one trainer encouraged me to start moving again, to just walk. I was still on the track. I started walking slowly, then to jog, slowly. I was doing it, but oh, so slowly. My head started to pound again. My legs didn't feel like they wanted to move. The Trainer started to jog with me. That helped. He was now my personal coach, running beside me. His only interest was seeing me finish and achieve success. As muscles I didn't know I had ached, I looked ahead. Everyone had finished and they were standing at the finish line cheering me on. They were calling my name. "Come on Helen, you can do it. Come on!" More than 30 people cheering just for me! It was overwhelming. I had to keep going now. It took everything I had. I drew close to this crowd, which now flanked either side of my lane, and I was caught up in their cheering, and I just willed my legs to move forward. As I passed through this throng of supporters, waving and cheering madly just for me, in a flash I had a thought. This was just like 'the great crowd of witnesses' in heaven, described in Hebrews 12, who cheer us on in our Christian life. It would be just like this! All the saints watching us, gasping when we falter, "Hoorays" when we get up again, and cheers to bring us Home! And these witnesses in Canberra brought me home that day, with tears running down my face. A huge cry went up when I crossed the finish line. I collapsed on the grass. I had done it!

We debriefed after this sprint challenge, and the run was related to other challenging activities in life that daunted us. Did our response to the run mirror our response to the difficult things life holds, for example difficult relationships. I told them all how much I had appreciated their encouragement at the finish line. But I was not able to share how those final moments had been huge for me, because of the agreement I had made of not talking about religion. That deeper experience was to be mine alone. What did I learn from this sprint challenge? I learnt that I need to say, "*I can*" more frequently. I learnt that my inner voice could defeat me before I even started. I learnt anew that simulations can teach us very deep things. I learnt that I needed to get fit. And I learnt that God can turn up in the most unexpected of places, even during a 500m sprint.

Each night I would write in a journal all that I had experienced over that day; the content and the techniques. I didn't want to forget anything. I used an exercise book and my coloured felt pens, and enjoyed the process. My day would often end at midnight, or later, as I sat on my bed recording all that filled my head, and heart. God was a part of my day, in this quiet alone time, before falling into a sound sleep.

Another task was also deeply moving that same day. We were all asked to imagine that we only had 12 months to live. One year left on this earth. That being the case, "How would you spend your time?" We each had to write down how we would spend that final 12 months; what and who would we concentrate our attention on. Then we were asked to write a letter to ourselves. This was very hard and I remember being moved to tears as I pondered the things in this life that were important to me. But they weren't things they were people. My family first; Mum, Dad, Geoff and Megan, and dear little Heather and then friends. Not having a husband or children to devote my time to I wondered if I would keep working or travel like so many others might? But I had already seen much of this amazing world and I decided I would continue to teach. It was a valuable thing in itself, my teaching. Such a short time! I wondered if I would tell anyone I was dying? I would want to relate in a natural way, spending quality time with them, being appreciated just for who I am; but then having to say goodbye. This was so deeply moving. And tears came. I remember wanting to leave something significant behind, something I could be remembered by.

I decided I would leave, something I had made. I envisaged making a patchwork quilt for the people I loved; first for Heather and then for others. This would be a tangible link to me. Yes, I could do this. I had made a couple of quilts, but that pastime had faded into the background these past years, and I had become unproductive. I would need a new lease of creative life to achieve this. How many could I make before I died? I also thought of making some more calligraphic works, which could be framed and hung as a piece of art. It seemed important that I could *do* something. I wrote all this into my letter. I had really been in touch with my mortality on this day.

On our final training day, **Day 3**, we were surprised by a revelation at our regular early morning reflection time. One of our participants had decided to go home. One in our group of trainees wasn't coping too well. Some of the deep personal stuff we had covered had really affected him. He knew he had work to do on himself, and his life, before he could help young people with their lives. He told us all this with tears in his eyes. How very brave he was. He was going home, but he said he would come back another time, to complete what he had started. We all gave him a huge clap, and hug, and he left feeling very affirmed.

We were briefed for the next activity, one that would determine our placement for the coming week with the teens. When the signal was given we had to 'let go of ourselves' and our inhibitions and just totally celebrate to the max when the usual music played. Hhmm! I wasn't sure about this. I didn't think it was helpful to totally lose control in real life. I wasn't in the habit of losing control of myself with alcohol or drugs. Could I do this? Would I do this? I felt very suspicious of this activity. And I knew this would be difficult for me, especially as we would be 'watched' the whole time, as part of a selection process. So at the given time, with wild music playing, everyone just focussed on being wild and out of control, while the trainers looked on. Very strange! Some people were getting right into it. I let loose a bit, but I knew I was very reserved in my version of 'out of control'. And I tried to watch other people to see where this was all going. I should not have been surprised at the outcome - I would not have a group of teens to lead. I was placed on the Production Team! I would have a 'behind the scenes role' in getting the meeting room ready for each activity. Apparently I didn't have enough 'let loose' to lead a group of teenagers! I felt very ripped off, considering I worked with teenagers every day. But Production Team it was to be. I didn't realise then that this would be invaluable training for me, and by not being emotionally involved with the teenagers' personal journeys I was able to watch and observe the proceedings more carefully, learning much at a distance.

After each changing activity the Production Team was needed to set up the learning space for the next event. All the Facilitators' needs were placed at the front of the room, for example new flip charts, chunky felt pens, or other resources. We had to take the most recent flip charts that Michael or Jo had produced and place them on the wall. The chairs might need to be rearranged to better cater for the next activity. If it was a life skills event, rather than a study session, there might be no chairs at all. The room had to be immaculate. We had spent time earlier removing items that were broken or not working in the room, e.g. ripped blinds, that served as visual distractions. The rows of chairs had to be symmetrical. The room itself must reflect the excellence that Michael was calling forth in the young people. We were creating a visually pleasing room that would also be educationally inspiring. This creative environment was working its way on me. I was absorbing it all. Academic sessions included skills in note taking, how to increase memory and concentration, and speed reading techniques. This was done by Jo. This is where I first heard the concept of 'whole brain learning'. Traditionally schooling has favoured **left-brain learning** including verbal and numerical skills, logic and analysis, being deductive and rational. This has been at the expense of the **right-brain activities** including visual and spacial understanding, seeing things as a whole, intuition and movement. I loved learning these new ideas and practise.

During the educational sessions, teens were encouraged to understand their own learning style, and to choose appropriate learning strategies to help them remember the content of their school lessons: did they prefer hearing information, seeing information, or writing down information? Note taking for greater recall was achieved through mind mapping. I had been using this method occasionally, but at *Discovery* everything was mind mapped. Multiple colours were used, as well as using pictures to represent whole concepts. Writing notes didn't have to be linear, down a page - boring! Students would choose words and symbols to summarise large sections of content. Note taking could be fun! I really liked this practise.

As I watched and helped with the program over the next week, I was amazed at the things that were brought up and dealt with. I made a list over that week of all the experiences the teens were given. Students had life lessons as well as school-focused ideas. Each word I recorded is a session; an experience, a call to live a life of excellence and integrity. I was watching the proceedings through my teacher's eyes. And when the Teens arrived, I was watching with my Director's hat on.

The single biggest impact Discovery had for me was learning, and seeing demonstrated, an interactive way of learning that was fun. Michael told the adults who were teachers,

"If you go into your classroom to have fun, then everybody else will have fun as well."

This was a **key** I would use to open a new door to learning in **my** classroom. I reflected on all the academic help being used to improve students' performance in their academic subjects when they went back to school, so they would do well in the exams. But at PHHS I was teaching content of **eternal value**, content that could mean LIFE for the learner. If I wanted **any** outcome in my classroom, it was simply that my students would **remember** what I had taught them. They could then draw on it at any time in the future. It was that important! I wanted to use these super-learning techniques in the Christian Studies classroom. I was already looking forward to my teaching year. I wouldn't change the content I taught, just **how I taught it**. I was looking forward to **making learning fun**.

But as I thought about a lot of this, I knew that the methods were not all new. Many of these techniques I had been using for years, outside the classroom, in my work with Scripture Union. I thought of Owen Shelley and his methods of making the Bible 'come alive' with children. His use of puppets, sketching, storytelling and audience interaction made his teaching come alive. Owen had been doing accelerated learning for decades! The creative methods of exploring the Bible with teenagers that I had used in ISCF for years, were like what I had seen demonstrated over these last 10 days, just in a bigger way.

The Teens were given some of the same tasks as we had done, including a 1km run. But during their longer program, a day was spent on a ropes course demonstrating the concepts of risk taking, team-work and cooperation. We members of the Production Crew were assigned to a group for that day, and we were able to be a part of this challenging activity with the teens. Over the week I observed much that was good, much that was life affirming, much that was challenging and life changing.

My growing coloured list contained so much of what we at ISCF Leadership Conference addressed and attempted to achieve in our week with Christian students. I thought deeply about it. But as I watched and observed I noticed some omissions, some areas *Discovery* did not address. I started another column on the same page. I had thought the obvious element left out was God, and I noted that. But I changed my mind, and later gave it a tick of approval. Michael and Jo would give us morning devotions, reading from spiritual writings of a variety of people, or inspiring sayings that had influenced them to aim high and achieve success. There was much spirituality at this Conference. Michael spoke of a higher being – he just didn't know his name. And then I realised that the thing missing from this secular leadership conference was a Person, and I wrote his name in large letters opposite my first list. Yes, Jesus was missing from this Conference. That was all. And that was everything.

In missing, or bypassing Jesus, these people offered no hope; hope of a life redeemed, a life lived in sacrificial service of others, a life that will continue into the next, for eternity.

There was one last task. It was for all *Discovery* participants, both teens and adults. We were told little of this until it was time. It was something that would be a big challenge. We would see if we had succeeded in relearning some of those internal messages that kept playing in our heads, the barriers we each had to achieving success. After a big motivation session from Michael, we were told what this last activity would be. The last task was to break a piece of timber in two, with our bare hands! Michael demonstrated it for us. We saw him prepare himself mentally, slowly and deliberately. We watched him stand in front of a one metre piece of a suspended timber, position himself, raise his hand slowly, steady himself, and then swipe through the air with great force. He received a great cheer when the piece of 2cm thick timber broke in two, with one blow from the side of his hand.

This momentous task was now to be *our* activity! We had seen that this was physically possible. The only barrier would now be in our minds. (I am recalling that another younger person also did this feat too, so we could see it wasn't just a 'super Michael' thing.) This was all getting slightly weird, I thought. This task was similar to feats attempted in the higher levels of karate. And I was expected to do it! I could already hear the excuses in my head. Had I learnt anything this week? Would I decide a negative outcome in my mind even before I started? It would be so easy to say, "I can't." But I didn't want that message anymore. I had decided that I wanted a new message in its place: "I can."

We all assembled expectantly in another room that had been prepared for us. Blocks of stone were stacked in two columns, with timber boards resting on top of them. About ten of these were ready for the first participants. We were able to watch others as they attempted the task, and encourage them on. I saw participants young and older break the timber. Each person who succeeded was visibly exhilarated by their success. We hugged them as they came back to the group of observers and celebrated with them. This was amazing! Some people faulted and the timber didn't break. They tried again. Some moved away unsuccessful.

I didn't want to wait till last. If I was going to do this I needed to do it early. I was ready to step up to a pile of stone blocks, where fresh timber had been laid. I looked at the timber.

"I can do this," I told myself. "I can do this."

As I psyched myself into the right frame of mind, I did one extra thing. I asked God to help me in this. I included Him. I didn't want to attempt this task on my strength alone. I closed my eyes briefly as I offered up my prayer. I opened them to look at the timber, and I began to concentrate. I followed the instructions we had been given and with everything I had, I raised my right arm over my head and brought it down with force. The timber broke into two pieces and clunked its way to the floor. I had done it! I jumped up and punched the air with my fist. I had done it! I don't think I have ever felt such elation at something I have achieved, as I did that afternoon. I was so proud of myself. I had done it!

And upon reflection, I knew then, there was nothing in this world that God and I couldn't do together! "I can't" had been replaced with "I CAN!"

I would leave *Discovery* a different person.

Teens were given the chance to express what they had learnt over the week. Some of them had come to Discovery because their parents had made them. Others had heard about the experience from friends, and they came of their own volition. Evaluative comments were very positive, and often spoke of transformation. One girl had been a concern over the week. I forget her specific details but by the end of the course there had been a breakthrough. She wrote a poem of a real journey of discovery, her own personal journey.

Parent's Day

After the teens had been farewelled on their buses, or in cars with their parents, the training team had a debriefing session. There was nothing new in this. (We had this as part of the process of ISCF Conference too.) We all sat in a big circle, on the floor, and were asked to share what we had learnt over the week. Where to begin? People shared deeply of their personal triumphs and how they wanted life to be different when they got home. Some were very specific about how they would start a transformation of their daily reality, to bring a personal excellence to areas of their lives. Others spoke largely of their new personal life goals. I said something like,

"I have experienced many good things in community here, over these last 10 days. Some of you have no such community to go back to, but I do. That community is my local church. We don't always get it right, but I am looking forward to living out many of my renewed ideals in their company."

(Oh my goodness! I was almost speaking about religion!!)

Later one of the younger women, whom I think had been part of a church in years gone by, told me she had appreciated what I had shared, and that there are perceived and real flaws in the church.

Then each person in the group was encouraged to give an affirmation to another, to tell them something that they valued about them. This began a very powerful time of encouragement for everybody present. People shared simple things, as well as very deep things. I remember Michael affirming Matt, and all that he had done over the week with the teens. He saw Matt as a new leader in the Discovery movement and gave him his outmost confidence and love. It was as if Michael had anointed Matt for the future of this Discovery movement. Everyone was deeply moved at what we had seen and heard.

We too were then farewelled onto our departing buses, our minds full of what lay before us. There was so much in my head that I wanted to bring into my classroom and my teaching. My classroom certainly needed a 'once over', with my new eyes. I needed to brighten the room up. It needed some more privacy from passers-by, and their distractions, and bright curtains along one set of windows would do the job. I would make them before school started. I wanted to start the new-year implementing all of these ideas. I would use posters in the classroom too and for every lesson, and my students would copy these concepts into their books with felt pens. I would buy multiple packets. And I would look again at EVERY lesson, to see how it might be improved. I would do this with Chris. I think I already knew that he would embrace these ideas and changes too. Chris had trained as a Primary school teacher, and in teaching young children he had readily used these methods.

I went to see my brother after I was home. He asked me how the course had gone. As I tried to find the right words to explain it, all I could do was burst into tears. He put his arm around me as I just cried. Such huge things had happened for me over the last 10 days. This was just an emotional release I had needed before I found the right words. Geoff eventually heard my story. Thankfully, I wasn't quite so emotional when I went to visit the O'Flahertys and told them of the experience that was *Discovery*. Chris listened to everything I had to say and smiled. He nodded his head to all the ideas I had. I knew Chris would 'get it'! I said I wanted to revise every lesson that we taught in our Christian Studies classrooms. Chris nodded that he too was in for the long haul. (Chris would be at Cherrybrook High for three days a week in 1993, and at Pennant Hills for two days.) We would need to get together every week to plan the next week of lessons for Year 7, Year 8 and Year 9. This was a huge task, but we knew we now had tools that would make even the planning of our lessons fun.

And so the pattern for that year, 1993, was set. Sometimes we would do the planning after school at Pennant Hills, sometimes at CTHS. Some of the best lessons I ever came up with came out of this time of review and rewriting. Sometimes it was Chris who would come up with an idea/activity that was fun, even outrageous; and sometimes I had the great ideas!

We talked and explored until we had each lesson reduced to one single concept; **one concept or statement that the students could remember**. Then I would draw a poster to go with the lesson. I had realised that all the work from each lesson got rubbed off the board at the end of it. I decided I would use the idea of flip charts from Discovery, but as **pre-prepared A3 posters** that students would copy and create a colourful page in their books at the end of a lesson. Each poster would contain the essence of what we had discussed in the lesson. These A3 posters of mine would then be placed at the front of the room, above the blackboard, so that any wandering eyes might wander back to biblical concepts we had previously discussed. I bought sets of coloured felt pens, collected empty tins and covered them with contact. In every lesson these blue and white tins of felt pens were ready on the student's desks. We would use them most every lesson.

To bring the youth workers up to speed on all the principles I had absorbed at *Discovery*, I wrote a philosophy statement to explain the new way of doing things.

I also made some curtains, bright curtains that would just cover the bottom windows, but still allow lots of light in. So the room changed from feeling like a fishbowl, to being a private, creative space where students were not distracted by passing crowds. Students noticed the difference straight away, many making comments.

"Miss, you made new curtains!"

But some of them had the distinguishing Aussie comment, the humorous put-down.

"Daggy curtains Miss," some Yr 8s would jest.

But I knew they were all quietly impressed.

There is a photo that shows my famous curtains. The back wall is wallpapered with the products of a Year 10 lesson, early Term 1. Can you see the Discovery difference?

ISCF

I arrived back at school for a new year, to a core group of Year 11 leaders who were keen to be involved in planning and leading meetings. This was very encouraging. They were organising ahead, and using the meeting material from the INPUT magazine, most of the time. We had a leaders' meeting, and young Robert from Year 7 turned up! He was as keen as they were. Rob is in most ISCF photos from here on in!

1993 School photos

Photo Day at Pennant Hills High.

I asked Chris to come to Penno for the early morning staff photo. It was a good opportunity to get a professional photo done to use for church promotion. This is the nicest photo we had taken together. Mrs Robinson was making funny comments behind the photographer while we were being photographed. It shows! I made sure we had a Music Staff Room photo again this year.

Year 10 listens to the music

A new book by an Aussie author made its way into our classrooms in 1993. **John Dickson** had published the essence of his talks as a singer-songwriter on his visits to many schools and youth groups. The slim volume is very much an autobiography, which helps young people look for the God John Dickson believed in.

"In Yr 9 me and my mates were the class clowns."

The quirky cover illustration uniquely captured the theme of John Dickson's testimony. As a teenager John had a sneaking suspicion that Christians were on to something and he was missing out. The topics John covers were ideal in our Year 10 program. Here again was an

Australian author who was hitting the mark. We embraced this new book to use as a resource in our Year 10 classes. This book would change what we did in Year 10 Christian Studies. Every chapter was packed with topics relevant to this age group. The Committee approved the book, and a class set was purchased. These funds, as well as our salaries, were available from the donations of faithful Christians in the local area, who saw this program as a valuable one. We were always grateful when big items of expenditure were approved.

John's clear and compelling style captured the students' interest.

There were a couple of funny stories early in the book before them, and my Year 10 students were carefully listening to the testimony of John Dickson, an ordinary teen at a Sydney High School.

John describes himself as,

"a selfish, 15 year old jerk " who discovered that "God didn't just forgive me… he was actively helping me change my life." P. 46

I knew every young person would turn to the chapter on sex first; clever thinking so John put that chapter first. I, on the other hand, started with Chapter 4 where John gives his very Aussie testimony - then we go back to the sex chapter, and then follow on to why God allows suffering etc. We occasionally slipped in an interactive lesson to reinforce a chapter that would be read, and this always worked well.

John Dickson has moved on to bigger and better things in the Christian scene, and now wears the title 'Doctor'. But he is still writing books; and none more basic to a Christian faith is *Sneaking Suspicion*, which is still in print. Thank you John, for this valuable resource that has informed and changed many young minds.

Romance 7 1993 February

I wish I'd had a sneaking suspicion about what was to transpire next …

School had begun for the year. I hadn't heard from him for a while. I wondered what was going on. I dared to phone. His plans were complete. He was leaving Sydney and doing some further study in another state. He wanted to get a ESL qualification. Then he was off to Europe to look for work in international schools. And that was it! He had made his decision without any thought of me. I was stunned. I needed to talk to him; with him. He was having his last day at church the next Sunday and then, car packed, driving to a friend's country home, for the night; one goodbye on his long journey. I wanted to catch him before he left. It would have to be on Sunday. I had told him I wanted to talk. I arrived after church and we sat in his back room.

"You were planning to leave without letting me know," I began.

"It seems you have been moving away from any idea of 'us', without communicating that to me. I don't think that is fair."

He was looking uncomfortable. This wasn't easy, but I needed to continue.

"I want you to do something for me before you go."

"Okay."

"I want you to think back over the last year or so, and the time we have spent together. I need to know if there would ever be any place for me in your life. I'll give you time to think it through. And I want to know today, before you leave."

An ultimatum of sorts! I could tell He knew he had gone about things the wrong way. I left, waiting for an answer to my question. It seemed like a long wait. I tried to busy myself that afternoon with things that needed doing, regularly casting my eyes to the front window to see if a car was arriving. It was a long afternoon. I was feeling quite anxious. This was no small interaction between two friends. One way or the other, this was it! What would 'it' be? I guess you don't let go of hope, until hope is really gone. I still had some hope, but not much. At least there might be closure and I would, for a change, know exactly where I stood. I needed that, after so long.

I don't really think I saw it coming. That seems crazy now. The sun was fading when he eventually arrived. He was due to go to evening church, to say more goodbyes, before the drive. "I have been thinking about what you said."

I don't remember much more, but that it was brief, and within a few sentences I knew. I knew from his words and tone of voice that he was leaving Sydney - alone. Whatever there was between us was over. And I knew I wouldn't see him again for a long time. I stood up to indicate it was time for him to go he didn't need to prolong this. I couldn't bear it. For the first time I wanted him to leave. I moved towards the front door, and opened it. He seemed somewhat awkward to follow my lead, but passed me at the door. He turned and put out his hand, for me to shake. I was stunned at his gesture. I shook my head and closed the door.

Somewhere between the front door and my bedroom the tears welled up. I watched him drive away. And then I cried. I cried long and hard. There was so much finality here that needed expression. I hadn't heard myself cry for a long time. It was a grief that had begun.

But I needed to stop. I had planned to go to church. I wanted to go, and to be in the presence of the God who knew my every need. So, I pulled myself together deliberately, as the 7pm service would soon begin. Leaders were all in place as I walked in, and I decided to sit at the back this week, right at the back. I moved into a back pew, where Rev Mark Eaton was already sitting. If I needed to leave it wouldn't be so obvious.

The service began with a song. That can be enough to undo you! The tears started, and I wiped them away. I did this a few times and Mark looked at me with concern.

"I've just had my heart broken," I offered, to explain the tears, when we sat down.

"Oh, I'm sorry. Are you OK?"

I nodded. Not really, but I would be OK for now. Mark was sympathetic and understanding. I needed that. I didn't stay long at the end of the service. I didn't want others to know I was upset. But by now the sadness hung like a mantle. I readied myself for school the next day, getting my folders together. Eyes that have shed many tears quite easily shut for sleep.

I woke the next day, and the memories from last night flooded my consciousness. I began the day as usual, and headed for the shower. As I stood under the hot flowing water I started to cry. It had caught me unawares. I was standing in the shower sobbing. I couldn't go to school if I couldn't control my tears. What would I do? I needed to ring up Rev Andrew Campbell and tell him I wouldn't be at school. But I just couldn't. I didn't know him that well. So I decided to ring Chris instead, although Chris and Peta knew nothing of what had been going on in my personal life.

"Hi it's Helen. I won't be in to school today," I said calmly.

Then the emotions took over and fighting back tears I said, "I've been in the process of having my heart broken. . . it was completed last night . . . and I just can't come like this. Can you ring Andrew? Just tell him what I told you. Tell him I'm trying to get my act together."

Chris's voice was warm and responsive. He would ring Andrew. That's all I could do. I went back to bed and found solace in not having to go anywhere, or be anywhere that morning. Later in the day I decided I needed to talk to someone, not sit at home and just be miserable. I rang Jenene to see if she was at home. She was, so I told her what had just taken place. She told me to come over. So I drove to Riverstone and I talked. We talked, over a cup of tea. There were still tissues needed, but to release it all in words was part of the healing process. That's what women do. After I left the company of my friend I didn't cry again. But a sadness had arrived to take the place of tears; an invisible sadness I would wear for some time.

With the reality of these final scenes I was somewhat sobered in my thinking.

Well I sure got that wrong! What a waste; a waste of so much time, and energy.

What was all that about, all the praying all the hoping?

I didn't have too many answers. The very thing I had dreamed and prayed about had just slipped between my fingers. I wondered if I would ever be able to pray about anything again, with certainty. But I decided one thing at least was necessary. I had kept postcards, letters, and personal entries in a journal full of hope. They had to go. They had to be gone completely.

I lit up a fire in the barbeque in my backyard. Page by page, paper letters, postcards and envelopes - one person's handwriting was engulfed by the flames. I watched it burn, slowly at first, then full of flames until it was gone. Now, it was really over. I could move on.

The End!

MY ROMANCE ended somewhere between the closed front door on Sunday afternoon and the fire I lit in the backyard a week later. I was now emotionally free and empty of all the hopes and dreams that would have seen me in a permanent relationship. I was now at the place of a new beginning; with empty hands. God was watching, and this was just where He wanted me, although I was too emotionally drained to recognise any of this at the time.

Yr 9 lessons on BIG ISSUES.

I started this familiar unit, slightly left of centre. I began with the use of some 3-D images that had just started to make their way into popular culture. As you look at the crazy, swirling patterns of a 3-D image in a certain way, a new image 'pops' into view. But it's not easy at first. You have to 'train' your eyes to see the real world behind the patterns. I had a number of these coloured images for students to use. Some students were really good at it, and demonstrated their prowess by coming to the front and identifying the hidden image behind a large 3-D page I stuck to the board. Many wanted to participate. I told them **my 3-D story**.

'I was at a meeting of teachers (SU Youth Committee) when someone (David Grover) pulled out a book. He had asked, "Hey, do you want to see something really amazing?" Everybody was interested in this new phenomenon, as he explained how we could see a hidden picture behind the patterns. You had to look at the patterns in a special way. This curious book was passed around the circle. Those holding the book held it in a certain way, right up close to their faces.

"Oh, that's amazing! That's incredible! I can see it," these were the comments coming from individuals who had deciphered the pictorial quiz. The book was passed to me. By now people were talking about other things. I held it up close to my face staring at the strange pattern on the surface. Nothing. I moved the book away from my face a bit. Nothing. Should I pretend I could see it? The pressure was on to be one of the people 'in the know'. Should I fake it? That was a very tempting option. For a split second I saw something different! I saw the hidden image part of a world map; and then it was gone.

"Oh that's great," I said enthusiastically, trying to hide the fact that I had not zoomed into this new world and walked confidently around in it, as other people had. I was disappointed. Why couldn't I see this?

I knew there was something to this from the other people's reaction. I wanted to know more. I wanted to see! I came across a gift shop that sold 3-D post cards. I purchased three cards with the aim of 'cracking the method' I had witnessed: *"hold it to your face , then move it away slowly."* It was like my homework. I had these cards by my bed, so that at the end of the day I could try to make the method work. I lay there, pulling these small images slowly away from my face. And finally I could do it - I could see the hidden image behind the psychedelic patterns on each card. Eventually I could hold the hidden image and 'walk around' inside this new world, and take in the detail. They really were very clever indeed.

I told all of my students of that story so they didn't feel so bad if they too could not see these secret images the first time, which ranged from capital cities, African Sahara with animals, a plane in flight, baby rabbits and antique cars, to name a few. I bought a book named The Magic Eye, which contained a number of 3-D images. I dissected the book, and laminated each page. I needed lots of these if this lesson was to work. Students enjoyed looking at a variety of images. Unlikely 'experts', who could quickly do this, became the class heroes for a lesson, and were quick to help those who were struggling.

What was the point of this lesson? I gave each student a small 3-D image to paste on a new poster page. The slogan that went with it read,

'JUST BECAUSE YOU CAN'T SEE IT DOESN'T MEAN IT'S NOT THERE! HOW ABOUT GOD'?

Many people find a belief in God easy, and have Him as part of their lives. Some people find this whole concept much harder, not seeing anything spiritual in their daily lives. With time, an interest, and maybe even some help from believing friends, you might begin to 'see' what is there.

A newspaper announcement

A classified in the newspaper would herald the news to a wider world. Lachlan Neil Jefferson arrived just at the end of April 1993, to Geoff and Megan. He was the first male baby to be born into the McNab family since his father, 36 years before. There seemed to be a favouritism towards males by my elderly aunt. But Mum would have none of it. She had experienced the same when I was the first born of Mum and Dad's marriage; like it wasn't quite good enough. But, none the less, here was a little lad who would carry the McNab name into the future.

Lachlan too, like Heather, would also fill my heart with a ready joy.

Back at school ...

Sometimes I would call into Christian Literature Crusade on the way home, to hire a video that I needed for the next few weeks. I could also cast an eye over its shelves for new items. I picked up a video I hadn't seen before:

Fury to Freedon: the true story of **Raul Ries.** *Raul had an abusive childhood. At high school his name stood for fear, for fighting, for fury. To his friends he was violent and dangerous. In Vietnam he was a top-notch fighting machine. To others he was a Kung Fu expert, but to his own family he was a time bomb ready to explode at any moment. Then one night, a miracle led Raul from inner and outer fury to an inner peace. Raul Ries was never the same. What could change the heart of a man who wanted to kill his father to a man with a passion to save him?*

This sounded fantastic! I borrowed the *Fury To Freedom* video and was blown away by Raul Ries's story. Raul housed a deep anger that found its expression in the martial arts. His excellence in Kung-Fu led to him having his own studio. However the inner fury was focussed, at times, on his young family. It was not a story I had heard before. He was like another Niki Cruz! God takes unexpected people, and makes them his own. This video made it very quickly into the Yr 10 classrooms.

It provided a good break from reading John Dickson's book.

The students loved this movie! Raul was played by a young, good-looking Kung-Fu expert. Sharon, Raul's girlfriend, then wife, was a beauty with a head full of gorgeous red hair. The movie was well acted too – I didn't have to apologise for this Christian video. Watching the video was the first time I heard the name of Chuck Smith, an evangelist in California (who helped establish the Jesus Movement in California). Chuck actually stars in the movie – as himself. The whole story was very compelling, and Yr 10 watched it over a four-week period. Again, I had to be careful to get the timing right for the last dramatic scenes. This Californian story was now echoing in the hearts and around the playground of students at Pennant Hills High.

SELF ESTEEM

It was Term 2 and the time had come to revamp the SELF-ESTEEM unit for Year 9. In it I used some of the previous lessons, also creating new ones. When I was finished it had a distinct *Discovery* flavour, and there were now enough lessons for two terms.

Term 2

1. 'Before' statements about myself; 'I' statements, creative writing

2. Self-Esteem overview

3. I'm Special; thumbprint

4. Games inside

5. Compliments- group activity (simulation game)

6. Compliments-how well can you do it?

7. Dead Poets' Society video

8. ... video

9. ... video

10. ... video

Term 3

1. Assignment based on Dead Poets' video

2. Suicide

3. Jesus and Self-Esteem

4. Conflict 1

5. Conflict 2

6. Group games outside

7. Conflict with Us/God

8. Twisted Mind video 1

9. Twisted Mind video 2

10. 'After' statements; Evaluation

Games

It was soon time to trial these new lessons. I got students to write some statements starting with 'I', and "I can. " and "I can't." With time left I anonymously read some of these out at the end. This was usually amusing as well as informative.

The next lesson was a profound, yet simple one. I had borrowed the heart of the content from an SU Input magazine. It fitted into my Self Esteem lessons well. I had blanked out many of the words so students had to add ME, MY, I in the spaces created. The message was overwhelming positive about being special in God's eyes. Then we read it, one at a time, around the room. A few students got to read out, because I'm special. And I would interrupt with "Yes, you are!" Students would giggle.

Then we played some of the games I'd learnt at *Discovery*. We laughed a lot as we did. One of them was a group juggling exercise. I divided the class into two groups. Into a circle I introduced a light ball that had to travel the same pattern as it made it way around the group, from thrower to catcher. Another ball was added, and then another one, following the same thrower and catcher pattern. How many balls could the group maintain? This was a big group challenge and those groups that could do it experienced a unique buzz to be working as a fine tuned group, for those last rounds of the game.

(But it seemed there was always one in nearly every group; always a boy who just couldn't do the group thing; who started pelting someone on the other side of the group with the balls. Sometimes I would try again, but mostly this one individual was not yet mature enough to cooperate to achieve something larger than himself. It was disappointing because the larger group missed out too.)

But there were **other games** as well. By now I was very familiar with the Cooperative Games Network that had begun in the late 80s. They were popular with community groups and a variety of youth groups. For some of these games I needed equipment, and asked Fred Gregson if he could knock these together. One highly popular piece, from Fusion Australia, was gheta boards; long pieces of timber with thick rubber banding across it. Up to four students put their feet under the rubber on either foot. Their challenge was to move the boards as one. The teenagers had to hang on to each other to help them balance, and there was much laughter as they made their way forward. This game was very popular. Much laughter as students embraced each other and fell over a lot until they got the rhythm going; then just big wide smiles and lots of chatter. (I took these boards to camps as well.)

Some of the games were inside, where the tables were packed up and moved to the edges of the room. These lessons weren't dependent on the weather. Inside we began with simple games such as tangles, and a variety of balancing exercises. Another was an aerial ladder using movable poles, up a line, the last pole becoming the first time each occasion. Here you had to trust your peers that they wouldn't drop you while you were in the air. Much laughter from all involved! Some of these gentler lessons were a nice lead in to those that needed some robust thinking.

Here is a quote from the program I prepared for the other teachers:

"This is not a hugely gospel-centred unit of work. There is not a lot of 'God talk'. But the fact that it is their Christian Studies' teacher talking to them about how special they are, you can look forward to making a huge impact in a student's life. Because of the relaxed presentation, when you do talk about God they are ready to listen."

Jesus and Self Esteem

This was it! This lesson was the hinge that all the other lessons swung on. It was here I could present a Biblical view on the topic of SELF ESTEEM. I didn't have a textbook to refer to. I started with a blank sheet of paper and some coloured pens. I sat at my desk and addressed this issue from my own experience. How did having God in my life contribute to my positive self-esteem? I knew it made a difference but I had never put flesh onto the framework I lived by. I began with a concept in a bubble, and when I finished I had a colourful mind map. With the concepts in front of me I now needed some Bible verses to consolidate each one. I delved into my concordance to find the verses I had in mind, and ended up with a full page of Bible truth. I drew this mind map up as a worksheet, leaving one blank word in each concept. The first thing we did in class was to complete each of the statements. They made powerful teaching:

KNOWING JESUS HELPS ME TO KNOW MY REAL VALUE

1. I know I am LOVED

2. I have been CREATED

3. I am a member of GOD'S FAMILY

4. My sins are FORGIVEN

5. I have the HOPE of HEAVEN

6. I am ACCEPTED just as I am

7. I have a FOREVER FRIEND

8. LONELINESS is taken AWAY

I reproduced all the individual Bible verses on A4 paper, mounted on coloured card. The student's task now was to find a verse that matched up with the above statements, and write it on their page. Some verses covered two statements. Then I read the whole completed page out loud, with some help from my young friends. This was a large resounding statement of God at work in an individual's redemptive story.

Here are the Bible verses I used. Can you, reader, match them up with the eight statements above?

*   "Come to me, all of you who are tired from carrying heavy loads of low self-esteem, and I will give you rest." Jesus   Matthew 11.28

*   "I will be with you always, to the end of the age." Jesus   Matthew 28.20

- "But by the free gift of God's grace all are put right with him through Jesus Christ – who sets them free. God offered him, so that by his death he should become the means by which people's sins are forgiven through their faith in him." Romans 3.24-25

- "Never will I leave you. Never will I forsake you." Hebrews 13.5

- "Greater love has no one that this, that he lay down his life for his friends." John 15.13

- "God created people in his own image, male and female he created them." Genesis 1.27

- "How great is the love the Father has lavished on us that we should be called the children of God. And that is what you are." 1 John 3.1

- "As far as the east is from the west, so far has he removed our sins from us." Psalm 103.12

Some of these verses had multiple uses. Did you notice that?

I loved this lesson. Without a fanfare, or any dissenters, after weeks of gentle focus on self-esteem, this loud Biblical statement was allowed to sit beside movie summaries, creative book-work and the memory of class games. This possibly is the most in-depth explanation of the gospel I had ever given at school. And Year 9 students were ready for this meat. I know at least one Year 9 student who took the mind map home and pinned it on her notice board. I didn't know this at the time, but young Christie would stand out to me for other reasons over the next 18 months, as she lived out the affirmations she had pinned to her wall.

Conflict

After *Discovery*, I had wanted to develop some lessons for teens on the topic of conflict. I had written to *The Conflict Resolution Network*, at Chatswood, and received a large envelope brimming with resources to work with. I was inspired by this remembering how little I had to work with when I first started teaching Self Esteem. Over two weeks in class we examined the idea of WIN/WIN, and how that looks different to WIN/LOSE and LOSE/WIN. The conflict theory was turned into practise, with skits the students could be involved in; on how not to do it, followed by the right way, while following the conflict resolution guidelines. The situations included conflict with parents, siblings and friends. This had worked really well. I had a sheet for the student's books called 'Fighting Fair'.

"I'm going to use this with my Mum," a boy commented as he left. Thanks Lord! My job satisfaction goes through the roof today.

Conflict Us/God

I had been wrestling with something in my head. Could I overlay conflict resolution on the Bible, when dealing with the problem of God and human sinfulness? Man and woman started off WIN/WIN in the garden, then LOSE/LOSE after Adam and Eve disobeyed. God would find a way to bring people back to Him, but it would cost Him big time. After following the conflict guidelines the students copied this statement into their books. The gospel in full flight again in this unit! And after the resurrection of Jesus we have WIN/WIN again. The students understood this simple yet profound Biblical teaching. The poster for this lesson was God had to LOSE so we could WIN a relationship with him.

I loved reading the student evaluations after the SELF ESTEEM unit. Apart from the fact that they all wanted more games (!), the feedback was very positive and I knew I was onto a good thing. Turning the camera lens to focus on their lives had stirred the students to be reflective about many issues they had to deal with. Their comments ranged from issues with friends, siblings and parents. They now had tools to use and they seemed appreciative about that. They also knew they were special, and that was important.

I loved planning and teaching this unit of work, and I realised that I had something to share with other teachers. I worked on presenting this long series of lessons in a booklet form for other Christian Studies' teachers to use. At the next teachers' event I shared the concepts behind the SELF-ESTEEM unit and an overview of the lessons. I had some of these SELF ESTEEM units ready for those teachers who were interested. Many took the opportunity to try something new, in a 'ready to go' form they could immediately use in their own classrooms. I became well known for the SELF ESTEEM unit among my colleagues.

My students weren't aware of this. I was just the teacher who had told them they were special, who encouraged them to laugh and who had given them tools to face life as a 15 year old.

A new beginning... Sometime in May

I had recently burnt my journal, a record of almost 10 years of relationship dreams. I saw that act as a closure for something that was not going to happen; an end; a letting go. I had got it wrong, so very wrong! This raised many questions for me. Could I ever pray about anything with certainty again? Could I ever put my heart on paper once more? Would I again dare to voice my dreams, my hopes, my desires only to have them laugh back at me from a page? I could hardly bear that thought.

Over this time a verse I had written in that burnt journal came back to me, from time to time, from its ashen grave.

The words of Psalm 37:4,

"Delight yourself in the LORD and he will give you the desires of your heart."

My mind began to turn over down these verses I had claimed as my own. I didn't know what to do with these words now. They seemed to mock me. I didn't get the *'desires of my heart'*. **He** had been so close, and then He had walked away. But I also knew God's promises didn't work quite as easily as that. I did know I needed to be careful with the use of scripture, and not to use it to justify my own desires. God wouldn't just give me everything I wanted. I hadn't meant to do that with this verse.

I kept thinking about those words over weeks, and months. And God's words, although burnt, were still alive and active!

"Delight yourself in the Lord..."

And one day it came to me. I began to understand this verse wasn't all about **me.** It was also about **God.**

It was about 'who God was' and 'what he wanted to do'. I think I looked at the verse from every angle, in my mind. In idle moments I was lost in the examination of:

"Delight yourself in the LORD and he will give you the desires of your heart."

Then eventually I understood.

This was not a statement but an *invitation*; an invitation from the LORD himself!

"Delight yourself in Me, and I will give you - **myself.**"

God wanted me to make **Him** 'the desire of my heart'. Here was a prayer that God would be delighted to answer!

"LORD, can I have more of you?"

"Of course you can!"

This was the only thing that made sense of it all! God was not mocking me from the pages of my Bible. He was inviting me to embark on a deeper experience of his love. God wanted to give me more of Himself, not just his big toe, but so much more.

"Let me be the desire of your heart, Helen. I will never walk away from you."

But an invitation needs a response. I kept turning this over in my head and my heart. What would I do with this invitation? It was kind of scary!

I had a prayer journal that I wrote in, sometimes. This was evidence that I did stop and give God time. But I didn't journal often, not often enough for an intimate relationship with my Creator. I knew that much. Some things would have to change if I were to respond to God's invitation in Psalm 37:4. It needed something more from me and I was balking at it for a while.

And then my eyes saw it, in a small book that I read, *The Guest Who Took Over*. It was a simple freehand drawing that triggered that 'something more' for me; a picture of a beautiful two-storey house, and a wonderful concept. I had heard the analogy before, of a house like your life, and its rooms were where Jesus comes to live. A powerful concept, but now it was the hand-drawn image of this house that spoke to my eyes and heart, and this drawing was the key to my deeper understanding of this analogy. I wanted to do this, to invite Jesus into my life anew, to let him change each room as needed. I embraced this with hunger. I copied the black and white picture and stuck it into a brand new journal. I bought the journal just for this purpose, to begin again with God. It was a journal with a beautiful cover. That was important. I didn't know what would fill its blank pages, but I hoped that it would be a thing of beauty.

15th May, 1993

Each page from my Journal is a fragment. These fragments will turn up from time to time on these pages, after the events and experiences that inspired them. As I hold my journal now, it is a mirror, and each page a picture and reflection of the journey I had embarked on with my God.

An invitation

Loris invited me along to hear a mission speaker at Thornleigh Primary School one Sunday afternoon. The meeting had begun when we arrived. We made our way to some empty seats in the hall and listened to what the speaker on the stage was saying. I heard of the civil war in Sudan, and how the Muslims in the north were persecuting the Christians in the south. It was heart-wrenching stuff. Children from Christian families were used as servants, and treated no better than animals. The poverty was extreme, and people were being killed. Yet in the midst of this God was at work growing his church. More and more Sudanese were coming to faith in Jesus and wanting to be baptised in his name. When there were enough people, a bishop agreed to cross a border and come and baptise up to 3,000 Sudanese Christians. These believers would come down from the hills to an agreed location, and there a mass baptism would take place. These Sudanese were finding hope in the darkest of times.

One time the bishop arrived to baptise a large group, but when he arrived he found a much smaller group waiting.

He asked, "Where are the others?"

He was told, "They are women and girls, and they have no clothes. They were too ashamed to come. They had to hide in the forest."

I was deeply moved by this story. Women in our world today were prevented from joining the church of Jesus Christ because they had no clothes! This was almost too hard to hear. I thought of my own wardrobe full of clothes and how I could even afford to use clothes as a form of expression. I have a double-wardrobe full! I felt some shame in this. I found myself thinking about this long after the meeting ended. And I wondered. I wondered if I were to make some dresses, could they, would they get to these very same women in need; in the hills of southern Sudan?

HELEN MCNAB

I rang **Sudan Interior Mission** and asked that very question. A week later I was phoned back with the answer, a simple one- "Yes. There was a link they had of delivering goods to the Christians in the south. The door was still open." That's all I needed to hear. I was thrilled to know I could be a part of a solution; the beginning of a solution. I needed to find some cheap fabric; cotton fabric that was cool to wear. I needed a simple pattern. I drafted one from a few patterns I had for women's tops - a simple sleeveless shift with a round neck. And then I decided I would need some help! And so a sewing project began at St Clements. I wrote up the project to give to interested women, and Mark allowed me to launch it in church. Many women said they would help. We had some afternoons where fabric was cut and some sewing begun. I bought a couple of rolls of cotton fabric from Spotlight in bright bold prints. It was just right! Many ladies produced fabrics they had in their cupboard. The pile was growing.

Some ladies took dress pieces away with them to make at home. I would cut out lengths of fabric for more dresses at home. At church the women would give me finished dresses and ask for more fabric. The number of finished dresses was growing. This was exciting. My spare room became the sewing hub for this project. All the finished dresses went in piles on the bed; some for women; some for girls; bright and colourful offerings to Christian sisters on the other side of the Indian Ocean.

When we had our first box full I did an announcement in church, wearing one of the new dresses. I wondered if people might be inspired to now sponsor the dresses so they could be shipped to Sudan? This is where the men could get involved! I set up a table on the lawn outside, after church, with the dresses on display and was pleased to receive more than enough for shipping costs. The first box was sent off. Hooray!

This activity continued amongst the sewing ladies and a second box of dresses was sent. At the '93 ISCF Leadership Conference the theme adopted was GO MAD_ Go Make A Difference. Chris O' encouraged me to tell the delegates about my sewing project. It seems he was impressed by what just one person can do. So I told these students, and team members, the story I had first heard that had drawn me to this endeavour, and of my response to their need. I was one person and I was making a difference. I had prayed a simple prayer, and God was filling up my hands with good works for needy Christian women, At the church Houseparty the following March sewing dresses for Sudan was one of the afternoon activities, and the sewers were quite productive.

Go M.A.D

I have mentioned that the theme for Conference 1993, was, GO MAD-Go Make A Difference. As usual, it had been chosen at the Director's Day the year before. This theme had so much potential. There was much talk about how this could be used. Into this new theme Greg Trainor passionately spoke on **'the gospel'**. As an Anglican I had heard a lot about 'the gospel'. There was *for the sake of the gospel, understanding the gospel, your response to the gospel etc.* From church I knew this concept, the gospel, to mean good news; this was also the frequently used definition. But it could also have some other meanings, and I rarely heard Jesus' name mentioned in the way Greg had spoken. The gospel was a person, JESUS. My heart had stirred at this proposition; and it said "yes" **the gospel was a person to be met and followed**. This fell in line with my desire to have Jesus take over my life, This word I came across so often had a human form.

These training days were always full of good teaching and fellowship, as team leaders turned up from across Sydney, and some from country regions. It was Greg Trainor who had given the opening address, and I was drawn to the theme he proposed. As an Anglican, I heard about 'the gospel' frequently; *for the sake of the gospel, understanding the gospel, know and tell the gospel, your response to the gospel.* Greg stripped the veil away, and shone the light on JESUS- the one to be met and followed. It was not a theoretical proposal here, but the offer of a living relationship with the living God, Jesus. This was the same message that I shared with the assembled team members, from Discovery. My discovery had been that one word, JESUS. It made so much sense, and this also fed into my desire to know Jesus better. I bubbled over with this teaching, and looked forward to implementing this also at our Conference.

GO MAD

- Your story makes a difference,

- Your smell makes a difference,

- Your availability makes a difference,

- Your discipleship makes a difference.

It was hard to know how to capture all that had happened at the Conference. So I just penned the Conference theme, and the title of each of Chris's talks; those titles were so full of meaning. A simple page, such as this, was all I needed to remember.

STORY: we each have a unique story that God can use.

SMELL: this was a funny bloke analogy, with a story about poo, when Chris was working on the Doulos ship. I'm sure all who heard it will remember it still. Chris used it to illustrate the fragrance our lives are meant to be, as we live for Him. He then shifted his analogy to the fragrance of fine perfume.

AVAIABILTIY: this was about being consciously available for God to use us in whatever circumstance we find ourselves, family school, church…

DISCIPLESHIP: is about the daily walking with Jesus, reading God's word, and talking to him like he was your best friend. It was about finding out what you are good at and offering that to Jesus to use.

This song was a ready hit in the church scene. Mark Eaton wasn't one of those Anglican ministers who refused to play Hillsong music, and as such we received a good diet of oldies, goodies and new music. Those same Anglicans criticised this song because of the line, **'I** will never let you go', commenting that a declaration such as that would be hard to keep. I turned this over in my head, and did agree with that point of view of the critics. When I penned this beautiful song into my journal I changed the line, to read '**You** will never let me go.' I tended to sing this version too. I'm pleased Mark introduced us to the Hillsong songs, let us experience the worship - centred lyrics and to make up our own mind on them ourselves.

God used Adam to highlight for me the areas where I was growing in Him. Thanks Lord.

This was a card of Thanks I received from the Conference. Alison Moor was responsible for the collection of these sentiments. I appreciated it because I don't remember Directors getting 'Thank you cards' in the past. Some short words were contained inside this card, but words of great encouragement for me. And if these words were not written down, well, you just wouldn't know.

We had an Evaluation Meeting, as soon as the students were safely on the train to Sydney. It was a very long meeting, because I included a session when each team member received 'I appreciate' from various team members. It was very candid, and very moving as individual team members had their gifts highlighted back to them. There was the odd tear. We laughed and we cried. It seems there was also the opportunity to write down a short phrase about someone else. I knew Chris's writing, and I was deeply moved by the things he observed in me. The first was a comment about my sense of fun, which I loved; the second an observation that I was giving myself away. I liked these little pieces of paper so much that I kept them.

I understood what some of the comments referred to. I had dared to do new things, in a very old SU environment. And here were my own candid comments about what the Conference (or I) had dared to do. I had delighted myself in the Lord's task, and he had given me the result, only he could give a successful event.

6/7/93

Dear Helen,

I just thought I'd write   little note to say how much I appreciate your thoughtfulness, compassion, your openness to the Holy Spirit etc, etc. You're a breath of fresh air in the Scripture Union scene! So often we get caught up in our own man-made structures and programs, so happy with how clever we are – not leaving any room for God to do what He wants to do, thus negating the reason for ministry!

Anyway, you are definitely going against the flow, a radical in this scene! I'm sure the Lord breathed a sigh of relief when you allowed Him to move – Helen, you're an awesome lady. I thank you for the way you make everybody feel special and important, and for your personal way of doing things. You constantly encourage me, and you always had time to talk on the phone and laugh about things, even on the busiest of days. Thank you for being a 'living sacrifice', giving all to Jesus even at personal cost. You truly do take up your cross.

I pray you grow closer and closer to Jesus, allowing His love to permeate every fibre of you being. Thanks for your leadership and friendship – know that you are loved and appreciated by me,

Love,

Adam

SPENDING TIME WITH JESUS July 93

Post-Conference

I returned home from Conference '93, not too exhausted, but definitely exhilarated. I had dared to make a change. We had moved from the mountains to the beach. I had been allowed to 'be myself' and bring freshness to the program. I was deeply satisfied to see God at work in the content and the context. I came home with one determination-to **spend time with Jesus** myself. No more distractions or tasks to be done. But when would I make the time, and where would I go, a tranquil bush setting perhaps? I knew it needed to be for an extended period, but when? Then time and circumstance presented a very unglamorous opportunity. During the next week of the holidays I organised to have my house sprayed to rid it of spiders and other creepy crawlies. I was informed that I couldn't enter my house for three hours after the treatment. Three hours! Where would I go? What would I do for three hours? Without too much thought I realised this was the enforced time out I needed. Yes, I would slow down; stop; spend time with Jesus, in my own backyard.

I wondered what would happen; just Jesus and me? I would come and wait. What would I hear? What would I feel? Would He come? Lots of questions and some anxiety filled me. I was stepping into the unknown here. Unknowns can be scary. But the appointment had been made – with the pest company, and with Jesus; He knew I was coming; He was expecting me.

The pest man came, with mask in hand, and sprayed all the necessary surfaces. Then the doors were closed, and he left. I could not go inside. I was alone on my back porch. I didn't venture into the garden I just sat on the top cement step. I sat and waited. I didn't speak out loud. The words I formed were made in my heart, as a prayer, an invitation. I waited. I just waited for Jesus to come. And in the waiting I was giving myself. I was surrendering. "I love you Lord." I waited.

I shouldn't have been surprised by what happened. Maybe I should have expected it; or seen it, but I didn't. As I sat in the quiet of the afternoon I started crying; slowly at first then weeping from somewhere deep inside. Tears welled up and flowed down my face; immensely wet tears; tears from an overwhelming impression that Jesus was here and in His presence I was deeply loved. Jesus had come. I kept crying. And I realised this is what had happened to me the night I had first become a Christian, over 25 years before. I had cried then. I was crying now. These two events were somehow linked. I was crying tears of being known, accepted and of being deeply loved.

When the tears were gone, but my hands still wet from wiping them away, I sat in the stillness and allowed Jesus to love me. And He did; quietly; gently; completely without words. Just with His presence. Or maybe I heard His gentle whisper somewhere in my being ,"I love you Helen."

I knew I had something to say to God in return. I needed a pen and paper. I wanted to write it down. Something had been playing in my mind for a while- ten wasted years, wasted on a man who hadn't loved me back. I dared to open the back door and reach inside to get paper and texta colours from near the phone. Thankfully my skin did not dissolve in the process!

I sat again on the back step. With pen in hand I drew and inscribed something on this small pad of paper in response to God's overwhelming love for me. Not lots of words to say today, but a drawing. I drew a set of scales. I wanted to somehow balance things up. I placed all my unfulfilled desires for a man on one side of the scales. On the other side I asked God to fill my next 10 years-with a desire for **Himself.** I wanted to be filled so full with God and His love that the scales would not hold it all.

There it was on paper. I had done it! The thoughts that had been rolling around in my head for a while were finally written down. And seeing it on paper I then asked Jesus for it. This drawing was my prayer. It was a big request, but a simple one. I knew I was being very bold. But bold enough to also feel scared. Would God honour this? Would He fill my life with blessings for 10 years? Only time would tell.

What a simple and blessed time this was when I finally 'spent time with Jesus'. I am pleased I have this page today as a memory of that afternoon in my backyard. I smile at this page now, and in what I did with it. But my seeds of doubt were reflected in what I did with this single leaf of paper. Would God come through?

In time I slipped this page into my Journal, loosely between its lined pages. I didn't paste it in as I could have, as I should have. That would be very daring indeed! If God didn't answer this prayer, if this turned out to be another disappointment, I could easily dispose of this single page that contained my yearning after God. But Jesus was there and He was listening. He loves prayers like this and He was pleased to do for me **more** that I could ask or imagine. Something was born that day that I wanted to continue with. I wanted to make space for 'spending time with Jesus' every day. I wanted to come, and wait, and listen for His still quiet voice. In my memory it's hard to put the pieces back into a timeline. But I can see it again through the pages of my Prayer Diary that are dated. I had pulled that Diary off the shelf, blown the dust off it, and begun again. I have two pages open now before me. I can see a change, the change that came as I spent time in the quiet stillness of being loved by God. I dare to open these pages too, so you can see what Jesus was pleased to do in me and for me, as I came to Him. These pages contain for me now the process of my coming and becoming.

High School Reunion... August 1993

There are some things that make most people apprehensive. I was no different. My high school reunion was marked on my calendar for a

Saturday night in August. It was many years since I had seen these people from North Ryde High. There had been one reunion for our group twelve years before, but nothing since. That reunion had been in someone's home. This reunion was a bigger event and was to be at Pennant Hills pub. At least I wouldn't get lost on the way!

The thought of meeting people you haven't seen for decades, and giving an account of how you have spent those years seemed a daunting task. It made me think back over my life to see what I had accomplished. Well no husband or children; no ring on my finger with accompanying photos in my wallet. My life hadn't been shaped by marriage and kids. Life had certainly been full, but it didn't look like everyone else's. This was what I wasn't looking forward to. But although I was apprehensive, I wouldn't have missed it for anything. High school and high school friendships are very formative and I had some wonderful memories of those friendships, which somehow had slipped away.

But I had a clash of events. I had already penned in a weekend away at Lawson with the Youth Committee, which Ridley Smith had generated for some major brainstorming and policy making. But I didn't want to miss the reunion. I decided I would come back for the reunion late Saturday afternoon, then sleep at my place, and drive back up the mountains again, in time for breakfast on the Sunday. I was looking forward to seeing old friends and seeing where life had taken them.

This wasn't a general high school reunion, for all years, just for the three-year groups who interacted together. In 1966, by the end of my 2nd Form a large group of us girls started hanging out with a group of boys from 4th Form. That was to become the shape of things for the next two years. Form 3 girls/Form 5 boys; Form 4 girls/Form 6 boys, with a slight overlap with people from other years. This had been the centre for our social lives most every weekend. We had adored some of these boys, and they had adored some of us. It was such a large group of friends, and it didn't matter if you weren't going out with anyone in particular, everybody went to the beach, to dances, parties and even church together. Stephen and Warren and Russell; Gary and Glen and Greg; Kerry and Lorraine and Cheryl; Chris and Denise and Anne; Lesley and Sharon and Charmaine; and many more! These were friendships that had made my teenage years so much fun.

Things changed after the boys left school in 1968. Many girls left too, at the end of 4th Form, to do secretarial or other training courses. Those of us who continued into 5th and 6th Form had quite a new experience in senior school, making different friendship groups and taking part in school leadership. I was especially looking forward to seeing Chris Pauling. I knew she was coming. We'd been friends from our kindergarten class at Truscott St Public School, right through to Sixth Form at North Ryde High. But I hadn't seen her since 1970, after we completed the HSC. The last I had heard of her she had been working at Ryde Library.

I drove down the mountain that night quite excited. What would I wear? A large group had already assembled when I nervously arrived at Pennant Hills pub. It was good to spy some familiar faces and have them smile in response.

"You haven't changed at all," said Cheryl and Lorraine; nor had they.

That was nice to hear! But I had long hair then; I was sure I looked different. I was soon talking and sipping a shandy. Drink in hand you sort of feel like you fit in. It was easy to scan the growing number of faces to see whom I recognised. Most of the girls looked familiar – not so with the boys. They had become men, some with many more kilos and much less hair! That was a surprise. Some people still lived in the local neighbourhood, others had moved much further afield. Many of the girls from our HSC year had become teachers, and we were well represented. One girl in particular, was now a primary teacher and she didn't have a good word to say about her job. It showed on her face. I didn't want to get like that. After talking to some less than close friends, it was easy to run out of things to talk about.

The room filled to over seventy people, and it was getting harder to see who was there. Our school captain Jean arrived, with one of our old teachers in tow- Miss Halloran! What a surprise. She had been a family friend of Jean's for many years, through Eastwood Rugby Club. It was so lovely to catch up with our favourite science teacher. Dale Halloran was still teaching, at Carlingford High School. So many of us were keen to make ourselves known to her, and she had a good memory for faces.

Cheryl asked, "Have you seen Chris Pauling?" I shook my head.

"She's over at the bar."

I set off in that direction and spied the familiar stature, face and hair of my dear friend. I was getting teary.

"Hello," I said first, as she hadn't seen me coming. She turned with a look of instant recognition and we had a long hug.

"I was so looking forward to seeing you," I told her.

"It's been too long."

And so we spent considerable time catching up on the last twenty years. Chris had travelled down from the Northern Rivers area, where she lived with her husband, Steve. Her Mum and Dad had moved to the north coast too. We exchanged addresses.

The one whom I'd adored was there too. He still looked good! I would definitely say hello. I did, but wasn't game until much later. It took an awful lot of courage to attempt it. Stephen worked for a newspaper as a journalist. I hadn't known that was his strength. But then we never did talk much about school lessons, at school or away from it. He was now married with a family, and living in Marsfield. He was with Ziggy, whom Stephen told me had become a millionaire. Quite an impressive credential to bring to your high school reunion! (Not that Ziggy would have mentioned that himself.)

There are people in friendship groups we now refer to as *gatekeepers*. Ron (I will call him) was one of ours. He was one of the dominant leaders of the larger friendship group, and his sister Anne was in our Form. Their parents were very generous and they always had an open house. He arrived well into the reunion night, and I knew I wanted to say hello. I would ask after Anne. And I wanted to find out where he was up to with God; I wanted to challenge him. Could I do it? Would I do it? Why would I bother?

Ron still commanded a prime place in this group of people and I would need to wait some time. It was getting late but I didn't want to leave before I'd had a chance to talk to this old friend and to talk about things of eternity. By the time I took the opportunity he'd had more than a few beers. I guess that's how some of these guys summoned the courage to be amongst school friends once again.

"Hello Helen," said Ron with a warm smile.

Standing with another friend, he was very open and willing to talk.

"I saw you across the room, and thought to myself, now there's a happy woman!"

I was almost stunned into silence. Ron could see that, just from my face. He must have seen me laughing and talking with old friends. Yes, I was a happy woman. I was known and loved by my God. I had a job that gave me so much satisfaction I could just burst. No ring on my finger; no photos in my wallet; but happy none-the-less. It was the nicest thing anybody said to me that night.

Ron lived on the northern beaches with his wife and children. I asked about Anne, and then I took my chance.

"Are you going to church these days, or are you still keeping God at a distance?"

Ron looked a little taken aback at my change in conversation.

He looked straight at me, and stood between his friend and me, so the conversation was just ours.

"We were converted at the same time, at the Billy Graham Crusade," I explained to him. "We went forward on the same night."

"How do you remember?" There was a look of being known in his eyes.

"It was an important night for me, and I just remember."

I didn't explain to Ron, how he had been a big part of that night for me, and the response of faith I chose to make. Ron had been the gate-keeper back then, and he was sitting behind me in the tiered stadium with other friends. I was so self-conscious of them being there. I knew I would respond to Billy Graham's message, even before it was delivered; I just knew. God had been tapping me on my shoulder for some time, but I had resisted. I knew tonight God would get my full attention, and my heart. But Ron and Ziggy were sitting behind me! It would not be cool to go forward. Would I dare to make that move in front of these boys who commanded so much? Would I? At the end of Billy Graham's message, and call to faith, people were moving to the end of the rows to move down the grandstand steps and onto the large outdoor oval in front of us. An inner struggle began in me; could I break through this perceived peer pressure and respond to the voice of God? Which voice would be the louder?

I heard and saw a movement beside me. It was Ron and Ziggy. They were going forward too. But they weren't waiting to go down the steps; they were leaping over the chairs and rows in front of them. They strode straight past me and leapt into the next row, and the next. There was some urgency in them that almost took my breath away. Eventually they joined the throng of people who now moved as one. I didn't have to worry about them anymore. I too was on my feet and moving down the steps to answer the inner call I had heard that night. It was then just God and me.

"My family goes to church," said Ron. "My wife wants me to go to church with her. Sometimes I do. But mostly I stay home. I'm really just pleased that my kids go as well. I'll get serious later in my life."

I was flabbergasted! It seemed Ron still wanted to have a good time with his friends; and yes, he too was keeping God at arm's length. Ron seemed to know that God would require more of him than that. He would wait till later, but how much later? When would Ron know it was time . . . to die? If you have been keeping God at a distance all of your life, do you know how to make peace with Him at the end? I could have said so much more. But I wondered how much he would remember, in the morning.

I had done what I had wanted to for Ron; I just started asking the questions. It was up to him to find his answers. I thought about making contact with him again later, but I didn't follow through on it. I drove home, warmed by the joy of renewed friendships and the reliving of good memories. I was reminded that, "I had a ball of a time at high school." Above all my heart was overflowing with the comment,

"Now there's a happy woman."

And with all my anxious thoughts about going to the reunion, I think that's what God had wanted me to know; to realise and to understand. I am happy 'in Him', and other people can see it. The eternal relationship that had been born one cold night in 1968 was alive and well and visible to others. It was God who had put a ring on my finger, and he carried *my* photo in *his* wallet. And, I knew I carried his love within me.

August '93

Turning up the heat

It was Wednesday night and, as usual, I went to Bible Study at the Stewarts'. Those nights were never early ones, as we would chat over tea and coffee for some time. When I got home all I did was get ready for bed, (unless) I had a class set of books to mark. I would never turn on the TV. Had I done so this Wednesday night I'm not sure I would have understood the enormity of what I may have seen . . .

I arrived at school on Thursday morning after lesson 1 had begun. I walked through a quiet car park and main entrance not encountering anyone. As I went to sign the attendance book a hand-written memo lay on top of the blue-lined pages for all teachers to read.

I stood perfectly still as I read this memo again, trying to let the words sink in.

3P4 burnt down overnight.
Lessons today will be in the Teachers Common Room.

That's what it said. That was my classroom!

3P4 burnt down!

BURNT DOWN!

I was instinctively drawn to the fire scene. I left the office area and made my way towards the canteen - a short, stunned, surreal journey. There was no indication that anything was wrong here. As I got closer I saw that the entrance through to the portable classrooms was closed; the metal gates locked. I stood and looked through the gates. There, through the bars, was all that remained of my classroom and its contents.

The steel frame of the room was still intact, but –

      Gone the windows,

      Gone the walls,

      Gone the furniture;

      all of it.

Charred chairs,

Deranged desks;

Mangled metal frames,

twisted sculptures against the ugly remains of a classroom- lost.

Ashen Bibles, blackened, burnt,

swept into a pile on the ground,

their papery, powdered form the only soft surface in the ravaged ruins.

I just stood and looked and ached. I didn't move, as the ugly scene made its impression on my eyes, on my mind, on my heart. Only **my** classroom had been affected, not any of the others standing nearby, where lessons were even now in progress. Why just my room? Could this have been intentionally, targeted? That would be just too awful. Much had happened here since I had walked out yesterday afternoon, and as I watched, much was going on now.

Men had already arrived on the scene and had started the clean up; men in steel helmets and overalls, sweeping away debris; men in collars and ties holding folders and walking around and through the remains, surveying, conversing. They didn't notice me. I watched for some time as the reality of what I was observing slowly sank in. I eventually turned and made my way across a deserted main quad to the staffroom. I almost appreciated not having to respond to anyone in those moments. Later a student said, "I saw you walk across the quad. It was so sad." My whole body must have spoken of the catastrophe my eyes had just seen.

I took a slight detour to the teachers' Common Room. It now looked like any other room in the school, with 30 desks and chairs filling the usual relaxed space. Today this was my classroom. I walked into the staffroom stunned. Ian was there. I spoke first.

"Looks like I've lost a classroom!"

He didn't know what to say either.

"I'm sorry."

I nodded.

"Some people saw it on the late night news," he continued.

I was stunned. If I hadn't been at Bible study last night I may have seen my classroom burning down on TV! I sat down. I looked at all my lesson resources on my desk and the book-filled shelves in front of me. At least I stored all my teaching resources in my staffroom. If I had lost all this it really would be devastating. How would you start again, if it was all gone? I had only lost a classroom and a lot of Bibles! That was at least something to be thankful for.

I needed to ring Chris, he would understand. He wasn't teaching and I got straight through. He hadn't heard about it; he said he would come over. That was the first thing to cheer my heart that day. It felt a bit like somebody had died. A few people came and went as the first lesson ended, and comments of concern were made to me by teachers and students. "I saw it on TV last night."

Chris arrived soberly at the staffroom door. He had seen the effects of the fire on his way in.

"How are you doing?"

I just nodded. It was like somebody had died. "I've got the best classroom in the school – with its own tea and coffee making facilities at the front of the room!" He smiled. "If I'd lost all this it would be so easy to just walk away!" I said, referring to all my books and lesson folders on my desk. He nodded. We talked for a while. PHCCEC was meeting that very night.

They would get immediate feedback and information about the fire to tell their congregations on Sunday. I had really wondered if someone would target my classroom, but in time the fire officials had indicated that it was not the work of vandals. This was so good to hear.

Then the bell rang for period 3. I had a class to teach! Chris said he would come with me, as I tried to pull my head together for a lesson. I had a quick look into the new 'classroom'. Thirty chairs and tables had been set up in the Teachers' Common Room, all facing towards the back wall. This had all been done before I had arrived at school! I was impressed by the efficiency and organisation. Thirty students lined up outside the room, very quietly. They made their way into the single rows of desks. All eyes were on me.

"I'm sorry about your room, Miss."

Many made similar comments.

"Now I've got the best room in the school. I can make tea or coffee anytime I like," I said with a smile, indicating the small kitchen at the front of the room. Chris was sitting up the back, and I made mention of him to the class.

The students had lots of questions, about the fire. Some of them lived close to the school, and had come up and watched my classroom burn to the ground. It seems it had provided local entertainment the evening before, with the roaring flames and the arrival of a couple of fire trucks and police vehicles. Some of the simplest comments said so much to me.

"Oh Miss, your curtains!"

"Miss McNab, I am really sorry."

Adam asked, "Miss, do you think the devil burnt your classroom down?"

I was amused at his black and white question.

"No, I don't think that was what happened," and spoke of the enquiry that was being made into the cause of the fire.

"Are you getting another portable?"

I couldn't answer that question as the Principal had not yet spoken to me, which in itself seemed strange.

"I don't know."

Lots of other questions followed and a lesson of sorts flowed. Not the lesson I had planned for that day, but conversations that were having an impact. I was enjoying bouncing some questions off Chris too, who was listening to the comments and leaning on the windowsill at the back of the room.

"I don't get it," said Adam. "I just don't get it! How come you're so happy, when your classroom has just burnt down?"

Was I? That was an interesting observation he had made.

"Nobody got hurt Adam. Nobody died in the fire! It could have been worse. The classroom was just a 'thing', and it can be replaced."

Adam nodded his head.

Chris eventually indicated he had to go. I nodded and knew I would see him that night, as there was a scheduled PHCCEC meeting. How timely. So it was just the students and me. Our discussion continued that morning on why God lets bad things happen.

Recess arrived, and so did many students at my staffroom door, from all year groups. They all came to offer their sympathy. I could tell that with the burning of my classroom, they had suffered a loss too. Some of their comments were so precious.

"It was my favourite classroom!"

"It was the nicest portable in the school!"

"We heard the fire engines, and came up. They were trying to put out the fire when we arrived," said one student who lived nearby.

They just wanted to talk to me, react to what had happened and encourage me. It was a lovely thing to be a part of. This was something that the principal did not do that Thursday – talk to me!

As recess ended, students left for class, and I was alone again. Thankfully I didn't have another lesson. I realised that I had my camera with me and I could take a photo of the remains of the classroom! So I returned to the scene.

The room looked less of a mess than when I first saw it, as much of the debris had been removed from the classroom, and now formed a growing pile of recycled metal just outside. The earlier horror had lessened as workmen moved efficiently to clean up the blackened mess.

More students arrived at the staffroom door at lunchtime. One young man appeared with something in his hand. He held it out to me.

"I found it on the oval this morning. I thought you might like it."

He was holding a singed page from a Bible, a single page that had escaped the flames. It was a scorched colour, singed on every side, now more an oval shape than a square-cornered page. How very precious. Fred Gregson found a page too, which he gave me. I ended up with about three of these feathery pages. I chose to keep just one – a souvenir for my Journal!

Of all my fragments, this one really is a fragile, decomposing page. It exists as a tangible link back to that August morning in 1993. The Bible fragment also bears testimony to the risen Jesus, whose body did not remain dead and broken, decomposing in a stone tomb. This page speaks of people who saw the risen Jesus and whose lives, as a result, would be forever changed. It was to this end that I continued that day.

I had other classes, and students wanted to talk and ask questions. I don't remember them in the same detail as that first lesson.

I now had a newsletter to finish!

The Committee was sobered that night too, hearing the story of my day. Some members had heard of the previous evening's fire, but not which part of the school was affected; others were just finding out about the whole event and loss. It couldn't have been any better, to be with my support group - caring, prayerful men and women from the Pennant Hills community. I felt very much cared for that night. I told them I now had the best room in the school! They asked me if I would get another room.

"The Principal hasn't spoken to me, so I don't know any details about that yet."

I would learn more at the Staff Morning Tea the following day.

I arrived at school, to get another shock. Expecting another day in my new classroom, I read a memo that explained 3P4 classes were timetabled in a variety of spare rooms around the school. Here was reality. I was immediately sobered by this, and my body may have spoken again of what I had just read as I walked across the quad to my staffroom. This would be really hard. Not the best room in the school anymore! I was in rooms all over the four levels. And here was the beginning of my love-hate relationship with my teaching rooms. I encountered them in a variety of conditions.

But I did have a lovely surprise in store that Friday morning, before my teaching day had even begun. Kate McPhail from Yr 9 turned up at the staffroom door with a splash of colour in her hands, a gift of an African Violet.

"I bought this for you. I was so sad for you yesterday. I thought this might help."

How very thoughtful of her to do that. I was deeply touched by this unexpected gift. What a lovely display of colour on my desk all day as a measure of one student's thoughtfulness. Thanks Kate!

Friday 6th August

The Principal did make reference to the fire at Morning Tea in the Common Room, now full of comfortable chairs again. An investigation was underway into the causes of the fire. I almost felt guilty. Did I contribute to this in any way?

"Miss McNab's classes will be relocated to a variety of available classrooms."

It felt very strange. I wasn't 'Miss McNab' to anyone else in that room. I was Helen. And it was **my** classroom. He spoke so formally, as if I wasn't even in the room. The Principal, curiously, never spoke to me personally in the aftermath of the fire. Not once. I worked out why in time. I heard on the grapevine, through Lyn M, that the 3P4 portable would not be replaced. The school needed to lose portables for the lowered anticipated student enrolments the following year, and the fire had just prematurely reduced the number of portables by one. It was natural attrition.

"But it was the nicest portable in the school!" the student's words echoed in my mind. Well that didn't matter. I didn't think it was fair. Not one bit. But nobody asked for my opinion. At that moment I grieved silently for my loss; some individuals, and the Committee, would also grieve with me.

At another full Staff Meeting, further reference was made to the fire. It seems the cause of the fire was litter that had been pushed under the oil bank heater, and it had combusted. I didn't know there was 'under' to those heaters, they seemed to be so close to the floor; not much more than a 1cm gap. Was it part of my job to look under heaters? No doubt cleaners had already been informed that cleaning under heaters was now part of their job.

And so began the love/hate relationship I had with my new accommodation. I taught in classrooms, quite literally, all over the school. Some rooms were fine, others not so fine. Level 4 English rooms, Level 1 Science portables, Level 2 Geography rooms, Level 3 Maths rooms, Level 3 Music rooms, and the Careers room. I had to carry heavy plastic crates of Bibles up and down stairs, along with my teaching folders and resources. I often needed to send two students back to the staffroom for the Bibles. I learnt a lot about what happened in each room, as I inhabited them with my classes. In spare moments I read what was on display boards and stored around each room; I noticed which rooms were cared for, and which rooms were not; which rooms spoke of the creativity of content covered, and which rooms didn't. But like it or not, day after day, week after week, I got used to this new routine, a routine that would last for many years.

It would be a long Friday this week. I had organised to take a group of kids to WINTER SLEEPOUT in Parramatta, an initiative of Sydney City Mission, to raise money and awareness of homelessness. A small but keen group of students had volunteered to be 'homeless' for the night and brave the extremes of winter in western Sydney. They had filled in permission forms and were excited for this extra curricula Christian Studies event. Parents delivered them to Church St Mall, well rugged up for this cold, clear August night. They were not only prepared with blankets and sleeping bags, but an abundance of snack foods for the long night ahead. It was a good way to get to know these young people better.

We gathered in the new amphitheatre in the mall, as speakers spoke their support and musicians sang their support well into the night.

As I surveyed the crowd that night I observed mostly young people, with young leaders. I was struck by the lack of adults at this event. Were the adults all tucked up in bed, supportive of a good cause only during the day, but not if it caused them discomfort? I wondered. How quickly we can lose the passion of our youth and move beyond this level of 'discomfort'. These good causes had their place, as long as we didn't lose sleep over them.

The music continued well after midnight. And then was replaced by the sheer excitement and tirelessness of youth as the hours ticked away. I didn't get much sleep that night, Parents picked up their sleepy, but satisfied, children early the following morning. This had been a great success. I was now very ready for a slow Saturday and the sleep I very much needed. I hit my bed as soon as I got home, fully clothed.

I found time later that afternoon to spend time with Jesus - to stop and reflect on the huge event that the fire had been for me. My room was gone and everything in it, the place to learn and experience something of God; the room I had made sacred. And as I reflected I realised that what I had lost was the environment for learning. But it's just a place, I decided, and God isn't confined to a place. His environment is something much larger than a classroom - it's people's lives he wants to be present and active in. And so I asked God that day to be just that! I asked Jesus to enable me to create a 'living' environment, that no fire could destroy.

SU National Conference

It was at a Monday night Council meeting that I heard of the **SU National Conference** to be held in Sydney, at Collaroy. These national conferences were held every three years, in various states, with SU staff travelling many kilometres to attend. I had only ever been to one other, when I worked for SU in the early 80s. We Council members were encouraged to attend the Conference and come to whatever sessions we could, over the week. As a Council member my participation would keep me up to date on what SU was doing in other states, especially in schools. We were also told that Philip Yancey had been invited to speak at the conference. Wow! And it transpired that Philip's Bible Studies would be given in the evenings, not in the mornings, as I would have thought. This meant I would get to hear them in person. Fantastic! So, after each school day, I could drive to the conference centre, join in an afternoon session, have dinner with SU staff and volunteers, and be there for the evening Bible Studies. I even planned to sleep there. After breakfast I could drive back to Pennant Hills for my teaching day. I was excited to again be able to be a part of this national SU training event. I wondered if PHCCEC would regard a full day at the Conference as a training opportunity for me. I could only ask them. I did, and they agreed. So, as well as attending every evening, I was released from my classes for one full day. Youth workers and ministers would cover my lessons. How gracious of the Committee to do this.

And that was what Philip was to speak about- **'Grace'.** I told my Bible Study friends that I would get to hear our man in person! They were excited with me, and envious. I decided I would be bold enough to show Philip Yancey the pictures we had drawn in response to his book. He might like to see what his words had inspired in us! So I copied more of the coloured Bible Study pages, and made myself known to Philip at the first afternoon tea gathering. Philip introduced me to his wife, Janet. This was their first trip to Australia, and they were both fascinated with the galahs feeding on the large expanse of lawn that we overlooked. He hadn't seen these colourful birds before.

The Bible Study I led at St Clements had studied Philip Yancy's book, 'Disappointment with God'. In our response we got creative with coloured textas and summarised what we had learnt in pictures and mind-maps. It had been informative and fun.

"How do you say that again - Gulars?"

And so it was that Philip Yancey warmly and graciously accepted my offering of our coloured pages.

"I will enjoy reading them."

That first evening was a themed opening session. The Bible Studies would not start until the evening of Day 2. I was very surprised the next afternoon, when Ron Buckland, National Director of Scripture Union, asked me (just out of the blue) if I would introduce Philip Yancey to the conference that evening. I was surprised and blessed at the same time. At least I had read one of Philip's books! It would be a great privilege to introduce him to the assembled SU crowd, of about one hundred people. I would speak about reading *Disappointment with God* and the blessings we had received as we studied it as a group. I rang Jill and told her, as our group was meeting that very night. They would be interested to know about my unexpected responsibility. I asked her to pray for my 'butterflies'!

So I gave my introduction to our American Bible Study leader, Philip Yancey, and then he took the floor. Philip began by telling everyone how I had 'drawn' his book, and how much he had learnt about his own book from my pictures!

We were ready for Philip to open God's word with us. We were expectant. Many, including myself, had pages ready to take notes. This would be rich fare indeed. Philip spoke of his first impressions of Australia. He commented on the coastal location and the view we had over the Pacific Ocean, which he found compelling. And then he began. Our pens were at the ready. But something happened that stopped us from writing. Philip Yancey told us a story, a story about grace. [But we weren't to realise that until the end.] And, as with any story, you can only help but listen. He wove a picture with his words. Philip retold the story by Karen Blixen, of *Babette's Feast*. The scene took us back to Denmark in the 1920s. Back to an impoverished fishing village where an austere Lutheran sect lived and worshipped. After the leader of the sect died, his two daughters attempted to carry on the work of their deceased father. [3]

Many of the audience would not have heard the story before tonight.

"One night the sisters heard a heavy thump at the door. When they opened it, a woman collapsed in a swoon. She spoke no Danish. She handed them a letter from a mutual friend, who urged the two sisters to take her in. This woman had lost her husband, and son, in the French Civil War. Reluctant at first, the sisters agreed to take Babette in as a cook and house keeper. So she cooked their daily meals of boiled cod and gruel. Babette did this year after year, bringing a new life to the stagnant town and its worshippers. Ten years later a letter arrived for Babette saying that a friend had bought for her an annual ticket in the French lottery, and the ticket had won. The prize was ten thousand francs

Babette convinced the sisters to allow her to cook a celebration meal, with her own money, for the occasion of the 100th anniversary of their father's birth. This would be a thank you to the sisters, for Barbette's years in their house. They agreed, but with heavy hearts, as they knew she would soon be leaving. Babette had to travel to France, to make arrangements for the dinner. Soon boats arrived at the fishing village and unloaded the gourmet provisions for the dinner. No expense had been spared. A sumptuous feast was prepared, the like thereof these people had never tasted.

And so the feast began, but these grumpy guests had all agreed not to comment on this lavish gesture. Although no one spoke of the food or drink that evening, this exquisite feast before them gradually worked a magical effect on the guests. Their blood warmed. Their tongues loosened. They spoke of the old days...they sang songs, and individuals

---

3 Used with Philip Yancey's permission

settled some long-standing feuds. Babette's feast opened the gate and grace stole in. The sisters were shocked to find out that Babette had been a famous chef in France. They are more shocked to find that she had spent all of her lottery winnings on their banquet. Babette would not be leaving their household."[4]

As Philip Yancey told this story my mind saw it in black and white. I had stumbled onto this story, as a black and white movie on the ABC, about a year before. I had not known what I was watching, having missed the beginning. But I remembered being drawn into the story as I watched. Yes, my mind was seeing this story again as Philip spoke. It was a story that none of our pens captured that night. We didn't need to, because it had been etched onto our imaginations. Philip told us it was a **parable of grace**: a gift that costs everything for the giver and nothing for the recipient. It was a parable to show how God the Father gave everything He had so we could secure a relationship with Him. God's extravagance had been the life of his precious Son.

Over the next three nights Philip would tell more stories, stories that again wouldn't be written down - stories that we just absorbed. He told a story about a modern family and the **ungrace** that had been handed down over three generations. [Philip Yancey coined the word *ungrace*, and it is now used in evangelical language to refer to the absence of grace.]

Four years later I would be reading a new book of Philip Yancey's[5]. There it was again, the story of *Babette's Feast*, in the opening chapter. I read the now familiar story with joy.

It wasn't until I got to the end of Chapter 3 that I remembered the other stories. I had heard them at Collaroy. I was reading the product of

---

4 Quote (and paraphrase) used with permission of the author, 2011
5 What's So Amazing About Grace, Philip Yancey, Harper Collins 1997

the studies Philip had given at the SU National Conference. But there was so much more in the book. More stories of grace and ungrace, inside and outside the church. There were powerful stories that would chastise the church for their lack of grace, the very place where grace should be demonstrated. I was to be quite moved when I realised that Philip had told us some intimate details of his own life, which he had chosen not to include in his book; details that made his experience of ungrace so very real.

Something happened for me that week in 1993. I was to understand the centrality of God's grace in his dealings with us, not for the first time, but in a new way. Grace was so central to God's dealing with His people that I had to make sure the young people I taught wouldn't miss it. Grace had to be the message they would take away - God's love and GRACE. And that's how I think of the word in my mind. GRACE is so important it should be spelt in capital letters! The same way GRACE was spelt on the cover of Philip Yancey's new book: in large, elegant Roman capitals.

There is an acrostic for grace that had been around the church for years, to help understand this important concept: *God's Riches At Christ's Expense*. But that didn't do justice to my new understanding of GRACE. I now have my own acrostic in my mind that helps me to remember GRACE:

- ***G**od's **R**ich **A**nd **C**ostly **E**xtravagance*

The extravagance of a generous God for me; the extravagance of a cross, so that I could feast at His banqueting table; an extravagance I didn't deserve; an extravagance that demands a response – a life of love, lived out extravagantly for Him. I needed to make sure this message of GRACE was coming through loud and clear in the lessons I taught.

5th November

I had experienced all week the unique creativity that SU brings to the theatre of faith. No more so that when a group gathers for worship. The presentation on the final night was very moving, and I captured it in my Prayer Diary, at home the following evening. This was such a fitting setting for Communion together. Our hands accuse us. Christ's outstretched hands bring us forgiveness.

Our hearts are broken

I have sometimes wondered why I stopped writing in my Prayer Diary. The fullness of this time in Term 4, and those November weeks in particular, give me some clues.

It was a Sunday afternoon in November. I was washing up the lunch dishes when I heard a news bulletin on the radio.

"Last night, at a dance Party in Castle Hill, a boy was killed after being stabbed on the dance floor. He was pronounced dead at Westmead Hospital a short time later. Police are interviewing young people who were at the scene. The boy's name has been released – he was Geoffrey B of Cherrybrook, a student at Pennant Hills High School. The person responsible has not been apprehended. Anyone with information is asked to contact Castle Hill police."

I was stunned. My hands were still immersed in water as I replayed the announcement in my mind.

Pennant Hills High School. That was my school!

Geoffrey B. I knew the name!

How awful, I knew the name on the radio.

My mind started to turn over this name, Geoffrey B, but I wasn't connecting it to a face. I felt bad about this. I taught so many students and this face was lost in the crowd. (I later realised why I didn't recognise his name straight away, as Geoff was now in Year 11, and I hadn't had him in class for 12 months).

I felt bad that a picture of his face was not coming to me. I went about my activities carrying this news as an unwelcome weight. My mind was working like a computer on the sea of faces I knew. And eventually a face rose above the rest – a cheerful blonde-headed boy with a smile. Yes, I knew Geoff B. Then the full extent of this news story hit me. I was stunned and saddened, as I knew Geoff as a quiet, polite young man with a nice group of friends. Here was another tragedy for our school that would devastate it, again. What a hard week it would be. I thought about the next day.

Geoff Barrett won't be sitting at his desk tomorrow.

There will be one empty chair;

In each of his classes, one empty chair!

Tomorrow one chair will be an unwelcome guest.

It will hold the grief of many.

That's what death means.

You don't get to sit in your chair anymore.

I went to evening church that Sunday, and over supper mentioned what I had heard on the radio.

"Yes, I heard that too," came comments of concern.

Monday 15th November

I walked into Pennant Hills High that Monday morning with a heavy heart. My senses alert to the students I was passing and very aware that this would be the beginning of a very hard week. The faces and the body language of Year 11 students betrayed if they had heard the news of Geoff, or not. It was hard to see someone join a group of friends, and after a brief interchange, observe the shock of 'knowing' settle over them. Students were wiping away tears. Some of the Year 11 students had been there; had been there with Geoff on Saturday night. They were distraught. And it wasn't just Year 11. There were other students who were being comforted too. Maybe they knew Geoff well, maybe not. This type of grief was a spreading kind, as our school well knew.

A note on the signing-on book gave details of a staff meeting before the start of the school day. I walked across to the staff room. It was then I remembered that Geoff had been from Year 11. This was Nikky Vanderhout's Year Group. How very hard this would be for her. The mood was very sober at the staff meeting, by now most of the teachers would have been told of the events of Saturday night by colleagues. Peter Noble, with a heavy heart, told those assembled, of the unimaginable – another of our fine young students had died. That Geoff's death had been a crime, with his assailant still at large, made the hearing of it so much harder. And to make matters worse Mr B was overseas for work when this happened. He had had to make that terrible journey home. Peter Noble mentioned Geoff's sister and brother, also our students in Year 12 and year 8, and that students in those years might also be affected by this news.

Nikky Vanderhout, the Year Advisor for Geoff's year has reflected,

"I recall that Peter Noble called me at home to let me know of Geoff's death before it hit the news. It was quite eerie watching the news broadcast that night and to see his school photo appearing regularly with each update."

We had experienced one student death each year for a number of years at Penno and so the Department process was quite well known to the staff but still, when it is one from the Year Group you have cared for over five years, the shock value cannot be minimized.

We had a special staff meeting on the Monday before school started but most of the staff had already been informed of the situation. Letting the students know is always difficult for it brings back all previous memories of loss for all students, not just special friends of the one lost. I must say that I have always been incredibly impressed by the quality of response provided by the Department of Education – there were numerous counselors present and they worked in conjunction with the Year Advisers, the Christian studies teacher and other staff. I think Greg Field was the counselor at that time.

Any student who wanted to was allowed to come to the Teachers' Common Room to talk to someone or just to sit with friends. Geoff's closest friends came as well as others who just needed space to think. The support people were incredibly good, taking some students to a quieter room as the need arose. It was a sad day and one in which the students grew noticeably closer as they comforted each other.

The press was not allowed on the premises but there were quite a few reporters at the school gate trying to get students to comment. We were careful to tell the students to walk away and not respond.

– Nikky Vanderhout

Nikky also recalls a comment made by the Principal during that morning meeting.

"At times like these, we wouldn't cope if it wasn't for Christian Studies." I understood I would carry a heavy load this week, along with others.

My classes wanted to talk about it. This was hard too, but it needed to be done. The students could sense the mood and were quieter than normal, after an assembly that relayed the news. Some asked questions and made comments, with a few students knowing more than others. Many of our Year 10 and 11 teens were regular patrons of this Castle Hill initiative. That a murder could happen at a well-run, under-aged, alcohol free event in the Hills district was shocking. This wasn't the western suburbs or the inner city.

Year 11 students came to my door at recess, and over the next couple of days a mix of eye-witness accounts filtered through;

"It wasn't Geoff's fault; they are saying Geoff started it; he was minding his own business; these two guys asked him for money; he didn't have any; I saw Geoff pushed and he fell to the floor; he had a knife; an ambulance was called; the guy who did it ran away; there were two of them; they weren't from the local area."

More so than when Chloe died, I watched many staff get alongside students in unexpected ways. Staff members were with students, in the morning, at recess and at lunch time; so many staff; just comforting kids. We were doing it again. At ISCF that Monday the group prayed; for Geoff's family, for the boy who did this to be found; for the week ahead. A funeral was being mentioned. By the end of the day students received a statement from the school to take home for their parent's information. An A4 sheet of paper indicates the magnitude of the message.

That night the news was full of the story again. There was a photo of Geoff with every news bulletin; his school photo; Geoffrey Barrett in his Year 11 uniform, a white shirt and school tie. This made the tragedy so much more real.

Morning papers contained the story on the **Tuesday**. By now the facts were becoming more evident.

This first article to appear in the papers also contained a large photo of Geoff's parents. Mr B was being interviewed by the press, for the first time, with microphones held in front of him as he spoke on behalf of the family. Their distraught faces told the story that November day.

The principal addressed the staff again, giving out details of Geoff's funeral and the arrangements being made for any Year 11s who wanted to attend. Peter Noble had offered a school memorial service for Geoff, when the family was up to it.

It wasn't necessary to continue discussing Geoff's death with classes by the Tuesday. Many students would not have known him, or the family, so most of my lessons continued with a new theme of the week before. If students asked questions I would deal with them briefly. It is important at times like these to know when to move forward. As the days ticked by, information was filtering through of the events of that Saturday night. Papers carried the story for a few days.

> A few days later Peter asked to see me and in his office he told me the family wanted the school to participate in the Funeral Service. We talked about what that would look like and who would attend. Finally all students were invited to attend, and I remember distinctly that it was during this Year Assembly, when I had to explain the funeral arrangements to the students, that my emotions became overwhelming, and I broke down. After the assembly, Martin Rees told me that he had written a piece of music for Geoff and so we let the family know and they included it in the service.

We would all hear about the events that unfolded in Blacktown, on that Tuesday night. Two youths had been charged over Geoff's death.

This was shocking news indeed, but also brought some sort of relief to this whole situation. One of the youths concerned had disclosed his actions to a teacher. That the assailant was also a schoolboy seemed such a sad detail to add to the events of Saturday night. Students talking later told me that these boys had gone to Blacktown McDonalds after the crime. This was such a poignant detail – a seemingly innocent choice after such a violence act. And they lived so near to me; Marayong, Prospect, Blacktown. Why did it have to be Blacktown, further fuelling people's negative image of the western suburbs? At school that day we heard that Nikky V, with the two new school captains, Martin and Elizabeth, would speak at Geoff's funeral on behalf of the school. This would be a very hard thing for everyone involved, impossibly hard.

Geoff B's Memorial Service, St Matthews West Pennant Hills

Thursday 18th, November

To say the mood in the church was sober that Thursday morning would be a complete understatement. But how do you describe the agony etched onto faces; faces known to you, young faces not yet fit to carry such grief.

> Peter Noble had asked me to speak as the school representative for he was quite unwell at the time. As I was afraid that I would be overwhelmed at the service, I had Martin Rees and Elizabeth Cox, the school captains, come to the lectern with me ready to read the rest of my speech, should the need arise.

Tribute from the school, written by Nikky Vanderhout

"On behalf of the students and staff of Pennant Hills High School, it is my privilege to share our thoughts of Geoff with you.

Geoff shared five years of his schooling with us and in that time, made many strong friendships. Geoff's friendship was of the utterly dependable kind, a good friend who'd stick by you no matter what. His warm personality and ready smile bore witness to his good sense of humour and his happy, easy going nature. His friends recall with pleasure the many of the fun times they have shared, laughing and joking together, times which will always be remembered with warm affection.

Geoff was a true peace-maker, having the special ability to calm others in the face of conflict. It is especially tragic that someone for whom aggression was so alien should be the victim of such unprovoked and inexplicable violence.

Geoff was a keen sportsman, tennis and soccer being the sports he enjoyed most. Everyone who competed with him, and against him, will remember his quiet enthusiasm and his sense of fair play. When Geoff represented the school in these sports, he always entered wholeheartedly into the spirit of the game and enjoyed the challenge of tough opposition.

All Geoff's teachers speak of his determination to do the best he could. Geoff was reliable and trustworthy, steady, polite and respectful. We could always depend on him to give his utmost to do anything he was asked to do. His co-operation, self- discipline and interest in learning made Geoff a pleasure to have in a classroom. After spending two weeks at work experience as a mechanic at the end of last year, Geoff was asked to comment on how work experience had affected his thinking about his time at school. In true Geoff style, he responded,

" ....to work hard and get a better job!"

This determination to make the most of himself was characteristic of Geoff's approach to his school-work as well.

Geoff was a mature young man who had the special gift of being comfortable with the person he was. He had no need to impress other people and didn't need to work at fitting in with others, for he fitted in so well. Geoff was always quietly confident and kind to everyone. He would never put himself forward, yet those who knew him best appreciated his sensible manner, the gentle way he dealt with others and his ability to make them feel valued as his friend. In the words of a close friend,

"He'd have made a great dad."

The school has been greatly saddened by the loss of this fine young man who was well liked by us all. We will miss his ready smile, his cheerful presence and the warmth of his friendship. We offer our deepest sympathy to Geoff's family, praying that God will surround them with His love and comfort them at this most difficult time of great sorrow.

Those who hope in the Lord will renew their strength.

They will soar on wings like eagles;

They will run and not grow weary,

They will walk and not faint. ISA 5"

Nikky's voice had been shaky in the middle of her tribute. It was obvious how hard this was for her, as she choked on the words, which added to the enormity of what we were all sitting through. Nikky stopped and quietly composed herself so she could continue.

Martin and Elizabeth stood behind me as I spoke. As my voice became unsteady I felt both of them place a hand on my shoulder - and that gave me sufficient courage to go on. I felt it was God putting his hand on me to help me continue.

Martin's cello composition for Geoff was so beautiful, and I was aware of what a deep effect Geoff's death had had on him. Martin was such a talented young man, in so many ways, and his music spoke deeply to all this day. But it made me think of Geoff and all *his* talents and dreams, which would never now find their voice or wings.

We transported all the students to the church by bus – and the students formed an honour guard after the service. The press was there in droves and tried to get student's comment but they walked by respectfully, to and from the church, without comment.

It is a very hard thing indeed to watch young people who are so very obviously grief stricken, say goodbye to a friend. They had loved Geoff dearly. It was hard too, to go back to school that day and take the afternoon lessons. Those staff members who didn't go asked about the funeral. Words were kept to a minimum.

I arrived home that afternoon quite wrung out. As an adult you keep it together when you have to. I could have so easily sat down and cried. Yet by now it was the middle of November and reports were due next week. I had a big deadline to meet for Monday – all Year 7 reports, and Year 9 by Wednesday. I knew if I stopped and reflected for too long I would end up in tears. I couldn't afford to do that. I knew from recent experience how wasted crying leaves you. So I girded myself, collected my mark book and a packet of blank reports, and began my Year 7 Christian Studies reports. I remember sitting at my kitchen table that afternoon and being sad because I didn't have time to shed tears for Geoff. And that seemed so wrong.

'Andrew is a polite and friendly student who enjoys Christian Studies. His book has been well kept. Andrew's assignment on the life of Jesus was creatively presented.'

All my reports were handed in, on time, that next Monday.

By the following **Monday** there were more details about a school memorial service for Geoff. A fellow teacher commented,

"The boy who did this should be made to come and watch this, and maybe realise what he has done!" I agreed with him.

Nikky came to see me, and asked if I would speak at this school farewell for Geoff. His parents, sister and brother would be there. As the Christian Studies teacher it seemed an obvious choice. I nodded and told Nikky I would do it, but wondered what on earth I would say! Where do you find the right words for a case like this? Did I have words that would bring great comfort? I didn't think so. I didn't know Geoff as a student with an active interest in Christian things. I couldn't say for sure that he was on his way to Heaven. I wondered if, in those final moments, Geoff knew that he was dying and called out to God to save him? I just didn't know that, so I couldn't even hint at it. Over a few days I turned this over in my mind. I knew I didn't have any answers, if that's what people wanted to hear.

And then I realised that I did have something. When life turns upside down and presents me with the most unimaginable events, like someone's death, it's like solid ground turns to an ocean. I don't know why a good God allows these things to happen, and I don't have answers for them. But in the midst of the darkness **I hold on to what I do know**.

I hold onto the fact that God is there; that He exists.

I hold onto the fact that He loves me and sent His Son to earth to show me His love;

I hold onto the fact that Jesus lived the kind of life I couldn't, and died in my place.

I hold onto the fact that God raised Jesus from the grave so that He might have victory over death, once and for all.

I hold onto the fact that Heaven awaits those who love God.

And by holding on to those things that I do know, I can trust God with the things that I don't know, things I don't understand.

And that helps me to get through.

And that's what I said to the assembled school, with Geoff B's parents, Sarah and Matthew, sitting to the side. There was absolute silence as I stood at the microphone. What would Miss McNab say?

I spoke those thoughts into an expanded tribute to the young Geoff B, who departed this life too early, and left his family, and those who knew him well, with a big hole in their hearts, that time has not filled.

As Nikky Vanderhout and I sat in an Eastwood café some months ago, and recalled Geoff B, and the details of that sad week, each of us had tears in our eyes. We shared things that were deeply personal for each of us, then and now; and in doing this our hearts gave voice to an unspoken prayer,

"Rest in peace Geoff, Rest in Peace."

A response from Sam Hilton, now 41, and a pastor of a church

I knew Geoff's death would have a huge impact on the Year 11s, especially on his friends. Many people in the church community prayed for these young people over those weeks. We were not to know then what impact these prayers would have.

Sam Hilton, of Year 11, wasn't one of Geoff's closest friends, but he and Geoff were neighbours and they walked to and from school together.

"In 1994 I became a Christian. This was after many years of faithful ministry through St Matthew's Anglican Church and the Christian Studies program at Pennant Hills High. I guess I never doubted the truth of what was being taught but it never really hit home for me until 1993, when I was in Year 11.

A friend of mine, Geoff B, was murdered at a local dance party. He was a good kid. He never did the wrong thing. And in fact Geoff was doing the right thing that night, while many of us were elsewhere getting drunk. I remember first the shock of what happened, but then being confronted with the reality that my eternal security was not contingent upon how good I am. This hit home for me at Geoff's funeral.

It took another year for me to take God seriously. I spent most of my year in Year 12 in denial of God's calling on your life and continued to live how I wanted, and in order to please the people around me. At the same time I started going regularly to a Bible Study at St Matt's. It was the end of that year that I realised I couldn't resist God any longer and I couldn't keep running from him.

At the end of that year I asked God to forgive me and decided to live for God. Praise God!!

The Christian Studies program at Pennant Hills High was brilliant. I remember loving camps, camping trips with Mr O', the consistent witness of Miss McNab and the teachers who boldly stood up as Christians in that school- namely Miss V and Mr Kneale. This all made exploring the person of Jesus a viable thing to do. It was not odd to be reading the Bible. It wasn't odd to have teachers who were Christians. It was completely normal to hang out with the Christian Studies teachers. I think if it were not for that valuable Christian presence in that school, investigating the claims of Jesus would have been much more difficult."

Sam Hilton, 2012

DAD

Phone calls can be a joy and a curse; a bringer of sweet news or an interruption; the conduit of a loved one's familiar tones or of their voice bearing news you don't want to hear. It was the latter phone call that brought the news, this time, the worst news. It was Mum to say that Dad had suffered another stroke, one he would not recover from. I had to come; we had to come, at once. I had to drive across many suburbs carrying such news.

Mum and Geoff were already at Bethany when I arrived. Mum was receiving an update from the head sister. They had moved Dad into a small room by himself, for the care he needed and for privacy. He was conscious, but lying in bed, now even more restricted as this stroke had left him almost motionless. We stood and watched while nurses attended him, our hearts heavy. We talked quietly to each other as we took in the full extent of his condition. A catheter drained urine into a bag attached to the side of his bed; his same metal bed, moved from his familiar room, now looking all together clinical.

I moved and sat on the edge of the bed, touching Dad's arm and speaking to him so he knew I was there. I kissed him on the cheek, and as I did, with his good arm he pulled me close to him in an embrace. I got such a surprise. Dad was hugging me. That's all that he could do, and he was hugging me. The hug said it all without words. Dad knew what was happening to him. He was telling me that he loved me the only way that he could. I hadn't had a hug from him, like that, for as long as I could remember. This was so very special.

"It's so sad," I heard Geoff say through tears. Mum was comforting him, as I lay in my father's spontaneous hug.

They were both watching. They understood this moment too. I pulled away. I don't know why. I wish I had stayed longer in my Dad's last embrace. I think it was too overpowering for me then; but now it's one of my most precious memories.

After some time Geoff left, and Mum and I went back home. She made a cup of tea, and then a few phone calls. Mum put our news on the Prayer Chain.

How long? We didn't know. They couldn't tell us. This was so hard. Christmas was just days away and there had been so much to look forward to, as we planned Christmas with the children. But now we would keep a daily vigil at Dad's bedside, waiting for him to die. It was awful, just awful.

"I don't even feel like having Christmas," Mum said to me, in a dejected voice.

I was stunned. Would we not celebrate Christmas as we had every other year? How awful! Was this said out of a selfish reason, I'm not sure. I think there was something much bigger at stake here. Mum's father died on Christmas Eve, some 40 years before. She had said previously that her family didn't know whether to have Christmas, or not. Here was another situation with so much similarity, and it was hard for Mum all over again.

"We **have** to have Christmas," I said to her. "It's because of Christmas that we have hope for Dad, because Jesus came that first Christmas!" Mum didn't say anything, but seemed to take it on board. The next day I overheard her on the phone telling Betty,

"Helen said we have to have Christmas!" And so we did.

Our Christmas plans were already made at Geoff and Megan's at Rydalmere; lunch was to be at Wentworthville. So at least Mum didn't have to prepare a lot of food. But as always Mum had lots of wrapping of presents to do, on the back verandah; presents for all of us, for her friends and their grandchildren, and for all the staff at Bethany; lots of presents. I was sewing in Blacktown, right up till the last minute – a pink tutu for Heather. I had guessed her size, and combined a few patterns to make a pink lycra tutu. Sewing on layers of pink tulle for a skirt was a challenge. At least it was all stretchy, and should stretch to fit her. I had also made an identical one to fit a small teddy bear. I got to Mum's on Christmas Eve in time to watch Carol's by Candlelight from Melbourne. This was a tradition we had. The carols were full of the reality of Christmas, and set the tone for the day ahead.

Christmas Day arrived.

"Happy Christmas Mum," I said offering a hug.

"Happy Christmas love."

We were soon eating freshly sliced ham and pickles on toast for breakfast, and then a dash to get to church. Mum had presents to give out, and if we got there early enough she could see people coming out of the early service.

We did our best to have a happy time together, the children setting the pace. The tutu was quite a hit! I named the two identical dancers as Heather Bear and Feather Bear. Our little three year old liked that.

I remember our visits to Dad over those next days, many days; sitting quietly by his bed; watching the staff attend to him. *Nil by mouth* said the sign over his bed. Dad's mouth was dry, but he couldn't swallow, so no water was allowed. They used ice to wipe over his lips, to relieve them. Some ice was left on the side table, and we would slide it over Dad's lips to moisten them when he needed it. We talked to him, quietly, speaking of what we did for Christmas and how the children enjoyed their presents. Sometimes the staff would arrive with a cup of tea on the trolley. This was hard for them too. Dad was one of their favourite residents. Sister Helen came in frequently to see him, and her gentle presence meant so much to all of us; and no doubt to Dad. With each visit we'd be wondering how we would find him the next time, although Mum kept us up-to-date by phone as well, ringing Bethany at the beginning of each new day. Sometimes each of our visits might overlap, and it was easier.

"His urine is getting darker. That's a sign his kidneys aren't functioning," commented Megan one afternoon, in a nurse's observant way. No, no! I don't want to know that, so I tried not to look at the clear bag that spoke of my father's failing organs. I tried not to look. But as the days wore on, the contents of the bag were almost dark brown.

On those hot days after Christmas Mum's phone rang regularly. When I was there I would answer it, to give her a break. The same questions would be asked, the same answers given. The repetitiveness was draining, but it needed to be done. Callers would finish with, "Give my love to Mum."

I was pleased to be visiting Dad there by myself this one afternoon. There were things I wanted to say to my father. I knew he was a fighter and he might respond to the things I offered.

"I know you were a soldier, Dad. And you know how to fight. But you don't have to fight anymore. It's OK to let go and say the fight's over. It's Ok to let go. You don't have to fight anymore."

I hoped it might help him in the battle his body was going through, the one his mind was also engaged in. I don't know if it helped, but I told Mum what I said. She seemed to think that it was a good thing to say. The next day I overheard Mum on the phone,

"Helen told him he doesn't have to keep fighting."

It was the Friday night after Christmas, and New Year's Eve 1993. I was planning on joining the Dunlop's and their church friends to see in the New Year. I had just finished dinner. Not a phone call, but a knock on the door this time. It was Mark Eaton. That was a surprise.

"It's your Dad. He's had a turn for the worse. You need to go. I'm driving you!"

My heart was in my mouth. We quickly set off on the drive to Marsfield; the journey Mum didn't want me to make on my own. She had made the phone call to Mark, and asked for his help. It was good to have Mark's company, on this my last journey to Bethany. The twilight was fading as we drove to Marsfield in Mark's comfortable Holden sedan. His well-kept car was much newer than mine. I was travelling in style and it felt like I was being chauffeured!

I didn't know what to expect at the other end. Mark told me he had brought some oil to anoint Dad with. That is a biblical practise for people who are gravely ill. I appreciated his forethought and smiled to myself that my father would have the last rights from the Catholics **and** the Anglicans. We walked through the quiet corridors of Bethany and into Dad's low-lit room. The change was obvious. Dad was lying flat in the bed and very still. He had slipped into a coma and would not regain consciousness. Dad looked at peace then on looking closer, I could hardly believe my eyes - the paralysis seemed to have gone from Dad's face. What a wonderful thing to witness. His smooth skin sat over relaxed muscles, and made him look like the Dad we had known before his stroke.

Mark took out the small flask of oil he had carried with him. He would have done this many times in hospital wards and in people's homes. Mark would do it now for my Dad. A prayer for the dying, and a small amount of oil was wiped on his forehead to claim him for the Lord Jesus.

"I'll give you some time," said Mark, as he moved to take a seat by the wall.

I felt a bit awkward, being watched. I didn't know quite what to do. Does anybody know what to do at the bedside of your dying father? It's not something that you rehearse for. But this was it. I was saying goodbye to my Dad. I touched his face and kissed him on the head. And I just gazed at him. His body was letting go. He seemed – at peace. I didn't say anything. I should have, but I felt too self-conscious at the time to do that. After a while I turned and nodded to Mark. It was time to go.

Mark drove me to Farrington Pde, as he had planned to do. It was well and truly dark by now. Mum was pleased to see us both; I was greeted with a big hug and Mark got one too. She was very grateful to him for his support of me. It was time for a cup of tea. Heather was there too. She was staying the night, so our attention was variously drawn to a little girl as we sat and talked in the lounge room. Mum reminded us that the first signs of an early New Year were about to begin - the 9:00pm fireworks in the city. We had a place of advantage at North Ryde, and our position at No. 34 was at the high point of the street. So we all went outside, into the cool of the evening, and into the middle of Farrington Pde. From here we could see the arch of the Harbour Bridge. Some people had also come to the corner behind us to get a view from there. Mark picked Heather up so she could see the coloured lights bursting into the sky. Heather was fascinated by Mark's beard, and now up close she began to run her hand over his whiskers. We all laughed at the spontaneity of a little girl. The fireworks were a tangible community celebration to experience together as our thoughts turned towards a new year, and its unknowns.

It was time for Heather to go to bed, and for Mark and me to drive home. There was Dunlop's New Year celebration underway, but it didn't seem appropriate to join in now. I wouldn't have been much company. So I just went home and to bed, before the noises of *"Happy New Year"* began.

1994

Chapter 6

My father died in the early hours of January 1st. I reflected that New Year's Day was a good day for a Scotsman to die. (My Dad was the first surviving child to be born in Australia of Scottish migrants, after the family left life in Dundee). The first of January was their day - *Hogmanay*. It is tradition in Scotland to visit friends and family in the first hours of the New Year. Dad's first visitor had been his God, who called to take him Home. Dad first-footed this year right through Heaven's door.

I was sleeping soundly when I was woken by a repeated knock at the front door. As I registered the knocking I wondered who it might be. I glimpsed my friend Rosemary, from church, through the curtains. I opened the door. She just said,

"He's gone."

And I knew. I felt tears coming, but caught myself because of Rosemary. Maybe I should have just cried.

"Your Mum rang and asked me to come round."

I nodded and must have said something. Rosemary asked if I would be alright?

"Yes."

It wasn't a long exchange, but one I won't forget. My Dad was gone. I understood Mum hadn't wanted to tell me herself, over the phone. It would have been too hard for her and me. I think she mostly did it for my sake, wanting someone to be there with me when I got the news. I picked up the phone to call her. Because Mum didn't have to tell me the worst, it was OK.

"Dad died about 3:00am. I woke about then and just had a feeling," Mum reflected. "Heather slept in bed with me last night, not something I'd usually do. I pulled her close and just hugged her." How very special, I thought, that at the very worst time for Mum, God had been working in that very detail. She had something of Neil in her arms the moment he was taken, and Mum had held their granddaughter close in her knowing.

I said I would come over.

"Betty is on her way."

It was good to know she was there for Mum now. After 43 years of marriage, a sister who had seen her fall in love with Neil McNab, say her vows, bear his children and live a full life together was there to help her walk this road too. When I arrived I gave Mum a big hug. She was doing OK.

"Hello love," said Aunty Bet. She made a cup of tea. We talked for a while, and I sat in the lounge room full of morning light, and collected my thoughts. Betty was in the sunroom, and Mum in the kitchen when Geoff arrived.

"Hi," he said to me as he walked through to the sunroom. He was quickly in conversation with this much-loved aunt.

Just "hi," that's all I got. We had just lost our father, I was his only sister, and I just got "hi." I had thought there would have been more. I was hurt; deeply hurt by that neglect. I sat and listened to their interaction, talking on all matter of things. Geoff didn't see as much of his aunt now that he was married, and he was just enjoying her uplifting company. But that set my mood for the day; one I disguised as the day continued.

And so the gathering of the clan began, and the relaying of the information to others started. That's what families do in the event of a death; they rally, they come, they help. Aunty Bet kept the cups of tea flowing, and made sandwiches. Much had to be arranged. Mum would make contact with Dad's priest at The Spirit of Sanctus Church after the public holiday. The service would be held there, in the church of Dad's choice, but Mum wanted her Anglican minister involved as well. In time the Catholic priest was happy for this to happen, and arranged to see Graham Orr to plan the service. The luncheon to follow would be held in St John's Hall. The church ladies would help with that.

I rang Shane with the news of Dad's death. With a broken voice she said, "I'm coming down." That was a surprise. I said we wouldn't expect her to come so far. Now, through tears she said, "Your parents have always meant so much to me. Your Dad was so kind, and always interested in what I did. They came to our wedding."

No more arguments from me. Shane was coming! This was so very special, and what I call the mark of friendship. She needed to make arrangements for a flight, and get back to me.

"We can't speak to the funeral people till Monday, but we think the funeral might be Thursday."

"Shane's coming down!" I said to Mum with a smile. Mum smiled back. This was special for her too. "She can stay here." Yes, that would work. And I would stay too.

"Janet's coming down too, but I wasn't supposed to tell you," said Mum. "You'll have to act like you are surprised." Oh, a double blessing of two best friends. I couldn't have asked for more.

Mum's friends came and went over the day. The house always seemed to have a visitor or two; Betty, Joy, June Jones, Jess Smith. June had arrived with hot scones. The phone kept ringing; family, neighbours and St John's friends. I would repeat the same information and asked them to keep their eyes on the paper for funeral arrangements. A representative from the funeral home would come on Monday. Mum wanted both Geoff and me to be there when she spoke to them.

"Hi," had been the only interaction I'd had from my brother all day. He was ready to go.

"Bye."

I'd wanted to ask him something, so I followed him out the front door. "I wondered if you'd wear your McNab tie to the funeral?" Geoff paused. "I'll think about it."

That sounded to me like a no. I was ready to snap, and I did. "Do what you like. You always do!"

That had surprised him, and he was now, for the first time that day, focussed on me. I walked back inside and shut the screen door. No one else had overheard our exchange that had left both of us hurt. *Not a great exit remark, Helen!* I thought to myself. This was now going to be difficult terrain to navigate.

Mark Eaton came to visit me at home that night.

"How are you?"

I said I was doing OK, and told him some of the arrangements that had been made already. He said he would be coming to the funeral, to support me. People were being so very kind. I found myself telling Mark about the exchange with my brother, and his seemingly ignoring me all day.

"It happens in a lot of families when someone dies," said Mark. "People find themselves arguing about all sorts of things, because they are thrown together and emotions are heightened." This was good to hear; so good to hear. It made sense and helped me to put today in a different perspective. There was much to think about as I closed my eyes to sleep.

Sleep led into Sunday, and it was a combined service at my church, being holidays. The news of my father's death was in the church bulletin. Jack Filby approached me after the service and offered his sympathy.

Jack asked, "Is there anything I can do to help?"

What a warm offer from this St Clement's elder. It didn't occur to me until later, when I was playing over people's comments in my head. I rang the Filbys and spoke to Jack.

"Can I take you up on your offer today? We need someone to play the organ."

And so it was arranged. I needed to get back to Jack with our choice of songs from the Catholic Hymnal. Jack, a church friend of mine would be involved in the funeral service. How very nice.

Monday: A man from the funeral directors arrived. This was just a process for them - a day's business. For us, we were making big decisions for the funeral of a husband and a father. You only ever do that once. Options were given; casket; flowers; decisions were made. Geoff and I would each write something. I said I would do a Bible reading. Mum seemed surprised.

"Now don't expect too much of yourself," she said.

"No, I'm not. I know I can do it. I'm used to speaking in public."

She wasn't convinced. But I was. I knew I could do it. And I wanted to do this, for Dad. Mum later said that nobody would think any less of me if I didn't do it, depending how I felt on the day. And she'd asked

Graham Orr to step in if I didn't feel up to doing it. OK, but I know I can! But I did listen to Mum, maybe she was right. Who would know how I'd be feeling at my father's funeral?

Geoff and I had similar thoughts in our minds for Bible readings; the passage in Isaiah 40, that speaks of,

'young men running and not growing weary, of walking and not being faint'.

It spoke of the hope we had for 'Grandpas' new 'legs', of our Dad standing straight and tall again in Heaven, free from the effects of a disabling stroke. But Mum rebuked us! She said with tears in her eyes, "That was only a small part of his life! We are not going to focus on that. There is so much more to be remembered."

She was right.

The passage in John 14 was large on my heart also, where Jesus is saying goodbye to his disciples, and explaining where he is going - back to be with his Father. Jesus gives the disciples a promise that he will also prepare a place for them, and come back to take them home. It is a very encouraging part of scripture, and it contained our desire and hope for Dad. We all agreed on John 14, and that, all being well, I would read it.

Geoff and I had similar thoughts on something else as well. He asked me what I remembered Dad saying. I'd been thinking about that myself. What were Dad's familiar comments? I wasn't sure. This had worried me; was there no one thing? My father had been a man of few words. And then it had come to me,

"As long as you do your best!"

Dad had always said that when I was young; for school tests and exams, physical-culture competitions or when learning to play tennis.

"As long as you do your best!"

I answered my brother's question without hesitation.

"There you go!" Geoff said with pleasure in his voice. "That's what I said too."

The RSL had made contact with Mum. They wanted to do an RSL tribute, with an Australian flag on the coffin and men laying poppies. Mum had said, "I couldn't cope with all of that," she said.

We understood and honoured her choice. As I reflect now on why Mum did that I wonder if it was the events of their early-married life that had fuelled this decision? Dad had had a breakdown after the rigours of serving with the 9th Division in both the Middle East and the Pacific. Mum had a new baby (me), to take every day to Concord Repatriation Hospital, to visit her husband, over a period of months. It was Mum that would help her husband get well, once he was home. I wonder if it was that less glamorous picture of war, that Mum had seen, (a service woman herself), that had stayed with her. Or, I wonder if "I couldn't cope with all that" meant exactly that. Mum would need all her reserved energy for the funeral, and this display of national pride may have just been too much.

What would I wear to the funeral? I didn't think I had anything appropriate so I would need to buy something. I wouldn't wear black, but just what I had no idea? I went into Blacktown. *I'm buying a dress to wear to my father's funeral*, I thought to myself, as I walked through the holiday shoppers. What a surreal thing to do. In Rockmans I tried on a cream suit, that was just the thing. I was grateful that had been so easy.

It was now Tuesday and all I had to do was write a eulogy for my father. This would be hard. With a very limited time frame, it had to be completed by Tuesday. I was also picking Shane up at the airport. I had just one time slot to do it. My brother was writing something too. I didn't know what. I would have thought we would discuss this and write it together, so we didn't overlap. But I heard nothing. I just had to write. I sat in my study, at my computer, remembering and writing, feeling and writing. There was nobody to make me a cup of tea, or offer me a cool drink or words of encouragement. Nobody. I have never felt so lonely as I did that January afternoon. Late that night I was satisfied with the printed page in my hands.

Wednesday arrived - **the day of my father's funeral**. Another hot day was expected. It was a strange feeling getting dressed that morning.

I'm getting ready to go to my father's funeral, I was thinking to myself, somehow conscious of my every move.

I needed to be at North Ryde in good time. As I drove over I had something on my mind that I wanted to do. I wanted to cut some of Dad's flowers to put on his coffin; the flowers he had planted and enjoyed years before, to add to the family flowers we had chosen. Would any of Dad's flowers be out? I told Shane what I wanted to do. I got the secateurs from the laundry and walked around the front and the back garden to see what was flowering. Yes, there were just enough blooms, including two small roses. I was back in the laundry, with my floral tribute, when Shane came in and took over,

"I can do that for you. I want to do it. Go and do anything else you need to take care of."

It was nice to have a friend at hand. Shane had buried her mother a decade before. She knew what this was like.

Eventually we were all ready. Shane would walk across to the church, just minutes away. The funeral car was picking them up.

Before she left Shane put the small posy she had made into my hands.

"Thank you," was all I needed to say.

The day of our father's funeral Geoff, and Megan, arrived looking very smart. They had earlier decided not to bring the children, having them minded by a friend. I didn't often see my brother dressed up. He still had his tie to put on, which he did in front of the long mirror in the hall. He had chosen his Robertson tie, the tartan of Dad's mother. Our words of just a few days before were behind us. Today as a family, we would stand as one.

A big black car pulled up out the front in ample time. We were ready. I carried my small bouquet with me on the short journey to the church. People were arriving as we pulled into the driveway and many were already seated inside. I smiled at Chris O'Flaherty, who was also just arriving. He had come. As we walked into the church I saw family; Lois and Colin, with Flora. This would be so hard for her too, saying goodbye to a much-loved brother. The Kerslakes were sitting together; Aunty Bet with Greg and Susan, Sallie and David. Jack Filby was already seated at the organ. I smiled. I detoured to the coffin standing alone at the front of this vast church. I placed my flowers on the coffin, as the others moved into their front seats.

This, **the day of my father's funeral**, I had time to think as we waited for the service to begin. I realised I had never been inside this church building before. It was a lovely building of light coloured bricks, with a high-sloped roof and a vaulting ceiling in the front. There was lots of space and light. The modern stained glass windows were quite beautiful. Why had I never come to church with my Dad? My work took me into every kind of church; other Catholic churches. Why had I not come here with him? Dad would have appreciated that so much. It was something I now regretted as I sat and waited for the service to begin. I gazed at the coffin the most unwelcome piece of furniture in the whole church.

There was a word of welcome from the priest, and then Graham Orr was introduced to the assembled crowd of friends and family. These two clerics both spoke as the service began and continued.

Then it was my turn; Jesus' words of comfort and hope. I knew I could do this. I felt so at home here, standing in front of a church, with my Bible open; standing in front of Dad's church, to read for him.

"Do not let your hearts be troubled. Trust in God; trust also in me. In my Father's house are many rooms; if it were not so, I would have told you. I am going there to prepare a place for you. And if I go and prepare a place for you, I will come back and take you to be with me that you also may be where I am. You know the place where I am going."

Thomas said to him, "Lord, we don't know where you are going, so how can we know the way?"

Jesus answered, "I am the way and the truth and the life. No-one comes to the Father except through me. If you really knew me, you would know my Father as well. From now on, you do know him and have seen him." John 14: 1-6

I did it! And I had heard my voice be particularly expressive, where it was needed most. God had been with me. Thanks Lord!

The only symbol we were not used to in the Catholic service was the use of an incense burner being gently swung over the coffin. It was only at this point I felt somehow uncomfortable.

Graeme Orr read out the eulogies for us.

1994 was not the era for doing visual presentations of people's lives at funerals. If it was I would have found many photos to use, some from the family collection of Dad's early years, and some photos I had taken over the years. Dad's interest in photography had been passed on to his daughter.

Neil McNab   1917-1994

There would be the photo of Neil as a child, holding a wooden horse,

A photo of Neil at the age of 12, taken with his Scottish family of six

There would be a photo of Neil on the tennis court.

There would be a black and white photo of Lance Sergeant Neil McNab, with his mother, striding down a Sydney street during the war years.

There would be a photo of an athletic Neil on the golf course,

And a photo of my young Mum and Dad at a dance, post war.

There would be happy photos taken on their wedding day.

There would be a photo of Neil with each of his newborn children,

A photo of a new War Service house, and the extentions Neil helped build.

And a number of photos of a happy relaxed Neil on family holidays.

There would be a photo of Neil dancing with his 10yr old daughter, at Lois and   Colin's wedding.

There would be a photo of Neil painting his house.

And of course, there would be a photo of Neil with his dogs,

As there would be a photo of Neil in his bountiful garden, at Farrington Pde.

There would be a photo of a proud Neil, in the family group, at Geoff and Megan's wedding.

And there would be photos of Dad with his much loved grandchildren, Heather and Lachlan.

But there were only three photos today that Shane carried for me, to use at the luncheon.

One was from Mum's dressing table taken on their wedding day.

The second was a coloured photo taken at the Nancarrow's home. Dad was wearing a red jumper, and it's possibly the nicest photo we have, of our happy, relaxed Dad.

And thirdly, the one I took of Mum and Dad on their 36th wedding anniversary, the last photo I would take of them, before Dad had his stroke seven years ago.

Jack's organ music pulled my thoughts back to the church. That indicated it was time to leave. Our family stood, as the coffin was wheeled to the back of the church, and outside. Geoff now took Mum by the arm, and they walked together down to the back of the church. Oh golly, this was going to be hard in front of all these people; I thought for a moment, *I'll have to walk by myself.* Then Megan slipped her hand into mine, and together we walked down the church aisle. How special, and not hard with help! For the first time I could see the gathering of people who had been sitting behind us. As I neared the back of the church I spied Ridley Smith, sitting on the end of a row. My face lit up in recognition. How nice of him to come! Ridley smiled back, a beaming smile and it filled me with a discernable warmth; a smile when I needed it the most. Thanks Ridley. And Joost had come, to represent PHCEC. How nice. Thanks Joost.

Outside it was such a glaring scene with the hearse containing Dad's flower laden casket. It was just then that I realised, we realised that Dad's younger brother had not come to the funeral.

"Hugh didn't come," we remarked in astonished tones. Surely at death the grudges and hurts of this lifetime can be put aside. If not now, when? Hugh's dislike of the Catholic Church had been larger than the ties to his older brother. It seemed unbelievable.

As guests started to leave the church the focus turned to greeting friends and family; the people who had come to encourage and support us. A hug for Janet, "What a nice surprise," I said, hugging her generously.

Rosemary and Karl were both there. I was touched that Karl had taken time off from 3M to come. "Thanks for coming. I know Lyndal would have been here if she was home," I said in recognition of my absent friend. They nodded. Karl was leaving for the drive back to Pymble. Rosemary would come across to St John's.

Chris came over and gave me a supportive hug. "I won't stay for the next bit." I nodded.

Others made themselves known to us, especially people who would not join us for the luncheon , people from North Ryde. It was soon time for our final journey – to Northern Suburbs Crematorium.

On the day of my father's funeral we were again all sitting in the big black car, for our journey to the crematorium. It pulled out of the Spirit of Sanctus Church into Cox's Rd, and turned left at the lights. We were in Wicks Rd, and the first street we passed had a sign on the telegraph pole. I consciously looked at the sign - FARRINGTON PDE.

I think we were all thinking the same thing. The drive to my father's last destination, a journey of about ten minutes, was past this familiar street, and his home of 36 years. The black limousine turned onto Epping highway, and then left into Delhi Rd; past the burgeoning business complex of recent years; past the long standing flower vendor, and the bush border of Lane Cove National Park. The stone gate of the Northern Suburbs Crematorium came quickly into view.

The green, well-kept gardens of the crematorium provide a soothing welcome to every visitor, each surrounded by their own grief. The chapel buildings stand as a landmark in the northern suburbs, with a distinctive Spanish roofline of red terracotta tiles, and a chimney that can be seen for miles. We made our way to the north chapel. A few others soon joined us, mostly family. We sat together in the front row, Geoff and me on either side of Mum. We were early. My father's coffin was already in position, in a curtained niche in the front wall; so close, in this small chapel. I smiled to myself as I realised, and said, "Dad always liked to be early!"

Mum and Geoff smiled and Geoff nodded in agreement. It was good to be amused by this small detail. Graham Orr took the service here, a short service of internment. So much had already been said at the church. Now just Bible passages and prayers! I probably shouldn't say 'just', as these words from Scripture were giving us great encouragement as Graham read them. We drank in every word.

Family emerged from the chapel into the sunshine of midday. It was done. We had farewelled our Dad, a husband, a father and a grandfather. Geoff lingered and didn't appear for a while. He told me later,

"I gave Dad a last salute."

A fitting tribute from a son, to his father, who endured the rigours of war to pass onto his children the gift of freedom.

We drove back to St John's where many were now gathered for a luncheon of sandwiches and cakes. I remember being in a very buoyant mood from having so many friends and family around. It was so nice catching up with friends like Donna Walsh, Joy's daughter. She had grown up through St John's as well. Her father, Gordon Mitchell, had been Dad's best friend, until his untimely death in 1972. They were both quiet, gentle men. She was reminiscing about our families shared memories. Donna commented on the photos I had displayed on the piano.

"I'm glad you put some photos out. That's a really nice one of Neil in the red jumper."

"Yes, I just thought of bringing them yesterday."

Not only had I brought framed photos, I had also brought my camera as I wanted to get a photo of Shane and Janet, to remember this day and their special gift to me.

On the day of my father's funeral Shane and I decided to go to North Ryde RSL for dinner. She was flying back to Queensland early the following morning. We asked Mum if she would like to come.

"No, I'm tired. You two go and enjoy yourselves."

We talked about lots of things, as we always do – equals in that department! We enjoyed our meal, and catching up in this unexpected way. As the night slipped away the conversation turned to more serious topics. Shane was reflecting on the suffering in peoples' lives.

"Your father didn't deserve what he got," she said, referring to the disabling stroke that he had suffered in 1987, almost seven years ago. She cared for Dad, and had visited him in rehabilitation, just after he'd had the stroke; one of the few people who did. That visit had reduced her to tears later. Shane had known Mum and Dad for years, and was deeply moved now.

"I know he didn't," I replied. "But it doesn't always work like that. I've seen a lot of good people get dealt some pretty awful stuff. Your mother was one of them." Shane nodded. Her mother had died of breast cancer, in the early 80s. Shane, her father and sister had nursed her at home, right up to the end. It had been hard.

"But why does God let it happen?" she asked, out of her own need to make some sense of it.

"He doesn't make it happen." I was searching my mind for the right words to say.

"We live in a world where bad things happen, and innocent people get affected. God doesn't cause the bad. And God *knows* what it feels like to suffer. He watched his Son die on a cross, as His own heart was breaking. He could have stopped it, but He chose not to, so that we could be forgiven."

"That makes more sense to me than anything, anyone else has ever said."

She was accepting the way I saw God at work in the world.

It was so very special, after years of friendship, to share something of eternal value with my best friend – on the day of my father's funeral. Friendships take years to grow and flourish. Some friendships see us through all the stages of our lives, and are to be treasured. I write these words in January 2010, in the beachside suburb of Kingscliff, northern NSW. Shane and Ron drove down from Bribey Island yesterday to visit me, a two-hour journey, with a chance to catch up. We have seen each other through many more of life's trials since that January night in 1994; hers and mine. Their children are young adults now, finding their own way in life. For Shane and Ron semi-retirement is now a planned reality. But I am getting ahead of myself.

It was getting quite late by now, on the evening of my father's funeral. Mum would be wondering where we were. As I pulled into the driveway, I could see the light was still on in her room. She was waiting up for us! We walked up the front steps talking, and I opened the front door.

"OK, you two throw your hats in."

Mum was aware of the time too!

"Where have you been? I've was getting worried. I thought something had happened to you."

Shane and I were laughing, like two schoolgirls getting into trouble for coming home late.

"We were just *talking!*" I said, something my mother would understand!

She laughed too, and we sat on the end of Mum's bed and talked some more about events and families - a debriefing of sorts at the end of a Big Day; a very good day, in all - **the day of my father's funeral**.

An early morning trip delivered Shane to the airport for her journey home. We shared a very warm goodbye, tinged with sadness. Sometimes a hug says it all.

It was a day to stop and do nothing. Our lounge room became the place for many visitors that day, from the closest of friends to the arrival of floral arrangements. Many cups of tea were consumed there, with the large windows offering views to the northern suburbs. Our lounge room also became the place where another drama was playing itself out. The day after the funeral I noticed billowing grey smoke rising into the sky from a very close location. It seemed so close I first thought a factory was on fire on the other side of Epping Highway. The thick plumes of smoke created looked like rubber could be burning. Then we learnt from the media that Lane Cove National Park on fire. We were very concerned. This had been our playground and picnic venue when growing up.

Over the next three days the smoke, and fire, increased to alarming proportions. The daily news was updating people on the real threat to homes adjacent to the National Parks, to the north and south of Sydney. Residents and fire fighters were battling to keep the flames from their doorsteps, and from the roofs of homes. We could see from our vantage point on the hill, helicopters flying over the smoke laden sky dousing the flames with water bombs. Thirteen local houses, 225 all up, were destroyed in those New Year flames, as fire fighters battled blazes all over Sydney. The worst of these 1994 bushfires was in The Royal National Park where 97% was burnt out. Four people were killed as a result of these fires. The fires had almost surrounded our city, and had made the international news in many countries.

As the fire raged something in us settled; the understanding that life without a husband and father was our new reality. Life might be simpler now, in some ways, especially for Mum, but still the quiet grief remained. 'Half' of our Dad had been our reality for almost seven years. Now his absence from our lives meant our God had made him whole. And that understanding is what got us through.

Many cards of sympathy were sent to Mum. Most were addressed to all of us. It was comforting to read them all, when I visited. They kept arriving over a period of weeks. They were greatly appreciated. I found cards arriving in my letterbox too. Most were from my church family. Jill organised a card for me, from our Bible Study group. Others arrived separately. It was something very special to tear open an envelope, not knowing who it was from, open the card and read the verse and handwritten messages. People were so kind to take the time. They were cards I would keep. Below are some of the written messages:

To Helen, from Ken and Ivy,

Please convey our sympathy to your mother whom we met at Gilbulla.

To Dear Helen and family,

We were sorry to hear of the sad loss of your dear father. Our thoughts and prayers are   with you at this time. Love, Michael and Sandra Iverson

To dear Helen,

Our thoughts and prayers are with you, with love from, Andrew, Deanna, Jonathan and Caitlin

To Helen and family,

May it comfort you to know that special thoughts and sympathy are with you.

From Bob Watling and family.

To dear Helen & family,

Thinking of you at this time and praying that the Lord will comfort you and give you his peace and love. Love Heather

To Dear Helen,

I pray you have the strength to get through the pain of your loss. Our thoughts are with you. Love Nicky and family

And one from an old school friend. How nice!

Dear Helen,

So sorry to hear of the death of your father, our thoughts are with you. Kind regards Julie Whitelaw (nee Selby-Adams)

Others cards arrived from families and individuals. It was something very special to tear open an envelope, not knowing who it was from, open the card and read the verse and handwritten messages. People were so kind to take the time. They were cards I would keep, so that one day I could remind myself how thoughtful people had been.

DAD

When the funeral was over, I noticed something unusual. Unlike the grief I had expected, I was surprised to feel a load had been lifted from my heart. That mantle of grief I had worn lightly for the last six years, had been shed. I didn't feel as sad as I'd thought I would. I think that was true for Mum and Geoff too. The sadness, the grief, of having had Dad disabled and away from his home, for years, had taken its toll. *'When Half is Whole'* the book had said. Our understanding now, as Christians, was that Dad had been made whole in Heaven, and was living a renewed life with his creator. I could see him walking through Heaven with his 'new legs'. Yes, Dad was whole again. Knowing he was in a better place was a sure part of our reality now.

I went to the Crematorium to visit Dad's last resting place. Mum had made the arrangements to have his ashes interned at Northern Suburbs Crematorium. I found Dad's niche among flowers and garden beds in the Returned Servicemen section. It had an outlook over the leafy boundaries of the grounds. Dad's fresh forged metal plaque announced his presence on the top row. And it was Dad's presence I was seeking that day.

I had heard my cousin Lois say that she went to the cemetery to talk to her father. I wondered if I might do this too. Could I connect with Dad here? I started a conversation, speaking out loud, only ending up praying to God. I hadn't expected that. But my out loud conversations with God were firm in my litany of habits. This place wasn't going to work for me. Oh, I'd come here to give my respects, of course. What about the place Dad had last been; where I had experienced him; one of his favourite places – the Spirit of Sanctus Church? This made sense. I could go to the church that was so often open; to the church I had never attended with my Dad, to find him. I had so meant to go... but, when all was said and done, I never did.

It was good to have four weeks of summer holidays left to enjoy, to enjoy some of the summer holidays. Mum and I spent a few days at the new SU property at Faulconbridge, that SU had just purchased. It was good to be able to use this facility, and give Mum a break from all that the past few weeks had held.

I could now start my new year at school in a good place.

Time heals; and so with January behind me I was able to start this new year at school in a positive way. I'm sure the prayers of many enabled me to do this; though many would not have known how I spent my 'Happy New Year'.

It was an evening at the theatre with Jill and Geoff a few years later. They were keen fans of Andrew Lloyd Webber, and often had a CD of musical highlights playing at home. I was invited to join them for a night at *The Phantom of the Opera*.

Phantom was one of their favourites. On the night we enjoyed a Chinese meal on the edge of China Town before walking down to the recently renovated Capitol Theatre. Unlike the Stewarts I knew little of the storyline of this musical, save the *'Phantom'* music theme. The music of the production was rich and resounding, and the costumes evoked scenes of the opera from another time.

In the darkened theatre a new scene began on stage. The heroine Christine, during a troubled moment in her life, visits the tomb of her father. She comes alone and starts to talk (sing) to his departed presence, seeking advice for her difficult situation. The words were raw with the emotion of a daughter separated from her beloved father and longing to speak with him again. I hadn't been expecting this, and when I realised she was talking to her father, in a graveyard, just as I had done, something welled up from inside me that needed to be released- tears; lots of tears.

Uncontrollably tears coursed down my face. I knew if I gave in to them I would be sobbing such that I might not stop. I couldn't do that, not sitting in a theatre in the quiet of the performance. It took every ounce of self-control I could muster to just sit in my theatre seat while the tears wet my face and dripped onto my clothes. I didn't want to draw attention to my plight from anyone near me. I managed to conceal my tears from Jill sitting next to me, just brushing some away as they reached my chin. Jill never knew the effect that scene had on me that night, the scene where heaven and earth came closer to each other and I wished that my Dad was 'somehow here again'.

Anzac Spirit

In Australia and New Zealand the 25th April is ANZAC Day – 'Lest We Forget'. On that day two nations remember all who served in their armed forces in any theatre of war. These two Pacific partners have been fighting alongside each other since the landing at Gallipoli, Turkey, in 1915. In Australia marches by veterans of all past wars are held in every town and city across the nation.

Today I wanted to march through the streets of Sydney– to honour my Dad's memory, and all he achieved as an Australian soldier. I had never done it before. I'd seen on TV that children of veterans had started to be involved, and could march either with, or for a parent. I wanted to do this. I didn't really decide to go until the night before. It had been in the back of my mind for a while, and now here was the opportunity, and I wanted to seize the day. I would have liked Geoff to do it with me, but I had left it a bit late to ask him. But it wasn't too late for me, so I decided to go by myself. I rang Mum and told her what I was going to do. Her response was warm and positive. I asked her if she would get Dad's medals out. I knew where she would look to find these precious war medals, in the second drawer of their dressing table.

As a child I was impressed by the size and colour of these medals that Dad would wear on his coat. He wasn't a regular participant in the Anzac Day marches, but I do remember as a girl watching from the crowd in George St one year, and waving when I saw him march by. Some years Dad would go alone to join his fellow soldiers, and we would watch for him on the TV telecast. Mum knew when he was coming when she saw the red banners of the 9[th6] Division, and we would watch carefully to see if we would get a glimpse of our Dad. Sometimes we were rewarded and we were very excited to see him march by, in formation, with his WW2 mates.

I called in to collect the medals and Mum helped me to pin them straight onto my navy blazer. They were heavy to wear and clinked together as I moved * praised by both Allied and Axis generals, as well as non-Australian war historians * being one of only a few Allied army units to serve in both the Mediterranean and Pacific theatres of war.

Mum waved me off as I drove to Artarmon Station where I parked my car. Proudly wearing my Dad's war medals I was entitled to free transport that day!

I arrived early and found O'Connell Street was surprisingly empty. As I waited the numbers grew, many men now who had once been a part of *The Magnificent 9th*. I asked where the Transport Division would gather and was told it was towards the end of the street. I waited and watched. I observed two men unroll a unit's banner from its large calico bag. It was navy silk, with gold fringing and tassels, with large white letters on it for all their combat destinations: Tobruk, El Alamein, Borneo, New Guinea. The banner also held the large, distinctive **T** for Tobruk that only the 9th Division banners carried. I knew I was in the right place now.

Family members stood on the footpath as the men from this unit formed small groups on the road, chatting informally. I started talking to a couple of brothers who had come in to watch their father march. Shane Curry was from Quakers Hill, not too far from me at Blacktown. He

---

6 The 9th Division was the fourth division raised for the Second Australian Imperial Force (2nd AIF). The distinctions of the division include it being: * in front line combat longer, cumulatively that any other Australian division * one of the Australian military's most decorated formations.

said they always came in for Anzac Day. It seemed we had more in common than locality as we talked about our fathers' shared war service. I told him my Dad had passed away earlier in the year and that I wanted to march. He introduced me to his father, Doug Curry.

"Your dad was an excellent tennis player. We had a tennis court set up in the dessert, where your father won many a match. The British soldiers wanted a game one day, not knowing how good your father was. As the game developed it became a national tournament, Australia verses Britain. Your father won for us!" I smiled. Yes, I'd heard of the tennis matches, if not this one. Dad was able to continue his favourite sport as a pastime while in Egypt. He had sent photos of these courts home to his tennis-playing mother, who rented out the family tennis courts over the war years to make an income.

It was these small black and white photos I carried today, in an aged album; images from the Middle East and New Guinea. Doug Curry nodded. Yes, they all had copies of these photos he told me; small black and white photos that held the memory of a shared time and place; now a unique piece of Australian military history. There were photos of other forms of entertainment, used by these men before me, to escape the reality of war.

Mostly the album contained photos of locations and military operations; tiny windows on the life and work of the 'Rats of Tobruk'.

"We called your father Jock," Mr Curry recalled.

This was something I hadn't known. Dad had a nickname; a Scottish endearment given to him by his mates. I felt like the layers were being peeled back. I was already feeling a bit overwhelmed.

As I watched these men mingling and catching up with each other in O'Connell St, I noticed something; they were all quite short, and not nearly the stature of my father. Then an image came into my mind from Dad's war photos. It was a larger photo than most of them, and not in the album I carried. It was a photo of Dad with two mates dressed in uniform walking in step with each other, shoulder to shoulder, along a broad paved footpath. Dad was the tallest in descending order. (It was possibly taken in Australia between the Middle Eastern and Pacific campaigns.)

In all of the war photos Dad is the tallest. These men in O'Connell St were those very same short men. I was taller than all of them too. It was like the old photos suddenly came to life.

Sydney was honouring her war heroes. Another man from the unit introduced himself, Barney Donnelly. He was the convenor of their Association.

"I heard that you want to march today. It's not RSL policy to allow family members to march. This is just for returned soldiers."

I was stunned! Was he really going to prevent me from joining the march? I had seen other family members do it! He was being unnecessarily officious. I was speechless.

"But if you go to the back row, I probably won't even see you!"

A gracious gesture, while being technically correct. I smiled a thankful response.

In time we assembled in rows, about three rows deep and eight men across. I was the only 'ring in' today; a daughter of a digger. Their former commander stood in front of the banner carried today by a young enlisted man, flanked by two other soldiers, one a young man the other a young woman. As each unit moved out of O'Connell St we got closer to the junction with Pitt St where a marching band dovetailed itself in front of us. We would march to their beat.

And so the march began for this 9th division Transport Unit, with these old soldiers falling into step again, in time with each other, and to the beat of the music.

We marched down Pitt St, and turned the corner, in formation, into Martin Place just after 11:00am.

Here the crowds were deep behind low railings, waving Australian flags and clapping. As we passed the Cenotaph, the Tomb of the Unknown Soldier, the marching slowed, as all these men had done over the years, faces turned to the memorial and they marched past with their heads turned to honour the fallen. This was extremely moving.

We rounded the corner into George St, the very heart of Sydney. George Street had been the life of Sydney for over 200 years. This was a major shopping street and thoroughfare that I knew like the back of my hand. Flora had worked in Angel Place, just off George St, and as a child we would visit her on shopping trips to town. I knew its department stores and shopping arcades. I had caught the bus from George St, to Sydney Teacher's College, on many a morning over three years in the 70s. But today it held no traffic save the military vehicles that carried aged veterans in a march they would not miss.

The crowds were bigger in George St, waving and clapping; children, men and women, mums and dads, everyday Australians giving honour to the men and women of our country who have served them in many theatres of war. It was a short march, down three blocks to Park St. But in those minutes the marching became secondary, and what I was representing became enormous. I was marching with my father's unit down George St, as he had done, many years before. He had fought alongside these same men in the Middle East and New Guinea to secure this city I loved. And in this moment I felt at one with Seargant Neil McNab. I was proud of him in a new way, so proud that the emotion caught up with me. As I marched past The Strand Arcade and Dymocks Building I was blinking away tears. And I knew also that in that moment my Dad would have been very proud of me.

We rounded the corner again at Town Hall and marched towards Hyde Park, where the march would end. These men knew instinctively where to 'fall out' and when the Anzac Day march for 1994 was over for them. They would meet soon for drinks in a familiar venue and be one again, reminiscing about times and places, about cobbers and commandants. It would have been good to hear some stories and ask some questions of these people. I looked for Doug and his family, but in the big crowd of people in Elizabeth Street they had gone. I didn't know where they met so this was where my Anzac day ended. I walked back to Wynyard with the rousing sound of the marching bands filling the air. I paused to watch the continuing procession of returned soldiers who were still in the march, with men from Vietnam and also armies of other nations.

The interest in Anzac Day ceremonies has grown over the last two decades and now seems more significant than our National Day, on 26th January. More and more people go to dawn services and marches in our cities each year, braving all kinds of autumn weather. I went back to O'Connell Street again, a few years ago, to see if I could make some contacts with these men again. I wondered if the Curry's would be there. But I didn't see any one that was familiar, and the group of men who assembled there was so diminished I was quite shocked. This last Anzac Day I returned again. There was no navy silk banner with its distinctive **T** to be seen anywhere. Although there were elderly men still marching from many of the other units of the 9th Division there were no men assembled from the Transport Unit. That made me sad.

"Probably too old to march anymore," suggested one man with whom I made an enquiry. Then I reflected that Dad would have been 93.

Most of these old soldiers I had met had hung up their marching boots, and made their journey out of the conflict of life itself. That being the case, I made my way down to George Street to watch the ANZAC[7] march- lest I forget.

Connect

It was a natural part of who I was as a person, to pull people together for community. It seemed an obvious thing to do this with Scripture teachers, for our own mutual benefit. It started simply with Chris and I meeting with Lyn Searle and Adam Ryan, on the same day that other teachers would be planning and consulting. We met in one of the local churches. It was reasonably helpful. But I knew we could maximise such an event with more teachers. With Lyn's and SUs help we tracked down all the high schools that had fulltime Scripture teachers. We sent out invitations, to coincide with the next pupil-free day. Our venue was the meeting rooms on top of the newly acquired Koorong building at West Ryde.

That's when I first met Philip Andrew. Philip worked at SCEGGS at Mosman, and had somehow heard of our new network. On the training day he brought a range of material to share that he was using with the girls at his school. I did a presentation too, and probably Chris as well, about our new method of approaching all our lessons. I shared the Self-Esteem model in depth. Philip, an Anglican minister, was keen to know more and to share it with another minister friend of his involved in schools' work. So Philip arranged a day for the two Christian Studies teachers to come to PHHS, hear my rational and follow me around to some of my lessons.

On the day Philip arrived with his friend, Ian Powell. In my time at Moore College I had overlapped with Ian. I had known of Ian Powell's work at the Department of Evangelism, working alongside John Chapman. He had great ministry gifts. Ian had just started as the Chaplain at Shore Anglican Boys School. He was open to all and any ideas he could use in his classroom. Philip knew he was bringing his friend to someone who really had a handle on Christian Studies classroom. I went through my rationale for teaching and some lessons. These two ministers came to my classroom and saw the posters and the arrangement of the chairs.

And they saw all the photos. We talked and shared ideas. I have recently talked to Ian about his 'best' lesson when he was at Shore. He told me and I smiled. Ian had changed a lesson slightly that I had shared with him on that day. I recognise it straight away. Ian had changed the lesson, as teachers do, when they borrow a lesson from somewhere. It was my 'best lesson' too. But the concept and teachable moments were the same. And they were born this day. Phil Andrew kept coming to our Teacher's Days and sharing and receiving good lesson ideas. I liked that we had some teachers from private schools.

A call to the garden

It was early in the school day, one Friday in May. There was a knock at the staffroom door.

"Is Miss McNab there?"

I turned from preparation at my desk, and saw Kate McPhail. I smiled as I stepped outside to speak with her; but the smile was not returned, which was unusual. Kate's big dark eyes looked worried.

She spoke with great anguish. "My Mum is in hospital having an operation. Something's gone wrong. The hospital rang. We have to go now. Can you pray?"

"Yes, of course!" I said placing my hand on her shoulder.

"Thank you. Please keep praying."

Kate didn't wait for me to pray as she turned and left, her whole body in haste to get home and speedily arrive at her mother's bedside. This did not sound good. My staffroom door had been the first place Kate had come after being called out of class. I'm pleased I was there to hear this sad news. I didn't see Kate again for a week.

By now she was dressed in the clothes of mourning. Kate's long hair fell loosely over her shoulders. I sat in St Matthew's Anglican Church, and watched her take a seat at the front of the church with her family. Kate now looked and seemed older by the experience of this last week.

Kate's friends had come to the staffroom to see me the next day, before school began.

"Did you hear? Mrs McPhail died yesterday!"

I was very shocked to hear this news.

"Kate rang last night. Something went wrong with the anaesthetic."

Kate's friends' faces wore their own grief, for the friend who had lost her very precious Mum. This was just tragic. Sharon, Liz and Carmen wanted to pray for Kate and the family. We met at recess in a classroom near my staffroom, just to do that. This was their first response, to pray. They had nothing else left to them. But they knew that the whole family would be needing help right now!

"Lord, we pray for Kate and her family. Be with them now."

I was impressed by this godly response to their friend's misfortune. I was impressed by their quiet faith.

Prue looked older too, dressed up. And there was a young David who had just joined us in Year7.

The news spread around the school, and shock waves gave way to a quiet sadness. The McPhails were well known to many being very active on the P and C, and in school musical productions.

The church was full very full.

Those of us from the high school staff, who knew the family, were encouraged to attend the funeral. I sat in a pew with Ellie and Gerri. We didn't speak. I wondered what each of these ladies was thinking, sitting here, at the untimely funeral of someone they knew; a wife and Mum, the same age as they were.

The funeral service began. An unspeakable sadness hung over St Matthew's as tributes began and hymns held hallelujahs for Him, the God whom Lee had known; hallelujahs, amidst the grief of unexpected loss. *Why's* were unspoken. Lee was so young; so loved by so many.

Rev Peter Taylor spoke of his certainty of Lee's personal faith in Jesus; words of hope offered to her family, and to her friends; words to hold on to; words to live by. He offered no easy platitudes, but a sure hope of Lee's safe passage from this world, into the next, where her Lord was waiting for her.

A song was played. Her mother had chosen it for her. The music began and a choral piece, not quite the style, filled the church. It had an old, dated sound. Not what I was used to listening to. But the words drew me in.

The words told a story; a personal story, of a woman and her Saviour. It was compelling.

> '*I come to the garden alone,*
>
> *While the dew is still on the roses,*
>
> *And the voice I hear, falling on my ear,*
>
> *The Son of God discloses.*
>
> *And He, walks with me, and He talks with me,*
>
> *And He tells me I am His own,*
>
> *And the joy we share, as we tarry there,*
>
> *None other has ever known.'*

The music marched the sombre mood out the door. It was replaced for me by a vision of Lee McPhail meeting everyday with her Lord, in quiet intimate places; and more so, of Jesus's own joy of meeting her there.

Eternity for Lee had begun in a garden...

a garden where her young Lord struggled with the choice He had before Him; the choice being played out in Gethsemane, a struggle for a cross and its burden, for death and its defeat. . . all so that Jesus could meet Lee every day in her garden.

This old song was so beautiful; so personal; so intimate.

It seemed we were overhearing the intimacy of a lover and His beloved. And in this packed church, it was as if Jesus was speaking to me.

> *"I want to spend this type of time with you Helen.*
> *Come to the garden..."*

We stood for the final hymn. The family left their seats at the front of the church and walked a journey of reluctant reality. They had said their goodbyes to a wife, a daughter, a sister, a Mum. Two younger children followed their father and the girls down the church aisle; a slim boy in a white shirt, young David, with the future in his eyes; and an even younger Elizabeth, dressed in a blue, smocked floral dress, looking so much like she needed her Mum.

It was still so sad; so very sad.

It was a few more days before we saw the children back at school, and Kate, into the care of her good friends.

ISCF Conference 1994

We were back at the Gerringong site this year, with the sea at our doorstep. A full program had been designed, including a Concert on the last night.

Chris had made the suggestion that instead of it being a concert for performers, it be a concert when **you bring your best to the Lord**, and not necessarily music based performances. We were looking forward to what people would come up with. Maybe they were, but I wasn't! I didn't know what I would do at the concert. I had no performance skills. I did think I could do a poem, but that would need some time to work on it, if it was to be more than a rhyming jingle. So I crossed that possibility off my very short list- and then there was none. I felt sad that I, as Director, had nothing to bring, nothing that was 'my best' for Jesus. Would I just stand to the back and not participate. Sad, if that was to be my fate.

One of our prime focusses for Conference '94 was mission. We had three team members who were planning to go to the mission field in the immediate future (plus two children). Adam Ryan had been led to serve in Mexico. He had started a relationship with a church in Chapultepec, and had already been serving for nine months. He was home to gather support and we were happy to have him on team again. Adam brought with him some greetings on tape from the pastor and his wife, Juan and Bertha. We learnt some Spanish and some Mexican praise songs. Adam had been translating some of our Aussie songs with his newly acquired Spanish.

Chris and Peta were planning to work with the Millet people in Bulgaria. We learnt about this people group and how they would serve them starting with language learning. The O'Flahertys were not leaving until the new year.

So, I had a few new heroes to add to my missionary list.

I wondered if I would ever be a missionary?

Then God planted an idea in my mind. I had been busy on Day 1 taking photos of all the delegates and team, including the children. I wanted to use these portraits in the chapel/gathering centre. I had drawn a large cross on a piece of cardboard, divided the shape into the number of

Bible Study groups we had. In each space I cut and pasted the members of each group. The finished image was big and strong. The concept was being one together in Christ. I put it up in our shared space where we had Bible Study and worship time. Conference people loved this colourful picture of who we were. This large Cross hung in the main hall for a week, as a statement of our unity and community in Jesus.

This new idea of mine, or God's, was to give each person a copy of the Cross, as a photo. Yes, this was it! This is who I was, taking and giving photos. I was thrilled that I had something to bring to the Conference concert, that was very 'me', and that the delegates had already had this image as part of their Conference event. So I took a photo of the large Cross outside. I looked for a place where I wouldn't get any shadows. Photo taken I needed a trip to Bulli to have the film developed. As Director I had the flexibility to visit the pharmacy to leave my film and then return for my multiple photos. I regularly cut many photos into the shape of a Cross. What a joy it was. I was quietly thrilled to be doing this, and didn't let anyone know what my gift was to be.

When individuals received their Cross they seemed delighted, As I put a cross into each persons hand there were expressions of delight. A very valuable image to take home indeed. Even those students who didn't take any photos, had an image of everybody's faces to take home.

What else was presented at this special Concert? Yes, there were performances of voice and instruments that took on new meaning as they were lifted to the Lord. James and Elizabeth did a recitation. Some delegates, even new friends, performed together. The families brought their best too; a rousing rendition of a chorus came from all the Fentons, with their Dad accompanying on the guitar; the very best Duplo building from Ben O'Flaherty and a drawing from young Kate; so very precious. I still have my little Cross inside one of my Bibles. Thanks Lord for reminding me that you have given me unique gifts that I can share with other people.

Mission visit, 1994

Serendipity: *gift of making fortunate discoveries by accident*

Our remodelled lessons continued to fill our classrooms. Our camps continued to fill young lives.

While all this was happening, Lyn Searle rang me one Sunday afternoon. She told me of some young people from an American Church who were in Australia to do evangelism. Lyn had met some of them at a Giraween High School the previous week. She told me of the pattern that was used in the Scripture classrooms. Lyn was hosting a group from this Disciples Church at Galston High this coming week. They were looking for another school to go into. I started to get interested. That it was Lyn offering this opportunity helped me make a quick decision. I respected her judgement, and she alone, out of many people, knew what the Christian Studies classroom was like. I said yes to a group from Disciples Church for Pennant Hills, and also a group for Cherrybrook Tech High. I let Chris know of this turn of events, and I will admit we both had a smile on our faces - no lessons to prepare for one whole week! Monday morning I cleared this event with the Acting Principal. Nila Lewis gave it her seal of approval.

They would be here for the first lesson, I was told. There would be three of them, I was told. Lesson one began, and Year 9 were getting restless. No one had arrived. I had nothing else up my sleeve for this lesson. I kept looking out the door to the corner of the next building. Then some people appeared around the corner.

"Are you Helen? Hello, I'm Doug. This is Laurie. And this is Greg."

"A class is waiting . . ."

The experts that they were, entered the Year 9 cauldron, introduced themselves, and Doug took the floor.

*Hi, my name is **Doug Hutchinson**. We are from Disciples Church in Costa Mesa, California. We have been invited to your school to share how God has worked in our lives.*

I grew-up in a church-going family. When I was a young boy we attended a large church in Grand Rapids, Michigan. The sanctuary had high ceilings and stained glass windows. I remember feeling a sense of awe and reverence in the cold sanctuary that was filled with hard wooden pews. I imagined that God lived high above our heads in the rafters of that old church. I thought of Him as powerful but distant.

When I was eight years old, my father died. I quickly became convinced that God was not only powerful, but He was also dangerous. In 1979, when I was 12 years old, I went to a Christian summer camp. At a campfire service, I first heard the gospel story and understood that the Lord is a God of love. I answered the call to give my life to the Lord. I remember feeling that something had changed in me, but I did not know how to make sense of it.

When I came home from camp, I told my step-father that "I got saved at camp." He responded, "Did you almost drown?" I told my Mom and she cried. Later that week, I was sitting alone in my room with my dog, Dusty. I began to reflect on my life. I thought, "How did I become me? How come I am not a dog, or even a chair?" Soon I was overwhelmed by a sense of awe, similar to what I used to feel in the sanctuary of our Church.

I realized, I had no part in my own existence. But then, in the midst of the awe, I was overcome by an amazing sense of love and acceptance. Before that moment, I had never known love in that way. That type of love was so foreign to me at that time. Now, after 16 years of relationship with the Lord, the love which was so foreign to me at the age of 12, has become the most distinguishing characteristic of His presence in my life.

Wow! That had been really good. The students had been very attentive too. Doug was the Youth Pastor at Disciple's Church, and he was working with local youth, while continuing with his studies.

Time for one more testimony . . . and Greg stepped up.

*My name is **Greg Dubose**. I live in Costa Mesa, California, near Disneyland, and I run a carpet business.*

My first years were marked by repeated loss and trauma. My Father died when I was three years old. He had been my world. Then, when I was four, our family dog and pet parakeet died. It was like I'd lost two friends. My Mom remarried when I was five years old, and as a result there was a loss of intimacy between us, because now I wasn't allowed to sleep with my mommy every night. My cousin was about four years older than me and was like a big brother and best friend. We would play all sorts of games and he had a train set that we would play with for hours. He died when I was seven years old.

Between the ages of five to 11, I would go to Vacation Bible School in the summer. My cousins and I would walk with our Grandma to church. So I grew up believing about God and Jesus, but like so many people, I thought that was all you needed to do!

Greg spoke of learning to guard his heart, and not letting anything in for fear of losing it. At school he became a loner and an outcast. In high school Greg's 'friends' encouraged him to steal his parents' whisky, and to get into more serious stuff. (Greg didn't go into details here, because of the young audience, but as I listened I understood he was alluding to drugs.) He quit school and joined the Navy, serving for four years. After leaving the Navy Greg got into a really bad scene.

Now one night, I was drinking, and assessing my situation. I was sitting on a beach on the San Francisco Bay staring out at the water and looking at the stars. I started weeping, feeling sorry for myself, wondering how I got here, and blaming everyone and everything for my situation, except me. I thought to myself that I'd probably end up drowning and the next day's newspaper would have a one-sentence story, about an unidentified body being pulled from the bay.

The weeping turned into outright bawling and with my face in my hands, I literally cried out to Jesus. I said,

*"Jesus, are you real? Is this what I am? Is this all I'll be? Am I going to be found dead lying face down in a gutter somewhere? Help **me** Jesus! **Please** help me."*

I know Jesus was there that night.

Greg's testimony was compelling, and everyone was listening intently. Year 9 students had not met anyone with a story such as this.

From this point on, for the next five years I always seemed to have some work and a place to live. During this time I was approached on numerous occasions by Christians preaching the Gospel. I would listen politely to their gospel outlines, then be thankful when they'd gone. I saw Christians as boring, who had no fun and who listened to really bad music.

But I knew I needed Christ.

I kept drinking, partying, and stuff. I was doing OK. I had a place to live, a girlfriend, a job, and I had my beer... I was having a great time. Then all of a sudden my brother shows up at my house. He starts telling me all about this Jesus guy who died for our sins and we're going to Hell if we don't accept Him as our Lord and Saviour. I'm thinking,

"Oh no, they got him!" I thought to myself.

It was through his brother that Greg started going to Calvary Chapel, Costa Mesa. He had been listening to Bible Studies on Revelation with Chuck Smith - Greg being interested in the relevant way Chuck Smith applied the Scriptures. One night it was Greg Laurie who Greg heard speak. Greg Laurie didn't do a Bible study that Wednesday, but spoke about the love of Christ. Greg heard Greg Laurie talking about a love that he needed in his life. He heard how we're all sinners, and that Christ had paid the price for our sins and all we have to do is accept Him into our hearts as our Lord and Saviour. And Greg Laurie asked if anyone would like to come forward and give their life to Christ.

Without realizing I was doing it, I got up and walked forward and said the sinner's prayer of salvation. Why? Because I knew I needed Christ!

I found out that those Christians have enormous amounts of fun, listen to some really great music, are full of genuine love, and I learned that God is a gentleman. He never forced me to accept Him, but He was always there, watching over me and keeping me safe, holding His hand out for me to take so that He could lead me through life. I felt forgiven and I felt loved. God was healing my heart that I had kept from everyone for so long. He has led me to this great church called Disciples Church where I continue to grow in God's word and be in fellowship with wonderful people."

* * * *

The Year 9 students weren't in the habit of hearing a Christian speak about their conversion experience. You could have heard a pin drop! The bell rang. We had run out of time for questions. Darn! Along with the testimony of Laurie Boon, these three members of Disciples Church took it in turn to speak to the rest of my classes that day.

"Are we having the American people?" I was asked at the classroom door over the following days. Good news travelled fast in this school; news of interesting Americans who lived near Disneyland and talked about God. We made sure there was time for students' questions at the end. Hands shot up.

"Have you been to Disneyland?"

"Have you seen a movie star?"

These questions filled every class that Monday, and every other day. The students' questions were definitely not deep and meaningful! We had to laugh. Though questions usually started with these simple ones, they progressed to some of a deeper nature. Doug was the 'wise man' of our three, and often gave the answer to questions asked using his small palm-sized Bible. He knew just where to find verses to answer a question or query. Doug's teaching was inspiring.

So ended our first day with Disciples Church; a very successful day indeed.

I drove Doug, Laurie and Greg home to Castle Hill. Laurie was staying with her friend Teresa, and the guys were staying with Val and Harry Dibley, and their sons Glenn and Rod. Val and Harry were members at

Castle Hill Anglican Church, Harry being on staff as the Men's Minister. Glenn was a PE teacher at Giraween High and heard of the need for accommodation when the team was in his school last week. It was a blessing to get to know this family and experience their hospitality over the week. It became a part of my routine to pick up these three gospellers in Castle Hill and drive them to school. Each day was very full. By Day 2, younger students were making contact in the playground, delighted to have further conversation, mostly about American culture. Above all it was fun! It seemed that the American culture was a very positive thing for our teenagers to relate to and it got these three evangelists a foot in the classroom door, and onto the interest radar of my Pennant Hills students.

Doug, Greg and Laurie came to ISCF as well, and were open to more questions. By now the juniors regarded these three people as friends, and numbers at ISCF had swelled this lunchtime. The seniors had not heard them speak, and Greg shared his story.

New friendships were in the making as I got to know these three Disciples better, spending time with them out of school hours. I was invited to some other activities for the rest of the team: a Bible Study, a dinner, a concert, and city sightseeing. It was fun getting to know these zany, refreshingly honest, authentic American Christians. I experienced real joy in their company and I was pleased to have their American accents in my classroom and in the staffroom. I was deeply drawn to the way these three Americans all spoke about their church. I had never heard anyone speak with such love about their church before. I was curious to know more about Disciples Church. Were they charismatic, I wondered? I met Adam Ayres and Wes Davis, both pastors of this youthful church. Both Adam and Wes had been to Sydney a couple of years before, to investigate the possibility of a mission trip; Galston High had been on the radar then but they said Pennant Hills and Cherrybrook were a delightful addition.

Over the week of talking to and relating to the students, Doug, Greg and Laurie made me realise how packaged our Christian conversation can become, how rehearsed and how banal it could sound. Their answers to difficult questions were warm and real and deep. They used the Bible mixed with a good dollop of themselves. I could tell they had been well schooled in the Bible and I began to understand that there was a discipleship program at Disciples Church. Everyone had to undertake Bible Study classes, at different levels, covering a variety of topics. The three representatives I worked with were a good advertisement for the effectiveness of the Discipleship training program.

I have to confess it took me till the Thursday to realise how important coffee was for American's wellbeing. It was still the era of instant coffee, in Australia, and I had been serving them International Roast in the staffroom, to less than favourable reviews. I eventually realised they needed some plunger coffee. So, on the Friday, there was ooh's and ah's over the strong cup of coffee I was finally serving them. This coffee experience was right up there with sausage rolls, their favourite lunchtime food.

On Friday, Chris O' was at Pennant Hills High, with his own three Disciple's visitors, Martha, Cherry and Brad, after a successful week at Cherrybrook. The experience continued at PHHS as Chris's team met all of his Friday classes. Wes Davis called by our school on the Friday too, to see how the team was doing. It was great to have him in our school and to hear his mid-west accent. Wes had been busy working with Lyn Searle at Galston High. Wes was able to sit in on a couple of our lessons.

Laurie was a little girl, with big hair and a big heart. She had endeared herself to the students over the week, and made some special friends amongst the Year 7s. Laurie was enjoying herself in Australia so much she was planning to stay longer! Her friend Teresa was pleased to keep her, and it meant we would see more of Laurie at school, from time to time. Greg wanted to stay too; so very much. But he was taking a little of

Australia home with him as a souvenir. He had got a tattoo of Tas, the Disney character of a Tasmanian devil, on his leg. Now that is definitely a permanent impression. We did some informal evaluation at the end of the week (over good coffee). Doug was talking of coming back next year to PHHS, but this time for two weeks, to maximise the relationships that are formed with the students. Yes, that would be better. I was all for it!

There was something else of a permanent nature that had been brewing amongst the Disciples. Glenn Dibley had spied, and liked, Kittren from the American team. Kittren had been working with Lyn at Galston High. They'd had a couple of chances to spend some extra time together, and as the team assembled to leave there was talk of a trip to California for Glen in the air. How very nice!

The last event for the week was a concert and barbeque at Galston High on the Saturday night and I had been invited. The GHS auditorium was full with many Galston students who had got to know the team over the week. Adam Ayres was a talented musician and, with the Disciple's music group, he led the mixed crowd of teens and adults in worship. And then Adam spoke. His style of communication was engaging and unique. I hadn't heard any sermon/message quite like it; erudite and skilful, stories told with humour, while engaging in the youth culture and leading the audience to things of God. Adam Ayre's passion for people and God was evident.

I loved these people. I had grown a special place for these three people in my heart. They had 'walked in my shoes' like nobody else had. They had been into every class, the good ones and the hard ones, and they had met every young person I taught. Not one person in the Pennant Hills churches had done that.

I was part of the cavalcade needed to drive these guys to the airport on Sunday morning. Boy, did they have a lot of luggage! Big hugs were shared and words of farewell to everyone, except Laurie. These young people had laboured hard for the gospel over two weeks in a country not their own. I knew they had already been blessed in the sharing of themselves, so sacrificially, and I was sure blessings would follow them as they went back home, back to jobs, and back to 'school'. They all wanted to come back next year! Time alone would tell. These young Americans had made an impact in my life, as I had followed them around, helping out with transport, spending time in their company and opening my classroom to them. My thoughts flew heavenward as they flew their way back across the Pacific. I had been so very blessed in their coming.

This experience with my Doug and Greg and Laurie inspired me to pull out my prayer diary again. I drew a picture of my three new friends. As I look at that page now, I'd recognise them anywhere!

I'd been challenged by these three people, and surprised at how quickly friendship can grow, genuine friendship. I had a deep joy that sprang from my interaction with Doug, Laurie and Greg; both in my school and in their extra-curricular activities. I was challenged to use my Bible the way Doug did, knowing his way around it so well. And I was warmed to know that we were co-labourers of the gospel of Christ, both here, and when they leave to go back home, and to their church.

Apart from our camping program, The Disciple's Church visit was **the best** thing that happened in Christian Studies in 1994. It was something that every student got to be a part of. I couldn't put a price on what Doug, Laurie and Greg had contributed; it was priceless. And for me, an often alone Christian Studies teacher, I'd had three people come into every lesson I taught. In a week they knew the school, they knew the classrooms; they knew the faces; they knew the scallywags and also the kids who were interested in talking about things of faith.

I'm sure there is a godly *serendipity*. And I'm quite sure I had been on the receiving end. My new friends had been my fortunate discovery.

Thanks Lord.

I continued to evaluate my classroom lessons, at the end of each unit. It was still a great way to find out what the students were thinking. Nothing compared to asking them a few questions and then reading the feedback. These comments came at the end of the Self Esteem Unit in 1994. In the middle of these lessons our visitors from Disciples Church arrived. What I read surprised me.

This was an evaluation about the SELF ESTEEM unit that ran over two terms. I didn't ask for feedback about the Disciples Church visit, which had occurred in the middle. But so many of the Yr 9 students commented on our American evangelists – favourably! This was quite remarkable. Those three young Californian Christians had made such an impact that the Year 9 students wanted to applaud them. What a lovely surprise months after the Disciples' visit.

If anyone had asked me, in 1994, how I enjoyed my job, I would have answered,

"I love my job because I can see God at work every day in the lives of the students. I can see myself bringing creativity and wisdom to each lesson, with a compulsory smattering of fun. I have never enjoyed any other classroom more."

Principal – Principle

Peter Noble continued on sick leave for a season. The school was being well run by Nila Lewis during that time. But as the new year came in it was obvious that Peter was unable to continue in his leadership role, and he took medical retirement. Peter had been the principle that Joost Gemeren had approached in 1984, regarding a full-time Christian Studies teacher. Without Peter's active support the program would not have flourished. Peter gave Marty the support and freedom he needed in the early years. It was Peter who assigned Lyn M, as our current 'go to' head teacher. He knew she would be right for the job.

Thank you Peter Noble, on behalf of all the Christian Studies teachers, both then and now, for allowing the good news of Jesus to flourish in your well run school. May you have a long, healthy and blessed retirement.

A large farewell event was held the following year at Pennant Hills Golf Club. It was well attended and Peter regaled us with his exploits from one school to the next. I continued to be impressed with Peter Noble's oratory skills.

ADAM RYAN

CALZADE JOSE MARIA MORELOS

ENSENADA Baja California

MEXICO

Another letter from Adam. How nice! I always enjoyed his letters – this one sent airmail from Mexico.

October 20,'94

Dear Helen,

How do you like the mindmap of my mind? That's exactly how it is right now – I have all these priorities and things that are foremost in my mind, you come out at the top! How's that 2/3rds of the way around this big green and blue ball, I'm sitting in Mexico thinking of my Helen McNab friend in Australia!

Let's see for you it would be about 2.37pm on Friday afternoon, October 21, 1994. For me it's 9.38pm on Thursday evening. Do I carry on with dribble or what? How the heck are you Helen? I've been thinking about you for the last few days, and wondering how you were. But of course every time I think of you I can't but get a picture of you in my mind. Then I think of your love. Your love – not just for kids at PHHS, but your love that encompasses everything!

Your desire to see kids fall into Jesus' arms, your desire for people to know Jesus, to hear Him, to feel Him and to experience Him. Your love for those needy women in Africa. Your love for those in your church, your family, your work etc. etc. etc. In fact Helen McNab, you're one big love bubble! One that will never burst. All this sounds strange (maybe) but I honestly admire you — and am challenged by your love — which I guess is behind the boundless energy you exert in sharing Jesus.

Know this, that the Lord sees what you do in secret, the planning, the agonising, the crying — He knows your heart, and He knows your longings, your desires, and your frustrations. In all this He is your stronghold, your portion, and He is your Shepherd — who will never lead you astray. And his love for you is as fresh and as strong as the first day you sensed it, and as you reached out to Him — He will pour over you the cool waters of refreshing that you've desired for so long, and the Holy Spirit will bring renewal and strength, and a fresh outpouring of His anointing will be yours. Not just in outward ministry, but in your life. Whether you realise it or not, your life, just in everyday living points to Jesus. I guess that all that love that you have comes or flows directly out of the love He gives to you — and I thank God, that He blessed me to be on the receiving end!

Thank you Helen for caring about me, showing me your love, and God's, through who your are. It really is a privilege for me, to be able to call you a friend — it's just a darn shame I can't see you that often! Oh well, there'll be a whole eternity to share in Heaven. Please know that you are appreciated by this missionary in Mexico — and you encourage me every time I think about you. You 'stink' for Jesus — seriously I want to 'stink' for Jesus as well (2 Corinthians 2:14-17).

Anyhow, you've probably got the message, things here are good. The guys in the US (Disciples Church) are so good to me — especially Brad (remember the young blonde guy?) and another guy Chris. I'm now an adopted missionary for their youth group. Next Thursday I'm going up to the US for a church dinner, then on Saturday we bring the youth group down to my place here in Mexico, for the night. (Can you imagine doing that at home, like driving to Melbourne for a day. Mad Chris and Brad!)

I can see you with a smile on your face. I hope I have contributed to that.

With love in the Lord,

Adam

 "…The creator of the ends of the earth,

 Neither feints nor is weary.

 There is no searching of his understanding.

 He gives strength to the weak,

 And to those who have no might he increases strength."

Adam's letter was the nicest letter I had EVER received. He certainly had a way with words, and encouragement was his second name. I did feel blessed to have someone mirror back the gifts they saw in me - love. The very thing I had asked God for, his love, was overflowing into the lives of others. How very special that Adam would take the time to encourage me like this, all the way from Chapultepec, Mexico. Adam Ryan could bless my socks off, even on the other side of the world.

Little did Adam or I know at the time, but I would be seeing him very soon.

I was slow at getting my tax return done that year. October rolled around and I finally stood with my tax cheque in my hand. The cheque was somewhere to the value of $2,000. What to do with it? I had in the past used these funds to pay off my car, but that debt had been cleared last year. What would I do with this money? Paying it off my mortgage seemed boring, so I just banked it.

Sometime in early November, as I mused over the Disciples' visit, and I continued to wonder about their church, it came to me. I could buy a plane ticket to California and visit these interesting young Christians. The excitement of the possibility surged within me. Yes, this was a good thing to do. I checked out the airfare prices for just after Christmas, and wrote a letter to Adam Ayres, asking if I could come over.

"We are so excited that you are coming to visit," was Adam Ayres' reply, after I phoned him to check that this was OK. I hadn't been on a plane since 1983. This was exciting. I had to get a new passport and organise winter clothes. I collected some Aussie souvenirs and asked Adam Ryan if he wanted anything from Oz. He was excited to know I was coming for a visit, and requested,

"10 display folders. They don't have them over here."

When I told my friend Janet where I was going she was very jealous. Travel isn't something you readily do with little children.

"Can I ask you something? If I gave you $100, could you buy me some patchwork material?"

Sure, I could do that!

"There's a well known patchwork shop that has this calendar each year, with beautiful patchwork images. I'd love to go there one day," Janet mused

"Where is it?" I asked.

It's called Piecemakers and it's in "Costa Mesa," came the unknowing reply.

I was astounded. "That's where I am going!!"

A cheque for one hundred Aussie dollars arrived in due time. I now had a project to buy some fabric for my friend. We had learnt patchwork together, over 10 years ago, when Janet too was single. We had spent many a fun evening together, in class, completing blocks for a sampler quilt. It seems she was keeping up the craft in her Alectown home. I on the other-hand, being so busy with school and church, had let this creative pastime fall by the wayside.

It was chocolate that Adam's parents wanted to send over to him- large amounts of Cadbury's chocolate as a Christmas gift. Apparently US chocolate just wasn't that good! I'd never seen blocks so large. This would be fun. Lyn Searle sent Adam some Aussie T-shirts. My bags were quite full.

As the plane taxied and took to the air, my excitement was real. As I said, I hadn't been on a plane since 1983. As I allowed my senses to take in all that being an airline passenger meant I marvelled that I was going to America because of my job teaching Christian Studies. This is something I never would have imagined.

One of the first things I did when I arrived was to visit Adam Ryan. He had been in the US since Christmas, and was staying in 'the guys' house. Adam sat on the lounge room floor, with sun shining in through a window, and opened his belated Christmas gifts. He grinned from ear to ear every time he opened a gift. He just laughed when he saw kilos of Cadbury's chocolate in his hands. That was very well received indeed. And because he was having more than 'a glass and a half of full cream milk', he decided he could indulge.

I was staying with Wes and Michelle Davis and their young family, Josh and Mackenzie who was three. I just loved Mackenzie's unusual Scottish name. To me it was a surname, but the lilt this name has when you say it made it perfectly fit this cute little girl. Wes took the kids and me to Laguna Beach to sightsee, there were plans to go to Disneyland and then there was Cornerstone. I had heard of Cornerstone Café from the Disciples in Australia. Two church members owned the Café, just off Harbour Blvd. A great deal of volunteer service was supplied by church members, many of whom had flexible schedules. Cornerstone was a funky place to meet, eat and drink coffee, of which there were numerous varieties. It was like an extension of church community, because that is exactly what the café offered, community, free of charge. It was the place for concerts, Bible Studies, discipleship classes and storytelling. I had heard of Adam Ayre's gifts in storytelling, and many said,

"Will you be here for one of Adam's storytellings?" It was starting to look like I would.

An Aussie accent was a draw card for many of these young people, as some were already interested in another mission trip to Sydney schools. Wes was planning an evening meeting for interested Disciples, for later in my stay.

New Year's Eve, 1994

I met Chris B at the New Year's Eve party. Chris ran the Disciples Youth group. He was tall and lean, with a personality as big as himself. Chris always had a smile on his face. Between Joe and Chris, Steve and I were organised to go visit Venice beach the following day. This was after my big shopping event!

I was now staying with Dan and Cindy, and Cindy was a patch-worker. She knew of Piecemakers, and told me where I could find it. Cindy also told me about the New Years' Sale. I had never heard of anything quite like it. The store opened at 6.00am, when everything was 60% off. At 7.00am everything was 50% off. At 8.00am everything was 40% off, and so on until 12noon. Adam Ayres had lent me his van, so I had transport. If I went at 6.00am I could get so much more value for Janet's $100.

I arrived in the dark at Piecemakers, to a line of women, and a few men. We were all early. There was an air of expectancy as we stood and waited for the doors to open. I was experiencing a unique American event here and I wondered what treasures I would find inside. As I stood in line in the dark morning mist, a thought occurred to me. If this was an early morning prayer meeting, would I be so keen to attend and be an early arrival? Hhmm! This was a sobering reflection.

My shopping spree at Piecemakers New Years' Sale lasted over two hours. To start with I just looked over the two-story country store. They sold both fabric and bric a brac, even furniture. I didn't quite know where to start. The fabrics were all so lovely. I realised that patchwork fabric production had come a long way in 10 years. They weren't just pretty florals any more. So many styled little prints and a vast range of colours. I was hooked! I needed some of these tactile textiles too. My passion for fabric had been reborn.

I decided to look through some patchwork magazines, to get some ideas of what to buy. That worked. I was like a kid in a lolly shop. A quarter of a metre of fabric, cut and rolled up is known as a 'fat quarter'. I met my first ones in Piecemakers. It was these I mostly collected for Janet. I knew the colours she liked, and gathered many prints and patterns.

My task was done. I carried two big bags of patchwork treasures back to the van. I had achieved my goal. But something else had happened. It was like I had met an old friend I hadn't seen for 10 years. And they had changed, for the better. This was a tangible gift that God gave me on my American visit. It has stayed with me these many years. This delightful craft of patchwork has bough me, and others, great joy. One of my latest creations was a quilt for lachlan when he turned 21! The pleasure goes on.

When Chris B learnt of my visit to Mexico to visit Adam Ryan, he said he would come too. He would drive me to the Mexican border! How very generous he was. Sue Wanke, my latest host helped deck me out with a smaller travelling bag, and a wind jacket. Early that Friday morning Chris arrived at Sue's in his pick-up truck. It was a two-hour drive to San Diego, straight down the F45. We drove past Camp Pendleton, and I noted this was where Raul Ries did his military training, and also past a huge white Mormon temple right next to the freeway. I got to know Chris better on that journey, and I heard his story. Chris had got mixed up with the wrong crowd, and had spent time in gaol for stealing. It was while he was in gaol that Chris became a Christian. His was an amazing story to hear. His life seems so full of joy now. Chris dropped me at the border, and planned to come down to Chapultapec the next weekend, to visit Adam, and drive me back!

I walked across the border from the USA into Tijuana, Mexico. There were many lines of cars and trucks all filing past immigration points, and many people carrying bags, and children. The extremes of rich and poor, of first world and third world were so dramatic here— all in just a few hundred metres. I hadn't done an international border crossing for over fifteen years, and never one quite as dramatic as this. Adam was waiting for me on the Mexican side.

We needed to catch a bus south. I watched and listened as Adam greeted a bus driver in Spanish and then bought tickets to Chapultepec. I was very impressed by Adam's use of Spanish, and this reflected the long hours of language study he undertook when he first arrived in Mexico. Adam was certainly at home in this new country of his.

Chapultapec is a small town 150 miles from Tijuana. The trip south was very scenic, as the road hugged the coast in part, and we drove just a few metres away from the Pacific Ocean. White washed beach houses were sprinkled along the sandy beaches. Adam explained that many Americans live just across the border from the US, enjoying all the benefits of a coastal Mexican lifestyle, where the dollar stretches much further, and then going back to the US, to shop and get medical services.

Adam lived above a shop, *de Todo Barato, (Everything Cheap)* in the main street. It was one room wide from front to back, open plan, and perfectly neat. In the US it would have been called a Studio apartment. Adam had furnished the apartment himself, buying furniture second hand. There were two couches, facing each other, to make a sitting area. And colourful Mexican rugs used as throws and curtains.

Adam's bed was a mattress on the floor, between the lounge area and the kitchen. It was always neatly made. The kitchen had been very makeshift, but Disciples friends had seen this, and supplied shelving and some cooking appliances for Adam's use. A big desk, made from an old door, was set up by the window, with a few besa-brick supports for shelves. From here Adam spent a large amount of time preparing Bible studies and sermons, translating songs into Spanish – and writing letters. The shelves were decorated with family photos, and an Aussie flag.

I was to sleep on cushions from the sofa in the lounge area. Adam had suggested I stay with Juan and Bertha at their house, but I wasn't keen on that idea. Adam worried how 'it would look'. I reminded Adam that I had been his teacher at Cumberland High, so he could tell everyone that I was his *nombre*, and as that role suggests a big difference in age, it would be acceptable for him to house me as his guest.

The bathroom in Adam's flat was the only real challenge. Plumbing seems to be the same in most developing countries. To get the water from the shower to go down the drain without splashing the rest of the floor, and the toilet, was an impossibility. You had to be careful your towel and clothes didn't get wet in the process.

I met Juan and Bertha the next day. It was a 15 minute walk to their house, in which they also held their church services. It was a new two-story house with modern décor. We sat near the timber kitchen and ate the burritos that Bertha had specially prepared. They were delicious. Bertha was a friendly, outgoing personality. Juan, was the quiet one of the two, and spoke only when he was asked a question.

Juan (or John) had been in involved in ministry in California. It was this small town of Chapultepec where he and Bertha had established a small Four Square church. Together they worked with local families, held church services and Sunday School, and ministered to poor families in the area. They spoke very good English. I was invited to speak to the church the following day, and Adam would translate.

Adam carried his guitar case on our walk to church that Sunday morning. He was leading the service and the singing today. Chapultepec is as flat as a tortilla, and the frequent walks, to and from the church, were great exercise. With some apprehension I approached my first charismatic Mexican church service. Would there be any speaking in tongues?

The big lounge-dining area was now cleared to accommodate rows of chairs. Many families had already arrived, and Juan was tuning his electric guitar. I was introduced to the church folk by Adam, in Spanish,

"Este es Elena. Ella fue mi maestro."

"Ah, maestro! Bienvenido Elena."

I sat by myself to navigate the service. The singing was done with much gusto and joy. Prayer time commenced, and I heard for the first time, people speaking in another language, a prayer language; many of them at once; soflty and intimately. It sounded very strange. I felt uncomfortable, but these people were used to this style of prayer and they seemed to pour themselves into it. More singing. Then Juan preached, in Spanish. Adam told me some of the points he was making, but it was impossible to get a full translation in that context. It seemed like it all went on for a long time!

Adam usually had a meal with Juan and Bertha after church, so I was also on the invitation list this Sunday. Bertha had been very busy preparing all this hot food the day before. Another Mexican feast awaited us. Adam would never go underfed as a guest at their table! The rice and meat dish we shared was very filling.

Adam and I, very full, walked the long flat walk back home, and had a rest . . . before we went back again - for the evening service. More young people came at night, some of whom Adam was discipling. These young people were very pleased to have another Aussie to practise their English with. As I listened, and watched I could tell what a fantastic job Adam was doing. The language learning in Ensenada had been a hard slog, but he had done it! The relationships with people took time and perseverance and Adam excelled at this. His careful planning and preparation of talks took discipline, wisdom and insight. Adam was certainly using his gifts here in Mexico, and being stretched.

There was one young man whom Adam had befriended, who he was spending much time with.

"I met Danny when the pastors suggested he could help me practice Spanish. He was 19 and was living in a tiny beat up caravan on his mother-in-law's land, with his soon to be wife and small child. He came once a week. We practiced Spanish, but mainly hung out, shared, and played the guitar. Eventually Danny and I led worship together. I was best man at Danny's wedding. He did eventually lead the service and give Bible studies. He now runs a computer repair business."

I remember one evening when Danny came around to 'hang out'. I just enjoyed hearing both of these young men praise the Lord, in Spanish, with their guitars. The familiar tunes, and unfamiliar language, were sweet praises to our God in my ears.

Adam had plans for a few outings, in between the ministry he needed to do. We walked down to **Estero Beach**, past the lion in a cage (!) and into the camping area. It was here, in one of the caravans that Adam had first lived when he came to Chapultepec. He pointed out his old van. Adam had felt this was the town God had wanted him to be in, and he was just walking around the town one day when he saw the Four Square sign for Juan and Bertha's church – and a friendship, discipleship and a shared ministry began.

Adam Ryan was Hillsong's first missionary. His youth group was supporting him in Mexico, not the main church. Adam was reliant on their donation each month to live on. Right now money was getting tight.

"I can't even afford to buy film, I'm that poor," Adam had commented on one of our walks.

Today we would visit the Estero Beach Resort, and Adam would use the ATM machine that was conveniently located there. But his checking found money had still not arrived. Adam decided to ring the leader of the Hillsong Youth to enquire about the money. I overheard the conversation.

"Hi Donna, it's Adam. Yeah, good! I was just wondering if you have put the money into my account for this month?

This was hard to listen to.

"I haven't got any money left and I need some soon!

Ok, that will be great. Thank you. I have a friend visiting me from Sydney at the moment, so it's good. How's everyone at Youth?

Good to hear. I'd better go now. Bye Donna."

This was not good enough! It prompted me to think of the care shown by CMS for their mission workers, providing housing and a regular salary. I doubt this scene would be encountered by CMS missionaries overseas, unless there was a problem with a local bank.

We enjoyed a pleasant, but expensive, cup of coffee on the terrace of the big hotel. What a lovely place Estero Beach Resort was to escape to for an hour or two. They also had an interesting small museum with Mexican artefacts and statues of ancient Mexico; with many Mayan masks, Toltec totems and an array of Aztec art. I enjoyed learning something of this ancient culture that I was visiting.

When Adam needed to do preparation, or do some planning with Juan, I was free to wander the town. Adam had mapped out shops for me that sold Mexican crafts. They were scattered all over town, so I got to see more of Chapultepec. The colourful weavings of ancient patterns on mats, rugs, and clothing were very distinctive. We had a big outing one day to **La Bufadora**, a blowhole an hour's bus ride south. The sound of the coast filled the air and a lazy atmosphere lay over the sun drenched trading area. Crafts vendors galore lined either side of the tarred road leading to the blow hole; shops and stalls selling jewellery, textiles, carvings, pottery, paintings and food. As we arrived midweek, there was almost nobody else around, so the shop-keepers were very pleased to see us.

"You my first customer today. I give you a special price!"

But the blowhole called us on. "This is more spectacular than the blow hole at Kiama," said Adam as we approached the viewing deck above the swarming sea.

I had to agree with him, as the shaft of water burst through the underwater cave below. You had to be careful not to get drenched when it blew, and we only achieved this by standing at a distance. This was fun!

This rugged coastal destination, with the sound of the waves, the smell of salt water, was a relaxing place for two friends on a day off. We enjoyed a leisurely lunch at a small restaurant and ate outside in the courtyard, overlooking the beach and the sea stretching into the distance beyond. The fresh air and gentle breeze encouraged our appetites. Today I really felt I was on holiday.

We also went into **Ensenada** for lunch one day. The bus journey north, hugging the coastline was now a familiar one to me. At almost the first food vendor we passed Adam said,

"You have to try these fish tacos Helen! They are the best in Ensenada."

Adam gave his order in Spanish, and we waited and watched as fresh pieces of fish were battered and fried, squeezed with fresh lime juice then wrapped in an avocado spread tortilla. Yum! They were absolutely delicious. No other fish taco I've tried in the US since then has even come close! It was fun to spend time around the wharves and fishing boats of this harbour town, seeing what had been caught by the men in their weathered fishing boats. We spied a seal swimming under the wharf waiting for its lunch. Not a sight I'd see in Sydney Harbour, then.

We ate lunch at what seemed a very posh restaurant this day: all white, with big wooden chairs, Black metal candelabras on the table, and Mexican scenes on the wall. Adam sometimes ate here on his day off. We ordered from the menu.

"There's a shop selling Ugg boots just across there!" said Adam, pointing across the road. "They import them from Australia. They're really popular here. I nearly fell over when I saw the sign."

We paid a visit to the Ugg boot shop. The long woolly boots made of Australian merino wool did seem so out of place in this coastal town in Mexico!

Chris and Brad arrived on the Saturday morning, and we went out for tacos, their reward after a long drive. These two Disciples were frequent visitors to Chapultepec on weekends, and were good friends to Adam, seeing what he needed and working towards meeting his needs. We drove back on the Saturday afternoon. It was hard to say goodbye to Adam. Who knows how long it would be before I saw him again. What an amazing job he was doing in Chapultepec. In a way I was proud of him! It was more like admiration, seeing up close the work he was doing here. It was such a blessing to have been able to visit and encourage him. Conference friends would be very pleased to hear news of Adam and his fruitful work in this small Mexican town.

We drove north along the now familiar scenic route to Tijuana, to another border crossing, this time by car. This crossing was very different. We joined the long queues of buses and trucks and cars. Immigration officers came over to the truck and looked it over. I'd been instructed not to say a word. They asked us questions about our visit. They looked at my passport. They looked at me. They looked at my passport. The uniformed men were very officious, but they needed to be. Many Mexican people want to escape to the USA for a better life, and many try to hide in cars and trucks to cross the border. Some, desperate for a better way of life, even climb the wall that borders the

US eight lane highway, and make a dash for freedom across the busy lanes. Chris told me many Mexican people have been killed doing just this. We were finally on our way, from the 'have-nots' to the 'haves', as the poor Tijuana scenes were replaced by curb and guttering, ashphalt freeways and well maintained houses. I was looking forward to going to Disciples Church one more time before I went home.

At a rest stop for food and fuel, I came out to the truck and found Chris sitting in the passenger's seat.

"It's your turn to drive!"

I was stunned into the realisation that he meant it!

"No, no. I can't."

"Yes, you can," said Chris, handing me the keys.

I was about to drive a geared truck, onto the four lanes of the San Diego Freeway, on the other side of the road to what I was used to! This will be interesting. So I reticently took my place behind the wheel and surveyed the dashboard and controls. Here we go! As soon as I had pulled out of the petrol station, and had driven around the corner to connect with the on ramp, I felt at home – it was just a straight drive now, and I mean straight, north to Costa Mesa. Chris had a Christian radio station on as we drove. We were coming into the outskirts of Orange County when I heard the voice of a man giving a Devotion. As I listened I slowly realised that the person I was listening to was Raul Ries! Our Raul Ries from the movie I showed in class was speaking on the radio! I felt like I knew him.

"That's Raul Ries!"

"Yes, he does a segment every day at this time," said Brad.

"I showed the video 'Fury to Freedom' to my classes."

I listened to his deep, gentle voice speaking of his walk with his Lord. This was special. I'll be able to tell the Yr 10s I heard Raul Ries on the radio.

Driving off the freeway and through Costa Mesa was another thing indeed. I was very relieved when I pulled up outside Sue Wanke's place. Lots of news to tell her of my week in Mexico!

Anaheim dawn

The 5:30am morning was dark and cold when I arrived at the Anaheim McDonalds. I pulled my coat around me. A tour bus pickup was arranged for 6 o'clock. I now had time for breakfast. There was no one around in the street and only an occasional car drove by. The only sign of life was inside the restaurant, where the bright lights spoke of the activity needed to keep a fast food chain functioning. I put my travel bag in the corner and found a warm space in what I thought was an empty restaurant.

And then I saw him, out of the corner of my eye; a homeless man who was seated inside the restaurant to keep warm. I could tell he was homeless by the state of his hair, all matted and dishevelled, and by the way he slouched at the table. He was sitting alone at a table at the front.

I ordered my breakfast meal; an egg and bacon sandwich, juice and a coffee. I was enjoying the breakfast aromas and the taste of the hot food in my mouth as the homeless man started to approach me, and my heart started racing. What did he want? What would he say?

As I might have expected the man asked me for some money. I looked away, shaking my head to indicate "No."

This served to remove the man from my table. As he turned to walk away I saw how torn and ill-fitting was the filthy coat he wore. I had never witnessed anything like this before.

There I sat with my bulging tray; there he sat at his empty table.

And slowly, but distinctly, I felt ashamed. Ashamed of my reaction; ashamed of the food I was eating; ashamed that I had turned a homeless man away, hungry. I had to do something. As I sat there I decided not to give this fellow patron money, but to buy him food instead. I lined up at the counter again and ordered exactly what I had ordered for myself, a breakfast tray.

I waited a few moments for the tray of food to be arranged and then I turned, and acted as a waiter to this familiar diner of McDonald's Anaheim. I surprised him as I leant over the table delivering his meal. He ate with gratitude. I could eat now too, not choking on my own food, but with a heart knowing that today, I had done enough.

As I bordered my pickup bus in the grey dawn of an American day, it was not lost on me that the man I had interacted with lived across the road from Disneyland- 'the happiest place on earth'.

While I was away Wes had organised a meeting for any interested Disciples Church members who might want to go on the next mission to Australia. It was scheduled for Monday night. The plans included the same time frame again, July/August 1995. I had a video-tape from a documentary from ABC TV on youth drunkenness, and binge drinking, in Australia. It gave a very real perspective into the hopelessness that seems to surround many teens, with so much family breakdown. I had given this video to Wes when I arrived. I hoped he would remember to bring it. He didn't! And so I had to speak to a roomful of people who were interested in coming to Australia in July. Doug was there, so was Glenn and Steve; and Joe. But there were many new faces amongst this gathering of Disciples. This was very encouraging. I spoke about our school system, about the right the churches have to go into schools; about the history of Christian Studies at Pennant Hills and Cherrybrook; about the impact Doug, Greg and Laurie had, six months before. Doug was speaking of a plan to go back to just one school, over two weeks, to develop relationships more. Glenn agreed with that.

People asked questions. It took up the whole time. Maybe just as well that the video got left behind. When the Team arrived in July, I was so very encouraged to see, almost everyone who had turned up to the initial meeting that Monday night, made it all the way to Australia.

Joe spent time with me on that last day. I think he took some time off work so he could!

"Would you like to go to Calvary Chapel Bookshop?"

That sounded like a good idea. Joe had been converted under Chuck Smith's ministry at Calvary Chapel, in the 70s. He occasionally went back to hear Chuck preach. The bookshop, attached to the church, was huge, full of Bibles, books, CD's and gifts. That's where I found a copy of 'Fury to Freedom' – the book. Raul Ries's story was also a book. How very exciting. I was already looking forward to reading it. I found some more Michael Card CDs, Joe buying me one as well. This little Mexican had such a big heart.

We arrived back at Sue Wanke's, for a final dinner she was holding in my honour, inviting people who had been on the Aussie mission team last July. Doug, Greg, Laurie, Kittren, Heather arrived as well as Chris and Joe. Sue had been cooking the night before and served us all a yummy home-cooked meal – Fried Chicken, good southern fare. These guys all made me feel so special. We talked and laughed, sang and prayed. They prayed for me and my flight, my ministry, and my walk with God. I don't remember being as nurtured at home as I felt in that community at that moment. I loved these people SO much.

I very much felt like a member of Disciples Church, on the Aussie continent.

Then, the final bag pack. Souvenirs took up most of the space: Disneyland treasures for Heather and Lachlan, Mexican textiles, patchwork fabrics, Michael Card CDs, and shoes (they made them big here. I even bought a pair for Mum!) My flight to Sydney was a late one, close to midnight. Joe drove me, and Doug, Heather and Brad Johnson turned up too. These people had showered me with hospitality, and now, right to the end.

My bag was very full but so was my heart. I had come out of a curiosity to pursue the source of these church member's joy. I had worshipped with them, been to discipleship groups, prayer meetings and social events. Their life was in and of God, each of whom had a living relationship with him. The love of God overflowed into their community life, and I had experienced this love, as hospitality and friendship, affirmation and encouragement.

'My cup runneth over.'

But, at the same time, after nearly a month away, I was very ready to go home. I was ready for what this new year would bring. I was also ready to go back to my favourite place – school, and my Christian Studies classroom. And I went home with my new found gift of patchwork, dusted it off and shined it up. Thanks Lord.

A reflection

Now that I have come to the end I have a new understanding of what this book is about. As I reflect on the story from beginning to the end I have realised that it is a book with substantive themes about life and death. I wonder if you too have noticed that?

There is much on these pages that embraces the fullness of life; young people with a joy for all things new, camps in the sun, canoeing on the lake, barbeques in the park, lives changed to live Jesus' way. There were adults with hearts full of love that they overflowed into young lives, both in schools and in churches. There were babies and toddlers to bring great joy, ball dresses and dancing partners to keep me on my toes. There were new ideas for the classroom and lots of creative energy. There were plane trips and unexpected cultural encounters.

There is also on these pages the theme of death. I hadn't realised when I began that the deaths recorded on these pages would number five people over a three-year period. But here they are, three young people whose lives were cut tragically short, the death of my own father at age 76, and the accidental death of a middle-aged mum. It's enough to shake you up a bit. Just like Sam Hilton was shaken up at the reality of Geoff B's death in 1993; so shaken up that he pondered his own death and having to stand before the Living God for himself.

Sam Hilton, and all his peers, were in the group we call the Class of '94. They were my first Year 8 group, and the first group I taught the Parables to. There was one Parable I used that year that I later decided was too advanced for my young Year 8's mind and experience. I had listened and assessed that these word pictures were for older lives. (You may recall the parable of the Sower/Soils on p.47.) It was hard for the students to decide what soil they were, as some students hadn't encountered God yet, nor had they been tested in their Christian walk. At the same time they were being exposed to Christian Studies lessons every week.

To my students, so many of you, I have some questions. **Let's go back to 3P4**, with all its posters and freshly made curtains for just one last lesson there.

Go back to the **Parable of the Soils**, which I put away as being too advanced for you then. Now you have tasted life as an adult and made many big decisions in your life: where you live, whom you live with, what you eat and wear, what career you will pursue, who you marry, how many children you have, what friends you keep, how you spend your money, where you put your political allegiance, how you spend your leisure time.

Christian Studies was **40 lessons a year, over a period of four years**. The seed of God's truth was definitely sown into your lives. What happened to the God-seed that was planted in you by this teacher?

I give you this parable now, for it is yours.

A teacher went out to sow some seed …

Some of you were the seed that fell on the **path**. You quickly heard the message of God's love and forgiveness, and just as soon, it was gone from your life. You were part of the scene for a few minutes during our lessons, but then you had those thoughts snatched away.

There were those also who represent the **shallow soil**. You participated in class. You came on the camps and had lots of fun and learned much. You may have gone to youth group for a while. But your commitments here were thin. And you didn't last long, once you made it to senior school.

There are **weeds** amongst some of you as well. These students too, were involved in class and on camps. Some I thought would last the distance. But God's word of life has been choked out of you. It was too hard for you to resist the charms of this fickle world. What kept you from God? Was it family and friends; was it work and making money; was it your spouse and children; was it moving house? Good things … but not as an excuse for giving God the flick. What weeds grew up and crowded God out of your life?

There was also **good seed** among you, even while you were at school. You will most likely know who these are. Their faith was a day-by-day walk with the Living God. They went to ISCF and may have even invited you to their church. These students knew how to laugh and smile out of a deep inner joy.

I can think of people I know when I describe the good soil both men, women and youth. These people live for other people in a sacrificial way. They give their time to Christian based events and pour their time into people who are seeking the kingdom. They may have been to Bible College because they knew they wanted to invest their lives in the kingdom. They may or may not own a house. They invest in overseas justice organisations, or they sponsor a child. They love to surf, dance, fish, listen to music and buy pretty dresses like other people. They play an instrument and like to cook. They invite people over and have a barbeque. They like good coffee. They love science, maths, IT and the arts. These things are just an expression of enjoying God's created world. Some of them are pastors; others are pastors' wives.. They plant churches and get alongside the new people who come along. They open the word of God with others. They give themselves sacrificially to their family and call themselves blessed. Others are active members in the church of their choice. When life gets tough they dig deep to an inner strength

These are people that you will know too. They were with you at school, maybe in the same class. You may have met them again recently. They hold eternity in their hearts and live life with the King of Kings.

My dear students, I wonder if by now, life itself has dealt you some tough blows, as it does for some. I wonder if you sometime think about the God you learnt about in high school. He has stood there these many years with arms opened wide, his still small voice whispering your name. He has felt your pain and knows the road you have trod. God can forgive your walk of faithlessness so you can begin to write a healed and forgiven story into your life. Jesus is longing that you do so.

What will you do with this parable of Jesus? Which soil do you belong to? Which seed do you long to be?

There is life and death, and Jesus is in charge of both. He offers life in all its fullness to those who would follow Him. Jesus beat death when He walked out of his rock tomb, and He offers the same to those who would call him Lord.

Life or death! Which one will you choose?